T0306141

"This fascinating book provides a vital bridge between both arts management and cultural policy, and between academics, artists, practitioners and policymakers. With conversations spanning the globe, and addressing a range of vital contemporary issues, *Cultural Leadership in Practice* is an essential addition to the field and should be read by anyone interested in how cultural leadership works in the real world." **Ben Walmsley**, *University of Leeds, UK*

"This excellent collection is important because it reflects the voices of practitioners from the field. It includes different artforms and cultural sectors, as well as practitioners in different nations, so its breadth is extensive. It is a timely collection therefore that every student of arts and cultural leadership should acquire." **Jo Caust**, *University of Melbourne, Australia*

Cultural Leadership in Practice

What do cultural leaders really think about the problems they, and the arts and cultural sector, face?

This book brings global leaders in the cultural field into dialogue with academics and experts to offer profound insight and perspectives on the complex issues the cultural sector faces in a rapidly accelerating and destabilising twenty-first century context.

The book engages directly with leaders in the arts and cultural sector, bridging the gap between academia, policy and practice. Each chapter sheds new light on national cultural policy contexts, offering different perspectives on arts subsidy, audiences, the cultural workforce, heritage, artform development and how cultural leadership functions in a fast-changing local, national and international context. Interviews are conducted by academics and experts with significant knowledge and understanding of the arts management and cultural policy field, who ask critical and probing questions. Featuring interviews with an impressively international range of senior figures from the cultural sector, from the Royal Opera House, BMW, Bloomberg and Onassis Foundation and covering countries including the UK, Germany, Chile, Singapore, Greece, USA, Serbia and Ireland, the book gives a truly global overview of cultural leadership from leaders who are open to question, critique and challenge. Each chapter offers a unique and fascinating insight into the mind of a leader in their field, with their experience ranging from huge participatory events featuring tens of thousands of people to the visual arts, opera, the Turner Prize and the #blacklivesmatter movement.

This book will be essential reading for reflective cultural leaders around the world, as well as a useful resource for students and scholars involved with arts and cultural management and policy.

Steven Hadley is an Irish Research Council Government of Ireland Fellow at Trinity College Dublin, Ireland, and a Visiting Lecturer at Leuphana University of Lüneburg, Germany. Steven also sits on the Steering Committee of the Cultural Research Network, the Editorial Board of *Arts and the Market* and is Policy & Reviews Editor for *Cultural Trends*.

Discovering the Creative Industries

Series Editor: Ruth Rentschler

The creative and cultural industries account for a significant share of the global economy. Gaining and maintaining employment and work in this sector is a challenge and chances of success are enhanced by ongoing professional development.

This series provides a range of relatively short, student-centred books which blend industry and educational expertise with cultural sector practice. Books in the series provide applied introductions to the core elements of the creative industries. In sum, the series provides essential reading for those studying to enter the creative industries as well as those seeking to enhance their career via executive education.

For more information about this series, please visit: www.routledge.com/Discovering-the-Creative-Industries/book-series/DCI

Cultural Leadership in Practice

Beyond Arts Management and Cultural Policy

Edited by Steven Hadley

LONDON AND NEW YORK

Cover image credit: isaxar / Getty Images ©

First published 2024
by Routledge
4 Park Square, Milton Park, Abingdon, Oxon OX14 4RN

and by Routledge
605 Third Avenue, New York, NY 10158

Routledge is an imprint of the Taylor & Francis Group, an informa business

British Library Cataloguing-in-Publication Data
A catalogue record for this book is available from the British Library

Library of Congress Cataloging-in-Publication Data
Names: Hadley, Steven, editor.
Title: Cultural leadership in practice : beyond arts management and cultural
policy / edited by Steven Hadley.
Description: 1 edition. | New York, NY : Routledge, 2024. |
Series: Discovering the creative industries |
Includes bibliographical references and index.
Subjects: LCSH: Cultural industries–Management. | Leadership. |
Creative ability. | Information technology–Social aspects. |
Culture and globalization.
Classification: LCC HD9999.C9472 .C845 2024 (print) |
LCC HD9999.C9472 (ebook) | DDC 338.4/77–dc23/eng/20231130
LC record available at https://lccn.loc.gov/2023042270
LC ebook record available at https://lccn.loc.gov/2023042271

ISBN: 9781032487731 (hbk)
ISBN: 9781032487724 (pbk)
ISBN: 9781003390725 (ebk)

DOI: 10.4324/9781003390725

Typeset in Calvert
by Newgen Publishing UK

For Francess, Aoife and Oscar.
First and Last and Always x

Contents

Contents

Contributors

Roaa Ali PhD is a Lecturer in Cultural Sociology at Birmingham City University and an Honorary Research Fellow at the University of Manchester, UK. Roaa is an interdisciplinary researcher focusing on race and diversity in the Creative and Cultural Industries (CCIs). She writes extensively on issues of diversity, inequality, and the politics of cultural production in the cultural sector. Her most recent publications include 'the trouble with diversity: the cultural sector and ethnic inequality' (*Cultural Sociology*) and a monograph titled *Contemporary Arab American Drama: Cultural politics of Otherness* (forthcoming with Routledge).

David Andersson is on the Arts & Culture Team at Bloomberg Associates, the *pro bono* municipal consulting arm of Bloomberg Philanthropies, based in New York City, USA. In this role, he advises cities around the world in their efforts to support their local creative sectors. He also manages Bloomberg Philanthropies' Asphalt Art Initiative and is an adviser to the World Cities Culture Forum. He is a graduate of Harvard University and a practicing visual artist.

Jennifer L. Campbell (University of Kentucky, USA) is a music theorist/historian whose interdisciplinary research explores connections between music, dance, politics, and cultural identity. Her dissertation, "Shaping Solidarity: Music, Diplomacy, and Inter-American Relations, 1936–1946" (2010) and article on the Office of Inter-American Affairs Music Committee (OIAA) in *Diplomatic History* (2012) offer seminal insight into the formalization of American musical diplomacy during the late 1930s and early 1940s.

Beatriz Garcia PhD is Senior Research Fellow in International Cultural Policy and Mega-Events at the University of Liverpool and Associate Director at the Centre for Cultural Value, United Kingdom. Beatriz has researched the rhetoric, impact and long-term legacy of culture-led regeneration interventions since 1999, conducting fieldwork on the cultural dimension of every edition of the Olympic Games since Sydney 2000. She is the author of *The Olympics: The Basics* and *The Olympic Games and Cultural Policy* (both with Routledge, 2012).

Steven Hadley is an Irish Research Council Government of Ireland Fellow at Trinity College Dublin (Ireland) and a Visiting Lecturer at Leuphana University of Lüneburg (Germany). An academic, consultant and researcher working internationally in arts management, cultural policy and audience engagement, Steven sits on the Steering Committee of the Cultural Research Network, the Editorial Board of *Arts and the Market* and is Policy & Reviews Editor for *Cultural Trends*. His recent published work has focussed on cultural democracy and inequality. His monograph, *Audience Development and Cultural Policy*, is published by Palgrave MacMillan.

Višnja Kisić PhD is Assistant Professor at TIMS Faculty Novi Sad, Serbia, lecturer at UNESCO Chair MA in Cultural Policy and Management Belgrade, and visiting professor at universities UIR Beijing, Lyon2 and Hassan II Casablanca. In her research, teaching, practice and activism she explores entanglements between heritage, social conflicts, cultural politics and more-than-human actors.

Olga Kolokytha PhD is the Director of the MA in Music Management and the MA in Music for Applied Media at the University for Continuing Education Krems, Austria. She is currently Senior Research Fellow at the University of Vienna where she was also lead researcher at the Horizon2020 project CICERONE (project co-ordinators University of Amsterdam), researching the cultural and creative sectors in Europe.

Leticia Labaronne PhD is a tenured Full Professor and the Head of the Center for Arts Management at the Zurich University of Applied Sciences, Switzerland. Before joining academia, Labaronne worked in the performing arts for over ten years. Labaronne serves on the boards of several journals and international associations.

Michelle Loh is Lecturer with School of Creative Industries, University of the Arts Singapore. She is a bilingual arts manager and researcher in arts management, cultural policy, diversity, audiences, music and the traditional arts. Her recent publications include 'Superdiversity and Cultural Policies in Post-Pandemic Singapore' in ENCATC Cultural Policy Tracker (2022), 'Language: Audiences for Singapore's Poetry Festival' in Routledge Companion to Audiences and the Performing Arts (2022) and Traditional Chinese Music in Contemporary Singapore (2020).

Jane Morrow is a visual art curator, writer, researcher, educator and advocate based in Belfast. Her practice-led PhD at Ulster University focuses on the precarity of artists' studios and workspaces. Jane's independent projects support artists, whilst her numerous jobs support organisations to resource, nurture, and profile artists.

Maria O'Brien is a lecturer in the School of Arts, English & Languages at Queen's University Belfast. Her areas of interest include film and digital games industry policy, with a particular focus on the role of tax credits within the European Union. She is a board member of Imirt, the Irish games representative body.

Tomás Peters is a cultural sociologist based in Santiago, Chile. He holds a PhD in Cultural Studies from Birkbeck, University of London. His main areas of research include sociology of art, Latin American studies and cultural policy. He currently is an assistant professor at the Faculty of Communications and Image of the Universidad de Chile.

Jill Schinberg is Associate Professor of Arts Administration University of Kentucky USA. An 'expat' from a 25-year career in arts administration, she has worked for music promoters, agents, international festivals, and performing arts centres in various capacities. Her consulting work with arts organizations, venues and dance companies led to her research in arts management consulting, arts programming, and equity issues.

Goran Tomka is a researcher and lecturer in the field of audience studies, cultural diversity and cultural policy. He is associate professor at the TIMS Faculty from Novi Sad, and UNESCO Chair in cultural policy and management from Belgrade, Serbia. He holds a doctoral degree in culture and media studies.

Acknowledgements

The purpose of this book is to bridge the gap between academic and practitioner knowledge in the arts and cultural sector. Giving academics and senior industry figures the platform to have intelligent, detailed and reflective conversations on contemporary, and often difficult, topics has been a revealing process. Both the subjects and the authors of each chapter brought significant levels of expertise, insight and knowledge to the process of each conversation and I would like to thank them all individually for their curiosity, tenacity and patience.

Chapters 2 to 14 in this book are gathered from the 'In Conversation' series published in *Cultural Trends*, a peer-reviewed international journal (AHCI and SSCI) which provides in-depth analysis of the cultural sector and cultural policy. This book would therefore not have been possible without the support and encouragement of Eleonora Belfiore and Hye-Kyung Lee. As Editors of *Cultural Trends*, they permitted me to introduce the 'In Conversation' format to the journal and encouraged me to develop the scope and range of content. Huge thanks to them for their permission to reprint the articles presented here, and for their support in nurturing and developing the format.

Sincere thanks also to artist Nina Cooke John and the city of Newark, New Jersey, for permission to use images of the Harriet Tubman monument, "Shadow of a Face", which was unveiled on 9 March 2023.

Cultural Leadership in Practice

Steven Hadley

Chapter 1

Cultural leadership is the new black. And, quite possibly, the old black. Though there are rarely new black cultural leaders. We'll get to that later.

Leadership in general – and cultural leadership in particular – are globally important fields of enquiry and interest. In the wake of #blacklivesmatter, #MeToo and COVID-19, questions have arisen as to how cultural leaders are responding to the issues and concerns of both the sector and society at large. All too often, leadership is taught and discussed in the abstract – as a set of theories, behaviours and competences. Uniquely, this book looks behind the veil and gives privileged access to the minds, experiences and often challenging beliefs of those in positions of power in the global cultural sector.

Cultural leadership manifests in a range of models, modes and discourses. Recent scholarship by, for example, Caust (2018) on *Arts Leadership in Contemporary Contexts* and Byrnes and Brkić (2019) in *The Routledge Companion to Arts Management* testifies to the variety of approaches to the topic. Frequently at issue is the important distinction between management and leadership.[1] Peter Drucker (1999, 1) for instance, argues (in his entirely unreferenced article in *The Harvard Business Review*), that "History's great achievers – A Napoleon, a daVinci, a Mozart – have always managed themselves". The fact that Drucker feels no obligation to substantiate this claim with empirical evidence

DOI: 10.4324/9781003390725-1

might tell us more about the academic literature on leadership than it does about leadership per se.

Recent work by Nisbett and Walmsley (2016) and Nisbett, Walmsley and McDowell (forthcoming 2024) on both charismatic and abusive leadership raises another interesting question with particular resonance in the cultural sector: whether leadership and moral leadership are synonymous. Capricious leaders are both effective and commonplace. As Kellerman (2005, 2) argues, "leadership is not a moral concept, and it is high time we acknowledged that fact … To assume that all good leaders are good people is to be wilfully blind to the reality of the human condition". Flawed leadership is commonplace, and the superhuman literature on leadership which frequently emanates from the management field does little to ameliorate this. Too frequently, the word 'leader' is associated with human qualities above and beyond any recognised norm. In this sense, it sets people up for failure. Indeed, the hyperbolic language of leadership – of 'peak performance' (Stulberg and Magness 2017), 'transformational leadership at the world class level' (Bass and Avoloio 1987), 'visionary leadership' (Dilts, 1996) – suggests that leadership cannot be commonplace. We should also be mindful that much of the initial canon on business leadership (see e.g., Bennis 2005) was written by people with direct experience of war.

But what is cultural leadership? The 'Culture and Creativity' website (funded within the framework of an EU Programme) describes cultural leadership as follows:

> Cultural leadership is the act of leading the cultural sector. Like culture itself, it comes from many different people and can be practised in many different ways. It concerns senior managers and directors in subsidised cultural institutions; public officials developing and implementing policy for the cultural sector; and a huge range of producers, innovators and entrepreneurs in small companies, production houses and teams. In the cultural world, nobody has a monopoly on leadership.

If, as John Adams had it, there are two types of education – one that should teach us how to make a living, and the other how to live – then cultural leadership occupies a strange middle-ground, where leaders working in arts and culture often do both. The 'Culture and Creativity' programme makes an important distinction regarding the duality of cultural sector leadership. On one hand, there is cultural leadership as arts management – financial viability, strategic and business planning, HR and governance – the internal functionality of cultural sector management. Hewison and Holden's (2011) *The Cultural Leadership Handbook* is, for example, entirely dedicated to this task. However, cultural leadership also encompasses the idea of making, developing and producing culture which will manifest in forms of social value which enrich and enhance the civic sphere.

Key to the task of developing the public realm are the variegated issues of diversity and representation. For several decades now, the subsidised arts sector has failed to successfully address structural concerns around gender, class, race and diversity more broadly. The individuals who occupy leadership positions in the publicly funded arts and cultural sector are not fully reflective of the demographic diversity of the UK. As the Arts Council England-commissioned review of equality and diversity within the arts and cultural sector in England up to 2013 states:

> It is also vital that the arts and cultural workforce becomes more representative of the society it serves. In particular, we need to do more to ensure that entry routes into employment, and opportunities for people to further their careers, are fairer and more accessible to all. This is as true for the leadership and governance of the sector as it is for those entering the workforce.
>
> (Consilium 2014, 1)

The report notes further that, "Establishing a clear baseline of Black and minority ethnic leadership is also complicated by the lack of a clear definition of what constitutes leadership in the sector" (ibid., 39). Arts Council England commissioned Consilium (2018, 71) to update the previous evidence. The follow-up report noted that, "many arts organisations don't have the expertise or resources needed to design and implement effective approaches to meet obligations outlined in the Equality Act 2010". The recent

Creative Industries Policy and Evidence Centre's (2021) report *Social Mobility in the Cultural Economy* further details the strata of inequality in the UK creative industries across class, gender, race, disabilities, skills and place.

Hadley, Heidelberg and Belfiore (2022, 260) argue that many of the access, diversity and inclusion initiatives endogenous to the UK and US cultural sectors are manifestations of a "performative liberal wokeness" and, as such, are "self-conscious symbolic public acts which largely fail to make a difference in the world" (ibid.). *Arts Professional* (2023a) has recently discussed the dismay at high turnover in diversity leaders, asking why it is that real and lasting progress on equity, diversity and inclusion (EDI) in the cultural sector remains such an elusive goal. Meanwhile, the proportion of staff at Arts Council England (ACE) from Black, Asian, and ethnically diverse backgrounds has fallen for the second year according to Arts Council England's (2023) Annual Report of 2022/23.

WHY LEADERSHIP?

The stereotypical components of 'a leadership education' can be found in works such as *teach yourself leadership* (Doherty and Thompson 2007) which outline many of the key debates (are leaders born or made?) and models (styles and building blocks of leadership, leading teams, overcoming obstacles – 'the hero's journey' – and carrying other people with you, amongst others). The need to continually reinvent such models and narratives can result in extremes such as Heifetz and Linsky's (2002) *Leadership on the Line: Staying Alive through the Dangers of Leading*. To be fair to Heifetz and Linsky, they bring a wealth of experience to bear in a book that is nuanced and humane, but the assumed need for Harvard Business Review Press to suggest such a title (with accompanying lurid yellow and red cover) speaks as much to publishing industry bottom lines as it does a developing field of academic inquiry.

Leadership (and management more broadly) is now such an extensive and developed field of academic enquiry that there are innumerable subsets: leadership and team working, behavioural analysis, emotional intelligence, vision-mission-values, change management, leadership types and styles, situational leadership, coaching, abusive leadership, relational leadership, action centred leadership, motivation, self-assessment, XY theory, funky business, adaptability, resilience, attitudes to risk, big hairy audacious goals, exemplary leadership, managing oneself, feedback loops, competencies and capabilities, emerging models, co-leadership, charismatic leaders, heroic leadership, distributed leadership ... The conceptual neophilia is endless.

Of course, if 'leadership' is anything, it is an industry. There are now so many books published about leadership (at the time of writing Google returns 2,660,000,000 results on the search term 'leadership books') that – whether one aspires to be the next Steve Jobs, Winston Churchill, Ernest Shackleton, Alex Ferguson or any other white man with substance abuse and anger management issues – a summary of the field is a huge task. The result of the need for the continuous production of books on leadership is the inevitability of contradiction. In the same way that many proverbs have an equal and exact opposite ('Good things come to those who wait' – 'Time and tide wait for no man'), the incessant need for yet more books on leadership means that to be a leader you must both stand bravely alone and bring your team with you, follow strategy and rules that you simultaneously disregard, consolidate your power whilst leading beyond authority and be unique whilst being admired by all. Leadership – like fashion – is now so heterogenous as to be all things to all people.

Leadership, then, is a nebulous concept. As a discourse, it frequently operates along what we might call 'the nature/nurture axis'. Dependent upon whether you are trying to sell books, recruit students, offer consultancy services or write the introduction to a collected volume of academic articles, your take on 'leadership' will differ depending on your standpoint. If you're selling teaching, then leadership is something that can be taught. If your target is the airport paperback book market, then leadership can be bought.

If the field of leadership studies has a unifying theme, it might be the underlying sense that it panders to its audience. Leadership – whether it be a year-long leadership development programme enabling you to take 'the next step' or sweeping generalisations on cultural history like Drucker's – wants to help make you, the individual, better. In this way, leadership can become a vessel for all and any unresolvable organisational problems and issues. Unable to be resolved at an operational or administrative level, these problems float to the top of the organisation to be addressed by the magical realism of leadership. In this managerial approach, 'leadership' both resolves and sustains structural issues within the sector that cannot be solved by leadership (alone). There is then a tendency to see leadership as the solution to almost any kind of organisational or societal problem (Alvesson and Spicer, 2011, 1). Moreover, most literature on the term is firmly – and problematically – grounded in white, western traditions of thought (Kolsteeg and Zierold, 2019).

The need for ceaseless reinvention of leadership in the arts is also noticeable, although my purpose here is not to provide a comprehensive overview of leadership in the cultural sector, an arena whose development continues apace.[2] Recent publications have included Morgen Witzel's (2022) *Post-Pandemic Leadership*, *Co-Leadership in the Arts and Culture* by Wendy Reid and Hilde Fjellværst (2023) and the second edition of Kenneth Foster's (2023) *Arts and Cultural Leadership: Creating Sustainable Arts Organizations*. These books – and many others – promise that we can learn how to rethink and reimagine being a leader and chart a course towards a new vision of leadership. But what does this tsunami ('Everest' would probably be a more appropriate metaphor …) of leadership advice, hacks, life stories and management guides tell us about our current age? Why so much focus on leadership, in the cultural sector as elsewhere? What is the context, condition, malaise, subconscious lack, managerial urge or liminal desire that brought forth this still burgeoning field of endeavour in the arts and cultural sector? And what if it isn't 'leadership' that's the problem?

In a now (in)famous article on the George Bush era in the US, *The New York Times* journalist Ron Suskind (2004) quoted a presidential aide as describing him and his peers as living in a "reality-based community". The comments (quoted in full below) articulate a view that latterly came to define 'post-truth politics':

> The aide said that guys like me were "in what we call the reality-based community," which he defined as people who

"believe that solutions emerge from your judicious study of discernible reality."

I nodded and murmured something about enlightenment principles and empiricism. He cut me off. "That's not the way the world really works anymore," he continued. "We're an empire now, and when we act, we create our own reality. And while you're studying that reality – judiciously, as you will – we'll act again, creating other new realities, which you can study too, and that's how things will sort out. We're history's actors .... and you, all of you, will be left to just study what we do."

Such sentiments are a precursor to our contemporary existential malaise. A malaise for which cultural leadership is often posited as a response, solution or balm.

Of course, scholars of cultural policy are aware that the field operates around a number of largely irresolvable binaries, which function to create a form of schizophrenia or cognitive dissonance in the sector, where perspectives are largely a function of subjective experience combined with an understanding/ appreciation of a particular artform. These binaries keep policymakers busy, cultural policy academics in line for promotion and those working in the arts sector in a constant state of emotional distress, hand-wringing and intermittent (though increasingly scarce) delight. Matarasso and Landry identified this condition in 1999 with their short work, *Balancing act: twenty-one strategic dilemmas in cultural policy*.

To suggest that leadership is the solution to these concerns is at best disingenuous. Where such issues are fundamentally ideological – and structural within the national policy framework – they can rarely, if ever, be solved by managerial or leadership approaches. Yet much of the rhetoric and discourse of 'leadership' repeatedly focuses on the broadly defined terms of an avowedly neoliberal managerialism: entrepreneurialism, resilience, adaptability and innovation. The ideas of capitalism have infused into political, social and cultural institutions at the national, state and individual level (see e.g., Harvey, 2007). Bourdieu (1999a) argued that – as a form of national governance – neoliberalism had become a *doxa*, an unquestioned and simply accepted worldview. By placing an overtly quantitative framing on social life (Bourdieu, 1999b), neoliberalism encouraged production, competition and profit above (often pressing) social issues. At the individual-level, neoliberalism promotes the idea that all actions are the result of rationality, individuality and self-interest (Navarro, 2007). Indeed, neoliberalism's individualistic focus has resulted in concepts such as 'the public good' and 'the civic realm' being discarded as unnecessary components of a moribund welfare state (Pendenza and Lamattina, 2019). Inequalities have resultingly come to be blamed on individuals – stigmatised within specific social strata – rather than on structural and intersectional factors (McKenzie, 2013).

A manufactured disenchantment with the role of community (and concomitantly the civic and the public) and an enhanced focus at the level of the individual, necessitates the promotion of the public-facing value of individual growth and self-development. This ideological framing deliberately obfuscates recognition of the fact that neoliberalism benefits only a very few (Harvey, 2007) with the majority of people misrecognising the economics and politics of neoliberalism as being in their interests (even when any given policy is to the denigration of millions of their fellow citizens[3]). Such a worldview also makes it easier to justify the thought that some people are more deserving of reward than others. As leaders who self-develop, self-police, self-govern and emotionally self-regulate, we become autonomous managers of our own affairs and solely responsible for our own transformation. In this context, 'resilience' means it's your fault if you fail.

WHY CULTURAL LEADERSHIP IN PRACTICE?

To address the above concerns, this book brings global leaders in the cultural field into dialogue with academics and experts to offer profound insight and perspectives on the complex issues the cultural sector faces in a rapidly accelerating and destabilising twenty-first century context. The book engages directly with leaders in the arts and cultural sector, bridging the gap between academia, policy and practice to ask what cultural leaders really think about the problems they, and the arts and cultural sector, face. Individual chapters shed new light on national cultural policy contexts, arts subsidy, audiences, the cultural workforce, heritage, artform development and how cultural leadership functions in a fast-changing local, national and international context. Each 'in conversation' is conducted by an academic or professional with significant knowledge and understanding of the arts management and cultural policy field, who asks critical and probing questions. Equally, each interviewee is a leader in their field with sufficient experience and standing such that they bring a depth of understanding and experience to their insights and perspectives on the sector. Featuring interviews with an international range of senior figures from the cultural sector, from the Royal Opera House, BMW, Bloomberg, International Olympic Committee, Onassis Foundation and UNESCO, and covering countries including the UK, Germany, Greece, Chile, France, Singapore, USA, Serbia and Ireland, the book gives a truly global overview of cultural leadership from leaders who are open to question, critique and challenge. Each chapter offers a unique and fascinating insight into the mind of a leader in their field, with their experience ranging from huge participatory events featuring tens of thousands of people to the visual arts, opera, museums, the Turner Prize and the #blacklivesmatter movement.

Too often there is a distance and discrepancy between the fields of arts management and cultural policy. What is taught on Arts Management MAs is not always a genuine or useful reflection of the reality in the sector. With that in mind, this collection brings together a diverse range of interviews to analyse leadership as a concept with many functions, applications and discourses. It considers artists, administrators, funders, politicians and policymakers equally, as leaders with both opportunities and constraints within their horizon of the possible. As such, *Cultural Leadership in Practice* aims to be a source of reflection, inspiration and insight for both cultural management and leadership scholars and for cultural managers themselves.

The chapters in *Cultural Leadership in Practice* are not presented in any particular order, and nor are they structured thematically. Deliberately, the book is designed to be a resource which does not require reading in a linear fashion and which offers a detailed and varied source of reflection and inspiration. Each 'in conversation' is unique, and yet each offers such a breadth of insight and experience as to have universal application. In such a way, each conversation – though defined by name, role, institution and nationality – *resists* categorisation.

CONCLUSION

Cultural leadership became a key concept in cultural policy (and subsequently across a range of funding and training initiatives) in the UK during the early 2000s. In 2004, at the inception of the Clore Leadership Programme, Robert Hewison published an article in the *International Journal of Cultural Policy* titled, 'The Crisis of Cultural Leadership in Britain' (2004). The crisis which Hewison (and Clore) sought to address was characterised by low morale produced by government underfunding, low pay, loss of status, ill-defined career paths and over-regulation. Hewison questioned whether the crisis of cultural leadership pointed to the emergence of new forms of leadership which embraced non-market driven values. Over the course of the past two decades cultural leadership has attracted significant public and private investment. It remains a major focus for development programmes, despite significant changes in sectoral needs and an increasingly fast-paced and worrying shift in the broader geo-political context.

The polymorphous nature of 'leadership' as a topic of research means that it remains eminently amenable to new sector discourses – whether around sustainability, resilience and progress or wellbeing and care. The endless crises of the arts sector are fertile ground for aspiring academics and lucrative territory for consultants. It is dispiriting yet necessary to state that if the sums spent on consultancy and cultural leadership programmes were as effective (indeed, transformational) as they claim to be, then labour conditions in the sector would surely have been considerably improved. That this is not the case raises an obvious question. Perhaps provocations like that of Adele Patrick (2019) on feminist leadership or Jenny Williams' (2010) writing on Black leadership and the white gaze can offer new and more tangibly progressive routes out of the current impasse.

As Price (2017, 13) succinctly states, "The discourse of cultural leadership which has developed over the last decade and a half continues to frame understanding among cultural professionals of what the concept is and can be." An observer

Steven Hadley

might then counter-intuitively ask, does the discourse and industry of cultural leadership allow for such things as modesty and reticence? The demand placed on actors in the field to be active participants in the narrative drama swirling around them seemingly disallows the idea that being a follower has as much utility value – is as much of a vocation – as being a leader. Perhaps we are now seeing the convergence of neoliberal austerity and the structural issues specific to the arts reaching a denouement as an 'exodus' of artistic directors hits the sector (Arts Professional, 2023b).

As a final word of introduction, it is worth noting that the conversations gathered in this volume took place over a period of time which witnessed not only the effects of COVID-19 on the cultural sector, but also the #blacklivesmatter movement and the inevitable range of international responses, compromises and contradictions that inflected the varying responses of governments and funders internationally. Much (perhaps too much) has already been written on the impact of COVID-19 on the cultural sector. As a result, the process of publication of this volume has involved little which was linear or predictable. For all involved this has been difficult but ultimately beneficial. Pauses in the process have allowed each author to reflect on where they placed emphasis in their questioning, and in one or two instances to revisit and augment the conversations with additional questions and new narrative perspectives. Much like cultural leadership itself, this volume is then the result of an adaptive and reflective process which has perpetually shifted to accommodate and respond to new contexts and challenges.

Notes

1   For an excellent discussion of this topic, see Zaleznik (2005).
2   For an overview of cultural sector initiatives see e.g., Shift Culture (2021) *CULTURAL LEADERSHIP Annotated bibliography* and the Creative Choices (2010) *A Cultural Leadership Reader.*
3   See for example Grogan and Park's (2017) discussion of confusion over Medicaid policies under Trump.

References

Alvesson, M. and Spicer, A. (eds). (2011) *Metaphors We Lead by: Understanding Leadership in the Real World.* London and New York: Routledge.

Arts Council England (2023) *Annual Report and Accounts for the Year Ended 31st March 2023*. Accessed from www.artscouncil.org.uk/our-organisation/annual-reports/arts-council-england-grant-aid-and-lottery-distribution-annual-report-and-accounts-202223.

Arts Professional (2023a) *Dismay at High Turnover in Diversity Leaders*. Accessed from www.artsprofessional.co.uk/magazine/news-comment/dismay-high-turnover-diversity-leaders.

Arts Professional (2023b) *Exodus of Artistic Directors 'Symptom of Sector Neglect'*. Accessed from www.artsprofessional.co.uk/news/exodus-artistic-directors-symptom-sector-neglect.

Bass, B. and Avoloio, B. (1987) 'Biography and Assessment of Transformational Leadership at the World Class Level', *Journal of Management*, 13(1), 7–19.

Bennis, W.G. (2005) 'The Seven Ages of the Leader' in *Harvard Business Review: The Mind of the Leader*, Boston: Harvard Business School Press, pp.15–35.

Bourdieu, P. (1999a) 'Neo-Liberalism, the Utopia (Becoming a Reality) of Unlimited Exploitation' in *Acts of Resistance: Against the Tyranny of the Market*. New York: The New Press, pp. 94–105.

Bourdieu, P. (1999b) 'The "Myth" of Globalization and the Welfare State' in *Acts of Resistance: Against the Tyranny of the Market*. New York: The New Press, pp. 29–45.

Byrnes, W. and Brkić, A. (2019) *The Routledge Companion to Arts Management*. London: Routledge.

Caust, J. (2018) *Arts Leadership in Contemporary Contexts*. London: Routledge.

Consilium (2014) *Equality and Diversity within the Arts and Cultural Sector in England: Evidence and Literature Review*. London: Arts Council England.

Consilium (2018) *Equality and Diversity within the Arts and Cultural Sector in England, 2013–16: Evidence Review*. London: Arts Council England.

Creative Choices (Sue Kay and Katie Venner eds) (2010) *A Cultural Leadership Reader*. Accessed from https://ntcreativearts.com/wp-content/uploads/2014/06/a_cultural_leadership_reader_201007051349381.pdf.

Creative Industries Policy and Evidence Centre (2021) *Social Mobility in the Creative Economy: Rebuilding and Levelling up?*. Accessed from https://pec.ac.uk/research-reports/social-mobility-in-the-creative-economy-rebuilding-and-levelling-up.

Culture and Creativity www.culturepartnership.eu/en/article/what-is-cultural-leadership.

Dilts, R.B. (1996) *Visionary Leadership Skills: Creating a World to Which People Want to Belong*. California: Meta Publications.

Doherty, C. and Thompson, J. (2007) *Teach Yourself Leadership*. London: Hodder Education.

Drucker, P. (1999) 'Managing Oneself'. *Harvard Business Review*, 77(2), 65.

Foster, K. (2023) *Arts and Cultural Leadership Creating Sustainable Arts Organizations*, 2nd edition. London: Routledge.

Grogan, C.M. and Park S.E. (2017) 'The Politics of Medicaid: Most Americans Are Connected to the Program, Support Its Expansion, and Do Not View It as Stigmatizing'. *Milbank Q*, 95(4), 749–782.

Hadley, S., Heidelberg, Brea and Belfiore, Eleonora (2022) 'Reflexivity and the Perpetuation of Inequality in the Cultural Sector: Half Awake in a Fake Empire?', *Journal for Cultural Research*, 26(3–4), 244–265.

Harvey, D. (2007) *A Brief History of Neoliberalism*. Oxford: Oxford University Press.

Heifetz, R.A. and Linsky, M. (2002) *Leadership on the Line: Staying Alive through the Dangers of Leading*. Boston: HBS Publishing.

Hewison, R. (2004) 'The Crisis of Cultural Leadership in Britain'. *International Journal of Cultural Policy*, 10, 57–166.

Hewison, R. and Holden, J. (2011) *The Cultural Leadership Handbook: How to Run a Creative Organization*. Farnham: Gower.

Kellerman, B. (2005) 'Leadership – Warts and All' in *Harvard Business Review The Mind of the Leader*. Boston: Harvard Business School Press, pp.1–13.

Kolsteeg, J. and Zierold, Martin (2019) 'Mapping the Meanings of Cultural Leadership: The Use of the Term in the Field of Arts Management'. *Arts Management Quarterly*, 6–11.

Matarasso, F. and Landry, C. (1999) *Balancing Act: Twenty-One Strategic Dilemmas in Cultural Policy*. Belgium: Council of Europe.

McKenzie, L. (2013) 'The Stigmatised and De-valued Working Class: The State of a Council Estate'. In: Atkinson, W., Roberts, S., Savage, M. (eds) *Class Inequality in Austerity Britain*. London: Palgrave Macmillan, pp. 128–144.

Navarro, V. (2007) 'Neoliberalism as a Class Ideology; Or, the Political Causes of the Growth of Inequalities'. *International Journal of Health Services*, 37(1), 47–62.

Nisbett, M. and Walmsley, B. (2016) 'The Romanticization of Charismatic Leadership in the Arts'. *The Journal of Arts Management, Law, and Society*, 46(1), 2–12.

Nisbett, M. and Walmsley, B. and McDowell, E. (forthcoming 2024) 'Abusive Leadership in the Arts and the Crisis of Accountability' in *Routledge Companion to Arts Governance, Leadership and Philanthropy*. London: Routledge.

Patrick, A. (2019) *Feminist Leadership: How Naming and Claiming the F Word Can Lead the Cultural Sector Out of Equalities 'Stuckness'*. Provocation Paper, Clore Leadership Fellowship (2018/2019). Accessed from http://womenslibrary.org.uk/moving-mountains/.

Pendenza, M. and Lamattina, V. (2019) 'Rethinking Self-Responsibility: An Alternative Vision to the Neoliberal Concept of Freedom', *American Behavioral Scientist*, 63(1), 100–115.

Price, J. (2017) 'The Construction of Cultural Leadership'. *ENCATC Journal of Cultural Management & Policy*, 7(1). [Online].

Reid, W. and Fjellværst, H. (2023) *Co-Leadership in the Arts and Culture*. London: Routledge.

Shift Culture (2021) CULTURAL LEADERSHIP Annotated bibliography. Accessed from https://cultureactioneurope.org/files/2021/10/SHIFT_Annotated-Bibliographie_Cultural-Leadership.pdf.

Stulberg, B. and Magness, S. (2017) *Peak Performance: Elevate Your Game, Avoid Burnout, and Thrive with the New Science of Success*. Emmaus: Rodale Press Inc.

Suskind, R. (2004) 'Faith, Certainty and the Presidency of George W. Bush'. *The New York Times*. Accessed from www.nytimes.com/2004/10/17/magazine/faith-certainty-and-the-presidency-of-george-w-bush.html.

Williams, J. (2010) 'Black Leadership and the White Gaze' in Creative Choices, *A Cultural Leadership Reader* (Sue Kay and Katie Venner Eds). Accessed from https://ntcreativearts.com/wp-content/uploads/2014/06/a_cultural_leadership_reader_201007051349381.pdf.

Witzel, M. (ed.) (2022) *Post-Pandemic Leadership Exploring Solutions to a Crisis*. London: Routledge.

Zaleznik, A. (2005) 'Managers and Leaders: Are They Different?' in *Harvard Business Review on The Mind of the Leader*, Harvard: Harvard Business School Press, pp. 73–96.

Public Monuments and Cultural Leadership

fayemi shakur, Director of Arts & Cultural Affairs, City of Newark, New Jersey: In Conversation (USA)

David Andersson

Chapter 2

fayemi shakur is the Director of Arts and Cultural Affairs for the City of Newark, New Jersey, in the United States. A long-time artist, arts administrator, and Newark resident, fayemi stepped

DOI: 10.4324/9781003390725-2

into this role in January 2020, just before the COVID-19 pandemic destabilized the creative sector internationally. In the summer of 2020, following calls for social justice across the globe, Newark joined many other cities in removing monuments depicting individuals associated with racial injustice. After removing a prominent statue of Christopher Columbus in a downtown park, the City commissioned a new monument to replace it that will honor abolitionist Harriet Tubman, who escaped slavery and helped many others do the same through the Underground Railroad, which passed through many sites in New Jersey and specifically in Newark. Designed by New Jersey-based artist and architect Nina Cooke John, the new monument was installed in March 2023 and is intended to serve as a gathering space for community events, learning, and reflection. In the fall of 2020, the City of Newark engaged the Arts & Culture Team at Bloomberg Associates, the pro bono municipal consulting arm of Bloomberg Philanthropies, to develop a commissioning process for this major new piece of public art and provide ongoing guidance as the project developed.

This conversation took place on 26 January 2022, and the text has been adapted from the original version that aired on Bloomberg Philanthropies' *Follow the Data* podcast on 25 February 2022.[1]

DAVID: There's a lot to unpack about how you got to this moment, and we will, but I want to start with the new Harriet Tubman monument itself. Tell us a little about this monument that's to come and the amazing design created by artist and architect, Nina Cooke John.[2]

FAYEMI: Nina Cooke John's proposal took our selection committee by surprise, pleasantly. It was unique in that it was designed to be a gathering space, someplace that's not just a statue, but a place where community can come to as a site of meditation, or protest, or community programming. She was very thoughtful in how she thought about not just the design, but about different uses of the space (Figure 2.1).

The monument is circulatory, it almost looks like a circulatory ramp, and it has a larger-than-life portrait of Harriet's Tubman's face on the side that's made of a concrete mosaic. It also has a metal sculpture outlining Harriet's figure, and at the top it will be

Figure 2.1 View from street. (Rendering)

Source: https://www.cookejohn.com/harriet-tubman-monument

illuminated similar to the north star. The learning wall will include audio stories that will be collected from the community. Working in partnership with Audible, we're putting together content that will elaborate on the history of the Underground Railroad. And it will also be surrounded by concrete benches, so it won't be a space where people will just walk by and look at it, but a space where people can actually sit and reflect and gather (Figure 2.2).

DAVID: This monument is really the first major public art commission by the city of Newark in many decades. How did the city decide that the Underground Railroad was the right subject for a new monument? And what does the subject mean for the Newark community?

FAYEMI: We've been thinking about monuments for a while. In 2019, we had an exhibition in Newark called "A Call to Peace" that was organized by Monument Lab and New Arts Justice at Express Newark.[3] I participated as a co-curator of community engagement for that exhibition. We really started to look at the monuments in

David Andersson

Figure 2.2 View from park. (Rendering)
Source: https://www.cookejohn.com/harriet-tubman-monument

our city that were prominently from a Confederate era.[4] People didn't really know the history of some of those monuments.

One of the questions that was posed for residents to consider was: what would be a timely monument for Newark? We had a lab, a little shipping container in the Military Park, where residents and visitors could come, and we'd talk with them, and they could complete a worksheet where they could either draw a monument or a statue or write ideas for what they thought they'd like to see in the city. Many of those proposals specifically named Harriet Tubman as a figure they'd like to see honored in the city of Newark. So, when the Mayor decided we would remove the Christopher Columbus statue from the park, Harriet Tubman was the first name to come to mind, and he said we should put a statue of Harriet Tubman in the park.

DAVID: Let's talk for a moment about the process for getting to this design. To start, you held a national open call for artists, and then you chose five of them and commissioned them to create conceptual designs. What was that process like? And what were the different designs that were proposed?

FAYEMI: It was super exciting to be able to put the call out nationally. Our top five choices that were selected were from Vinnie Bagwell, Jules Arthur, Dread Scott, Abigail DeVille, and Nina Cooke John. All of their submissions were pretty unique, and even when we put out a survey that enabled residents to provide their feedback, there was no clear winner. Some of them were figurative, some of them were traditional statues on a pedestal. I think that Nina's stood out because she really presented a way for us to reimagine what a monument in public art could be.

DAVID: The community feedback element of your selection process was really well thought-through, and it's been a critical part of the project. How did that feedback inform the selection and why was it so important to you to include?

FAYEMI: I'm always taking a look at what's happening nationally when projects like this are done, and we really wanted to avoid some of the challenges and pitfalls of the community feeling like they weren't engaged. And they really want to be. The community wants to be informed and a part of the process. It also helped build some of the excitement. Part of the website that was created included video presentations for each artist to talk about their projects, as well as a short description. It wasn't a voting process, it was more like a comment survey. So people could say, "I really like Vinnie's; Vinnie is my favorite artist," or "Dread Scott's looks pretty unique, I'd love to see something like that." That was really helpful to us and was a sigh of relief to the panel of artists, arts experts, historians, and community stakeholders, because there didn't seem to be any conflict there in who we were going to select.

DAVID: An interesting element about how you've structured this commission is that you've paired Nina, the winning artist, with an emerging Newark-based artist, Adebunmi Gbadebo,[5] to support the project as an apprentice. Why was it important to include this apprenticeship structure and what is Adebunmi's role in the project?

FAYEMI: Celebrating our local artists and giving them opportunities to learn is a really important part of our public art program. We often encourage collaboration even with our murals, with maybe an inexperienced artist who hasn't been a part of a larger scale project with someone who's more experienced. That's typically the way we've been working the past couple of years, and it really has a benefit to the entire team that works on the project. Adebunmi is an amazing artist in her own right, but she's never done a public art project before. She primarily works with hair, but also around themes about slavery. She's been tracing her own family's history and has even visited some slave plantations down south, and she had a residency at a clay studio. She's interested in sculpture. So that was just a perfect opportunity for her and for us. Even though Nina is also from New Jersey, we wanted a Newark-based artist to be able to learn from this experience too.

DAVID: The monument is scheduled to be installed later this year, but in the meantime, you have been working on a whole host of community programming where the artistic team will engage directly with Newark residents, including inviting them to actually create art elements that will be incorporated into the physical monument itself. What does the Newark community have to look forward to in the coming months?

FAYEMI: We've had a couple of workshops so far. The first workshops were at Express Newark and the Newark Museum. They are opportunities for residents to create clay tiles that will be part of a mosaic on the actual monument. We're also hosting workshops at the Harriet Tubman Elementary School and also in the city's recreational spaces for youth called Centers for Hope and our senior centers. Those are a couple of the sites we're looking at to have new workshops, where even if you don't have an art background, and you don't think that you're an artist, it's a way for you to be a part of it too.

And then there's the audio stories, where, in partnership with the Newark Public Library and Audible, we'll be capturing interviews from people, reflecting on themes about liberation, courage, and Harriet Tubman's legacy. We wanted to be kind of personal too. I really love the way that Nina is framing the prompts for people to respond to, to reflect on their own personal stories of struggle and what helped them get through difficult times.

It really also just makes me think about art in general, right? And how during this pandemic, I can't think of anyone who hasn't benefited from art. Whether it's a piece of music or a painting, a photograph, or a poem. I think this is a profound contribution that artists give us, to heal and be inspired. So I'm really glad that we have all of these elements for community to engage with.

DAVID: You're exactly right. We're at this time when we've been lacking connection, and so being able to come together, be creative, and participate in this community narrative that's being shaped is special. There aren't that many opportunities to do that.

Let's stay on this subject for a moment. The pandemic and concurrent lockdown changed the way people experienced culture, and in many cases brought in new audiences as people sought new experiences in a challenging time. How can arts organizations and funders harness that new interest and energy moving forward?

FAYEMI: Community engagement and social impact seem to be buzzwords when it comes to measuring and evaluating this work, but supporting individual artists and small to midsize organizations is critical. At the height of the pandemic, I appreciated those who recalled a time when artists helped lift America out of the Great Depression as part of Franklin Roosevelt's New Deal and its Works Progress Administration, which hired more than 10,000 artists to help stimulate economic recovery.[6] Moving forward, we should have more funding in place to continue supporting artists, artistic programming, and cultural institutions through local, state, and federal budgets. We should be committed to this more fully now.

Right as the pandemic was starting, Mayor Baraka launched the City of Newark's first ever municipal arts grant program, called the Creative Catalyst Fund.[7] This financial support was a lifeline for our artists who struggled to find paid work and for smaller cultural organizations that had to close their doors without a safety net. All but two of the applicants to the fund estimated some amount of pandemic-related monetary loss in 2021, and over half of grantees were forced to shift some or all of their in-person programming to a virtual setting. And yet, with City support, 134 artists and organizations received grants in 2021 for programs that served over 250,000 Newark residents and visitors and paid over 1000 additional artists for their work supporting these projects. Our program was only a part of the equation, and there are many learnings to take forward in helping the creative sector in challenging times to survive, adapt, and continue offering enriching experiences to our communities.

DAVID: So, backing up a bit, the new Harriet Tubman monument first came about because, in June 2020, the city removed a Christopher Columbus statue in what was then called Washington Park in downtown Newark. Tell us a little bit about what drove that decision to remove that statue and what that meant to the Newark community.

FAYEMI: Oh, yes. That period of unrest during the George Floyd protests[8] on top of the pandemic was so super intense. Here in the city of Newark, we had about 12,000 people that flooded the streets. I was there with them, and everyone marched with the Mayor at the head, leading everyone to City Hall. The police actually led motorcades alongside the protestors and really gave space for people to express their anger, their justified anger. The Mayor signed an ordinance banning hate groups in the city of Newark and said that he would close the first police precinct, which was the site of the 1967 rebellion here in Newark.[9] We had a lot of dialogue about what it means to abolish white supremacy. It was a challenging time to be in conversation with people, but it was a time, I always say, for a lot of unlearning about racism.

Amid all of that, we also saw monuments being toppled all over the place. The Mayor asked me if I thought we should remove the Christopher Columbus statue in Newark. He was concerned about public safety and whether artists would attempt to topple it and then be hurt in some way. And I said, absolutely, we should remove it. What a profound opportunity. For so long, we have been talking in our own community about the false narrative around Christopher Columbus, and we want our children to learn the right history and we want our children to be able to see representations of themselves in their own history and be proud of that.

The Mayor said Harriet Tubman will replace this statue, and we will rename this space Tubman Square. For a Mayor to lead something like that ... We're really fortunate, because Mayor Baraka is an artist himself, and he just gets it. He is just so in tune as an artist who comes from such an incredible family himself. So, I think we're a little lucky there.

A few weeks later after our conversation, he called me around 9.00 pm and he said, we're ready to go tonight; you can call a few people, don't call too many, just a quiet gathering down there. I called some poets and drummers and community activists, and it was about two or three dozen people that showed up. Some brought candles and sage and flowers. We have video footage of the drummers out there. There were people chanting at the statue of Columbus as it was being removed. Some people cried, people were hugging, some people laughed and cheered. It was highly charged and emotional, a beautiful moment that we never really thought we'd see, to have that opportunity to challenge that history in this way.

DAVID: It sounds like such a powerful night. Many cities around the country and around the world have had monuments removed these past couple years, and from what I've seen, most cities haven't yet figured out what's going to replace those monuments, if anything. So, as one of the first to commission a permanent replacement, what advice or insights do you have for other communities that are thinking about the ways to grapple with the past and what that might mean for the future of designing their public realm?

FAYEMI: Definitely make sure you include community engagement. Definitely make sure you have some type of feedback process. I've heard of community meetings that have gone awry. Maybe we were lucky because it was during the pandemic, so we had to think of ways to do things virtually, and so certain obstacles that others had, we didn't have. I would say definitely study the work that other people have done but also really take seriously the themes of representation in your own city and find ways to connect with stories that resonate with the residents and the kind of cultural history that exists in your own community. It always helps too to try and align with what's happening now, what we see happening politically, so that art can be used as a tool for conversation.

DAVID: That's wise advice. So, what is the broader policy context – in Newark and nationally – that you're seeing develop in terms of heritage, representation, and shifting narratives?

David Andersson

FAYEMI: One of the things I'm seeing is some dialogue that the Monument Lab has prompted around collective memory and trying not to think of monuments or statues as celebrating one individual.[10] We tried to think about that with Harriet Tubman, not just honoring Tubman as a singular figure, but what she represents, and being able to take a look at our history of the Underground Railroad in our own city, all the different safe houses that existed here. It just allows for deeper storytelling.

And it is always great when you have the support of local government and your local art agencies and art institutions in your city, working in partnership and collaboration also leads to a greater impact. I think the Tubman monument will also give us a chance to think about other issues like voting rights, the carceral justice system, reparations, police brutality. There are so many entry points using Harriet Tubman and her legacy to talk about those things.

DAVID: You mentioned some of the partners that you've been working with, and this project has gathered a fair amount of attention and active participation from local and national funders and institutions. How did this project develop into such a significant public–private partnership for the city of Newark?

FAYEMI: I tell myself affirmations daily every day. I've had a dream that I really wanted some national funders to support this. And I knew immediately that it would be so wonderful if we could partner with the Mellon Foundation.[11] I really love the work that the Mellon Foundation is doing around public art and monuments in particular. We were so fortunate that we made that connection with them and they are now one of our funders, as well as Audible, which we're lucky has its headquarters right across the street from the park. Their expertise around technology and storytelling is going to be a really important component. The Newark Museum of Art is also right across the street from the park, so it's situated in just the perfect place for residents and visitors to have a great experience.

DAVID: You described the support you've had from Mayor Baraka and the Department of Public Safety in Newark's racial justice efforts of the past couple years, but not every city is so lucky. What are your thoughts on how to undertake this kind of work in the face of opposition?

FAYEMI: I've certainly been observing how communities are navigating the take down of confederate era symbols down South, particularly in Louisiana and the opposition they have to face. It takes time to build relationships with residents, organizations, and leaders who are like-minded in mission and vision and create safe spaces for civic engagement. If safe spaces to express ideas and values in support of humanity and racial healing don't exist, we can't wait around for others to create it. It's important to make space for dialogue and discussion. Art, culture, and public spaces can be utilized in meaningful ways to initiate dialogue, move the needle, and draw more support. Non-profits like Monument Lab have been really instrumental in facilitating some of those critical conversations. I have had the pleasure of working with them and they are a great resource.

DAVID: How do you think that your experience and the administration's experience with this project will shape how public artists are commissioned in the future in Newark?

FAYEMI: I'm very new to local government. I'm entering my third year working for the city. Before that, I worked as an artist myself and as an arts administrator for 20 years, so it's really interesting to be on this side of things and to see how things work. Like, oh my God, there's so much honestly that I want to change. I'm really just internally stressing why art needs support and funding, why artists deserve to be paid for their work and not considered as volunteers, and advocating to demonstrate the municipality's commitment to public art and how it enlivens our neighborhoods and enriches our city. I think you have to be strong in advocating and making sure that funding is in place.

DAVID: So what's your pitch? I'm curious when you're trying to make the case for art as a public service, how you convince people.

FAYEMI: We have an arts Mayor, so I don't have to work that hard. I'm really lucky. But my pitch really comes from our local arts agency, Newark Arts, that created a cultural plan that highlighted an in-depth study that found that the Newark arts sector contributes $178 million to our economy and supports 5,000 jobs.[12] I think that when we had that cultural plan, it really opened the eyes of a lot of people to say: wow, we really need to value this sector and what they contribute.

David Andersson

DAVID: The arts have clear economic benefits, as you laid out, but arts practitioners know well that culture has many other positive impacts on communities – in public health, education, public safety, and other sectors – that sometimes are harder to quantify, though increasingly these benefits are being studied.[13] How have you seen the myriad benefits of arts and culture play out in Newark?

FAYEMI: In Newark we've definitely seen how the arts can breathe new life into our communities and help revitalize our neighborhoods, particularly through growing our partnerships, collaborations, and public art program. But also, supporting local artists by providing spaces to perform, learn new skills, gather and meet other artists ultimately benefits the community.

Artists need places to experiment, practice, and grow. No one did more to model the value of cultural work in Newark than Amiri and Amira Baraka when they created spaces like Spirit House[14] and Kimako's Blues People.[15] It's an enduring legacy and contribution to the Black Arts Movement[16] that can still be felt in our city. Through Mayor Baraka's arts initiatives, we are intentional about the ways we value and celebrate artists in the city of Newark.

DAVID: You have a lot of experience as an artist and an arts administrator, and you brought that with you when you took this position in the city. What has it been like to carry that expertise into public service?

FAYEMI: Yes, because before I was on the outside yelling at city hall, "you're not doing enough," and now I'm on the inside! But the wonderful thing is even from day one, when we convened inside municipal chambers with the Mayor and our arts community, maybe a hundred people came, and he announced my role. It was really beautiful. My own community came out and applauded because we've never had this type of coordination in our city before, a person that's in place to make sure that not just art organizations but also artists are being supported. It's something that people have called for, for a long time. Now being in that position, I feel an intense amount of responsibility for the community that I love so much. We have an amazing village here in Newark.

DAVID: And you are not just any person in this role. You're somebody who has done so much work in this community and is really trusted. It's a testament to everything you've been able to do in these two years that you've been in this role.

FAYEMI: Well, maybe more artists should be hired to work in these roles.

DAVID: Absolutely. A last question for you: looking forward, what's your vision for the future of public art in Newark?

FAYEMI: Well, we are taking advantage of these American Rescue Plan dollars, and the Mayor has allocated $500,000 for public art alone. We really want to go deeper into our neighborhoods to do some of these projects. We're looking at some of the hotspots in our city that have issues around public safety or gun violence or blight and vacant lots. We want to contribute to neighborhood revitalization in the city.

One initiative this year I'm super excited about is our Art Space Initiative. The Mayor would like to provide three to five city-owned properties to artists and art organizations who want to do programming in the city. Again, the purpose of that is to go into the neighborhoods. We can see even around the spaces where we have community galleries, how much they uplift the surrounding community. So, we want to have more of that type of energy throughout the neighborhoods, not just downtown, but in as many communities in Newark as we can.

DAVID: This is such an important topic and this conversation is ongoing across the globe. Keep up the good work, and thank you for sharing your wise words. I'm sure they will be an inspiration to many other cities that are trying to figure this all out too.

Notes

1 "Not Just a Statue: A New Monument Rooted in Community and History in Newark, NJ", Bloomberg Philanthropies (www.bloomberg.org/blog/not-just-a-statue-a-new-monument-rooted-in-community-and-history-in-newark-nj/).

2 www.cookejohn.com/.

3 "A Call to Peace", Monument Lab (https://monumentlab.com/projects/a-call-to-peace).

4 The Confederacy included 11 states that declared secession and warred against the United States during the American Civil War from 1861 to 1865.

5 https://adebunmi.carbonmade.com/.

6 "The Forgotten Federally Employed Artists", Hyperallergic (https://hyperallergic.com/610071/the-forgotten-federally-employed-artists/).

7   "Bolstering Newark's Arts and Culture Sector While Faced with the COVID-19 Pandemic", Bloomberg Associates (https://associates.bloomberg.org/cities/newark/bolstering-newarks-arts-and-culture-sector-while-faced-with-the-covid-19-pandemic/).

8   https://en.wikipedia.org/wiki/George_Floyd_protests.

9   The 1967 Newark rebellion was instigated after a Black cab driver was beaten by two white police officers for a minor traffic offense. During the five-day uprising that took place across the city, 26 people were killed and hundreds were injured.

10 "National Monument Audit", Monument Lab (https://monumentlab.com/audit).

11 https://mellon.org/.

12 "Newark Creates: A Community Cultural Plan for the City of Newark", Newark Arts (https://newarkarts.org/newark-creates/).

13 One great example of effective research on the social impacts of arts and culture is the Social Impact of the Arts Project (SIAP) at the University of Pennsylvania. Completed in 2017, the three-year study of the impact of the arts on social wellbeing in New York City neighborhoods found that in low income neighborhoods, the presence of cultural resources is significantly associated with improved outcomes around health, schooling, and personal security. "The Social Wellbeing of New York City's Neighborhoods: The Contribution of Culture and the Arts", Mark J. Stern and Susan C. Seifert, Social Impact of the Arts Project, University of Pennsylvania (https://repository.upenn.edu/siap_culture_nyc/1/).

14 "Recovering The New-Ark: Amiri Baraka's Lost Chronicle of Black Power in Newark, 1968", Bright Lights Film Journal (https://brightlightsfilm.com/recovering-new-ark-amiri-barakas-lost-chronicle-black-power-newark-1968/amp/).

15 "Allah Mean Everything", Newark Review (https://web.njit.edu/~newrev/v2s4/ed.html).

16 "The Black Arts Movement (1965–1975)", Black Past (.www.blackpast.org/african-american-history/black-arts-movement-1965-1975/).

Philanthropy and Cultural Leadership

Christos Carras, Senior Consultant, Onassis Stegi: In Conversation (Greece)

Olga Kolokytha

Chapter 3

Christos Carras was born in London (UK) in 1962. He read philosophy at Cambridge University and then at the Sorbonne where he earned his PhD. From 2000 onwards, he has been working in the cultural sector, initially as the Project Manager of the EU-funded MediMuses network. In 2006, he became General Manager of the B&M Theocharakis Foundation for the Fine Arts and Music. From 2009 to October 2022, he was

DOI: 10.4324/9781003390725-3

the Executive Director of the Onassis Stegi (Onassis Cultural Centre).[1] He continues to collaborate with the Onassis Stegi as a Senior Consultant developing European networks and the sustainability programme as well as pursuing other projects independently.

This conversation took place online on 17 May 2022.

OLGA: How do you see the role of private foundations in the domain of culture and what is the philosophy of the Onassis Stegi with reference to culture?

CHRISTOS: Those are two very different questions. So just to make sure the question is, how do I see – in other words, what do I imagine – their role ideally to be, or how do I see that their role is?

OLGA: Could be both, they are both intriguing questions.

CHRISTOS: The role of private foundations is difficult to quantify to start with, and not just in Greece but throughout Europe, especially in Europe. In the US, perhaps things are a bit more public in terms of numbers, but in Europe, there's very little data available, generally speaking, about the specific contribution of private foundations to culture. I remember reading recently a survey that was carried out in 2019, by what was then the European Foundation Centre, which has now merged with the Donors and Foundations Network in Europe and become Philea. They did a survey amongst their members asking them about their contribution to culture. I think 170 something members were contacted, about 40 answered and their contribution was about 22.5% of their annual budgets amounting to something like 900 million EUR per year.[2] That was in 2016 or 2018, but there's very little specific data, for example, in Greece available about, just to start with this basic fact, how much budget is there made available for culture. So that's one problem.

The second question, the second issue, also involves drawing some boundaries around what we mean by "contribution to culture". Do we include contribution generally speaking to civil society, which may or may not touch upon specifically cultural issues, for example, issues of social innovation, which may have a cultural dimension? So that's also something that's not quite clear cut.

And I think a third area is the precise boundary between what one might consider to be CSR[3] activities and what are foundation activities, because you have, for example, a bank in Greece that is connected to a foundation that runs a network of museums. So the foundation runs museums, but the foundation is basically a CSR action of the bank. So all these things make it difficult to have a very precise opinion about what the contribution is and where it is. That having been said, it's fairly obvious that there is a very, let's say, visible presence of foundations in Greece as in many countries.

OLGA: Can you speak a little more about the situation in Greece?

CHRISTOS: So in Greece, there tends to be a very small number of large foundations at one end of the spectrum and many smaller foundations at the other end. And obviously, it goes without saying that the action of the large foundations tends to be the one that focuses attention, has the most impact. As is also the case quite frequently in the south of Europe, foundations here in Greece tend to be what we call "operational foundations" rather than grant-giving foundations. So for the most part the foundations here run their own programmes of whatever kind, which doesn't obviously exclude them also giving grants, but the main model in Greece is the operational foundation.

Having said all that as an introduction, I think the areas one can see in culture are obviously infrastructure, I mean, contribution to the development of new infrastructure. Then there is the programme and programme support dimension. In other words, these foundations run their programmes, these programmes involve people from the broader cultural field, and so on. There is an area which has to do with capacity building, and scholarships perhaps specifically for the cultural sector, which is an issue in itself. Then there is a very big area, which is interaction with the public sector, with a broader public sector at whatever level – central government, regions, municipalities or whatever. And there is no doubt that especially at the level of infrastructure, one has seen over the years a very significant activity of the larger foundations in Greece.

This ties in, I believe, with a tradition of philanthropy in Greece. A tradition that to a very large degree was based, historically

Olga Kolokytha

speaking, on the weakness of the State and its inability to really develop cultural infrastructure or cultural policies in the past. And more recently, of course, with the crisis. The financial crisis in Greece[4] resulted, again, in a weakness of the public cultural sector to support as much as it possibly would have liked and therefore a greater call on private funds to play a role. Or perhaps these private funds play a more visibly prominent role precisely because the state over the years had actually reduced its contribution.

OLGA: How has this interaction between the state and the private sector developed since the financial crisis?

CHRISTOS: Now we're in another phase, when the state is back again. And I think it will be interesting to see what happens going forward. And that's perhaps another question, what kind of interaction can and will there be? Another point I'd like to make is that in Greece, culture has always meant something rather specific and perhaps different from many other countries, with an emphasis on cultural heritage, and also the reinforcement of a national narrative. In many states of Southern Europe, "culture" has predominantly meant "cultural heritage" in terms of state support. The major part of the state budget and also many regional funds go to cultural heritage in one form or another. And also until recently, the cultural sector in Greece was defined pretty much by the arts rather than a broader sector involving other types of cultural activities, what we might call the cultural and creative industries more broadly.

In other words, there was always a gap somewhere in the cultural scene in Greece concerning contemporary cultural creativity and, let's say, more innovative forms of cultural action and also forms that did not so directly concern the fine arts only, but were more broadly related to issues of cultural innovation and what have you. So in the field of contemporary culture, I think the private sector has played a significant role. It is difficult to quantify, but obviously, there are some very big examples. Two large foundations play a very significant role in the cultural sphere, primarily in Athens, but they're not the only ones obviously, there was an art museum created by a private foundation, a couple of years ago,[5] and yet another one that presents significant visual arts exhibitions in various locations.[6]

I think it's a prominent role that takes on various forms according to the programmes of the foundations themselves.

OLGA: And what about the philosophy of the Onassis Stegi with reference to culture?

CHRISTOS: The Onassis Stegi is specifically part of Onassis Foundation. So as a foundation, we have a view of culture as being something that has to be more broadly connected to society in many ways. We see our role as a cultural organization that is engaged in a conversation in the public sphere with, broadly speaking, cultural activities and formats as the medium for this conversation. The focus of Onassis Stegi is very much on what's happening today, and it's very much not a discipline-defined centre. In other words, we are really interested in whatever is happening today, in whatever connection we see relevant to culture in a broad sense. Culture can also mean issues that border on the political and the cultural, because they reflect the ways in which ideas circulate in our communities and our society. And we feel that is the connecting link between culture in the strict sense and a more political discourse on the other. We don't disconnect this, across the whole spectrum of forms of creativity from things that border more on social innovation, to things that are very solidly inscribed within a discipline, such as theatre or music. So we're not defined by a specific discipline.

A second thing is that we're not really defined by our space, even though obviously we have a space with performance and production infrastructure, but we do a lot of work outside that space. We really do see ourselves as being defined by the programme and not by the building. The third element is that we are very much concerned with trying to achieve accessibility for a large, broad spectrum of society both in terms of our pricing policy but also in terms of the range of programmes that we put on, but which we try to do without sacrificing what we consider to be relevant or innovative artistically or culturally speaking. The fourth element of our strategy is to really support and nurture the creative sector in Greece. Obviously, that is very much a priority both by producing new work, by financing new work, and importantly, by supporting the work of artists for example in touring or in providing fellowships and capacity building in various forms.

OLGA: You more or less answered my planned question on how programming is shaped. Attached to that is a question on the criteria for funding productions or activities, or indeed working together with other entities, for example, cultural organizations.

CHRISTOS: I can say something about the last part of that question, the collaboration side, because it's something that I'm also quite directly involved with. And it is to say that since the fairly early days in our history – we opened at the end of 2010 so we're a relatively young organization; we're not an infant but we're sort of an adolescent probably as a cultural organization, which perhaps explains our hyperactivity at some levels as an adolescent organization – so from the very beginning, to my mind at least, establishing international collaborations and working within networks of institutions especially within Europe was a very important policy for several reasons. The first being of course Greece. We sometimes forget Greece is a periphery, culturally speaking, of Europe. It's not one of the countries in Europe which is seen as a driving force of contemporary creativity. So, in order to get on the map and to be able to show what we're doing at the moment, being in networks is a very important step. And this has had the result that Stegi over the years has become a very frequent partner in networks, for example, working frequently in the borderline between scientific, technical innovation and artistic innovation. At the moment, for example, we are a partner in the STARTS Regional Centre "Repairing the Present" network,[7] working on themes related to sustainability.

A second rationale was to try and facilitate the circulation of artists and artworks, their mobility, and of course, networking is an important stepping stone for achieving this. And the third is knowledge exchange. Learning from our peers and the diversity of the European context has been very helpful for us, both to fine-tune our strategic thinking and to get ideas, to get input. So this collaborative aspect has been particularly important, especially on an international level.

OLGA: How do you see culture in Greece after the crises? There was the financial crisis of 2008 onwards and there is the COVID crisis, so maybe you could comment on both. And how private foundations played a role in the developments in the cultural sector during that time?

CHRISTOS: I think this is a very big question and it has very many levels and not one. I think obviously the crises did have a significant impact on the sector and that foundations did play a role. The private non-profit sector definitely played a role. But I think it's also fair to say that one witnessed a greater willingness and readiness to collaborate between artists. So, we saw examples of artists working together, finding innovative ways of producing nonetheless, despite the obstacles, despite the adversities involved. I think during these periods we've seen several changes in the way the Ministry of Culture has responded as well. For a certain period in the most difficult moments of the financial crisis a lot of funding was cut. There's been a renewed effort recently to establish a better understanding of what's happening through the Mitroo – I guess this is translated as Registry of Artists and Artists' Organizations. I think that was a positive step. Plus, the reintroduction of certain funding schemes during the COVID phase, for example, an incitement to produce digitally, as indeed was the case for the private foundations. So generally it's a lively sector, there's a lot happening.

I also think that after Documenta 14 in 2017, to talk about the visual arts side, we saw quite a few artists coming to stay in Greece, to create studios here. There's a more lively, grassroots type of creativity happening as well, without the usual institutional problems having gone away. I mean, it's taken years to get the Museum of Contemporary Art to start. Let's hope that now we're in a position when it will actually restart delivering its role, which is a very significant one in that sector. So I think it's an environment in which structural weaknesses emerged at several levels during COVID, especially the questions of the labour context of the arts in Greece. It became very clear that the precarity of people working in the arts sector was severe precisely because the art sector always had a tremendously significant informal element to it. And this is one of the areas that obviously needs to be addressed.

There are several elements that are still missing. There's a lack of transversal action at a cultural level. I would very much like to see a much greater connection between, for example, culture and education. There's a lot of potential to be explored between culture and innovation, or to better understand the role of sub-sectors such as design, video games or digital games. There's a need to really expand the understanding of what the cultural sector is, to take into account what the dynamic of the sector is today. I think there's a lot of work still to be done in working in that zone between amateur and professional production, which is where perhaps new talents emerge. So definitely, there's work to be done in the incubation of talents, in that intermediate zone.

And I believe that there's a lot of work to be done also in developing a better understanding of the role of cities in cultural production, and the role of culture in creating resilient and innovative cities that can capitalize on their potential through culture. There's a lot to be done. And the national scene is definitely dominated by Athens, so there's a need for a much greater regional spread of opportunities. But there's certainly a lot going on and in some sectors like contemporary dance, for example, there's significant work of an international standard being produced and toured abroad.

OLGA: Why is culture so attractive for private foundations?

CHRISTOS: In Greece, it's true that there aren't that many foundations that are active in other areas exclusively like innovation and research, but foundations tend to split their resources between social cohesion, health, education and culture. Perhaps from our perspective, from the cultural sector, we see the cultural action more. And certainly, there is a certain shine to the arts. Perhaps it's the sense that support for the arts can be up to the private sector because it's less constrained by particular needs. This perhaps indicates that there's not enough of an understanding of culture as a public good. Hence, it's perhaps "understandable", in inverted commas, that the private sector should be more deeply involved. My personal position is that culture is very much a public good, which doesn't preclude the private sector from being involved in its production, but it shouldn't be considered as being something additional to the public good. Like health, education, safety, and so on. It's very much part of the core services that one would call a public service.

OLGA: Do you think that private foundations are interested in and focusing more in promoting culture inside or outside the country?

CHRISTOS: I think, primarily inside the country and that's probably because the mission of most foundations is to be active in Greece. That's one thing. The second thing is – and this is a speculation on my part – that perhaps apart from some of the larger foundations or some of them which have a very specific focus on collaboration abroad, I'm not sure whether Greek foundations as a rule have strong networks abroad. Unfortunately, I don't have access to specific data about it, but for what it's worth, my feeling is that the institutions don't typically have very strong international networks. I mean there are exceptions such as one foundation which is quite active especially in the area of social cohesion and social innovation bordering on culture, which has over the years been particularly active in managing funds from abroad, from the European Economic Area (EEA), for example, so there's a network there between the EEA grant system and this foundation here in Greece, and they've done a very good job. But foundations, from what I know, have not been particularly present, for example, in the European cultural networks ecosystem.

Then there is Philea, the network of European foundations and I think there are four or five Greek foundations which are members of that, which isn't bad, but nonetheless, I'm not sure how strong these international networks are generally for foundations.

OLGA: How do you see the role of private foundations in funding public cultural infrastructure? How is this intervention articulated or justified in that sense?

CHRISTOS: Well, it's a question that goes at its root to the legitimacy of private organizations having this kind of impact on the public sphere, which is a very tricky question. My feeling about that, is that it's complex because private initiatives are extremely useful in that they often complement areas in which the State is not aware that there's a need, or is not concerned by a need. So, they develop projects and programmes that may respond to minority needs, but which nonetheless are very significant but which the state might consider not to be within its brief, and so on. So there's definitely a need for this.

On the other hand, the fact is that, in our kind of plutocratic societies, the more wealth you command the greater impact you can have on the public sphere, but that is not restricted to foundations. I mean if you are wealthy businessman and you own a newspaper, you have probably much more impact on the public sphere than a foundation. If you are a commercial company that fills the city with billboards, with advertising, you are influencing the public sphere as well in a sense that's commercial, but still you are influencing what's there, the trends, the discussions that are going on.

I think that generally the question of influencing the public sphere is a broader question. Now the fact is that foundations provide actions that one often associates with what would be a central or a local government action. So in that sense, they seem to be somehow occupying a space that would otherwise be occupied by the public sector.

And I have two things to say about that: first is, that the weaker the public sector, the stronger the private sector. This is my personal position: I very much believe that one should try to strengthen the public sector. Not in the sense of making it bigger, with more public servants, but making it better, more efficient, more proactive, more innovative, and so on. I think it would be a terrible mistake to say ah, there are private foundations that can substitute, or come in as contractors, so we don't need to do that. It's important that the public sector should be strengthened as an innovative, efficient organization, and we have a long way to go in Greece.

The second thing I'd say is that the public sector should really try to cultivate a more strategic discussion with the private non-profit sector. I mean, in view of the fact that there is this activity and that it is a positive contribution to society. Not that the state should be able to dictate what foundations do, but there should be more mechanisms on a voluntary and informal level perhaps, that enable a greater exchange of strategies, ideas and projects between these two sectors. So I would see that an important element in harmonizing this relationship would be the development of this kind of interface in a more formalized way.

OLGA: Which do you think are the differences in the approach of private foundations and the State towards culture in Greece?

CHRISTOS: In cultural policy, as I said before the main difference is that the State, rightly so, has responsibility for cultural heritage. Cultural heritage is generally speaking public property and therefore, even if private funds can support restoration projects or whatever, only the public sector can actually manage heritage. The other difference is that it's usually up to whatever interests the particular private institutions have, what they conceive their interests to be – which may or may not actually coincide with what one might consider to be real needs – that define their programmes. Conversely the State, theoretically at least, needs to strategically prioritize, through processes of data gathering and input from various sources, what a country needs and act in accordance with that. The private sector does not have this kind of constraint in a sense, and hence can pursue projects according to other priorities and other interests, which isn't to say they're necessarily bad, but let's say they start from a different position.

OLGA: So do private foundations share knowledge and networks with the State? Do they work in synergy or more in competition?

CHRISTOS: I would say that there is a form of synergy, but it's often a synergy that's a bit shallow, like a contractor's role. In other words, the State will request a private foundation to implement something because they'll do it faster and more efficiently and pay for it. So that's a kind of contractual relationship.

Or there's a kind of funding relationship. As I said earlier, there should be a deeper kind of strategic synergy between the two sectors. I don't see it really as being a competition. I don't think there's a competition between our private and public sectors. I don't see that. I think that the situation in other countries might be different. Where one sees very large private museums concentrating significant attention like in France for example, then there's a big discussion about the fact that private collectors who have the means to create these tremendously valuable collections, which the state cannot do, end up having a kind of competitive relation with State collections. I'm not sure that that's so prominent in Greece because the State's never been that present on the contemporary scene.

OLGA: Do you think contemporary culture is more promoted in the framework of private foundations in comparison to the state and how does this relationship with contemporary culture work? You mentioned earlier the state being more active in cultural heritage, but what does this relationship of private foundations and contemporary culture look like in terms of policy programming, outreach, and so on?

CHRISTOS: Well, I think it's worth noting that the first time that there's been a specific Deputy Minister of contemporary culture has been in the last two years. I think that in itself says something – that there is a renewed interest in this dimension. Not all private foundations are that interested or active in what we call contemporary culture but certainly some are, and it's because they recognize the significance of contemporary creativity, what's happening today, creativity in its living form, not a historical form of creative practice today, as being a very significant dynamic more broadly in society. Supporting creativity and supporting people's ability to develop their creativity has very positive spillover effects. Not in an economic sense, but generally in terms of the dynamism of a society as a whole. It's certainly the case for us that the focus on contemporary culture has to do with our perception of the significance of creativity more broadly for society.

OLGA: Do you think that there are any friction points between private foundations and the State with reference to policy, strategy and action? And if there are any, what are they?

CHRISTOS: I can't think of any particular friction points as things stand, I'm trying to think in what way there would be friction points in terms of policy. I can't think of something.

OLGA: Do you see private foundations as taking more risks in policy making as opposed to the State? And if so then what are these risks? What is risk in that context?

CHRISTOS: Obviously, there's a risk taken in developing an infrastructure and then having to keep it going. I think there are unfortunately several examples of very well-intentioned infrastructural cultural projects undertaken by the private sector that then don't necessarily have the full capacity to keep going, or to keep going at the level that they want. So there's a risk there that you create something and then can't continue it. And then perhaps the State has to come in and help or whatever. And there's a risk also when we're talking about support for contemporary work. There's obviously the risk of trying new things, of innovating, or trying new methodologies, or trying new performance practices, all these things are inherently risky. You try something new and it may work, or it may not. So in that sense, there's de finitely a risk.

OLGA: Given the increasingly important role that private foundations play in the cultural life of the country, do you think that national strategies for culture tend to be shaped more by them or by the State?

CHRISTOS: I think there are very high-profile examples for someone looking from a distance that obviously stand out. Generally speaking, the larger institutions are more visible, the larger museums, and the larger performance spaces – and those are relatively balanced between the private and the public sector. I mean, there are large public festivals, the Athens and Epidaurus festival, for example, very significant museums, obviously, the Acropolis Museum, the Archaeological Museum, the Pinakothiki, the National Museum of Contemporary Art, MoMUS, these are anchor institutions, there are also other regional museums, and so on. Those are very visible structures obviously, so I would imagine that from the outside institutions like those, perhaps have the greater visibility at that level. But over the years, the actions of the private sector either through large-scale exhibitions or performance spaces, are definitely present. Let's not ignore the fact that private institutions, the large ones at least, have perhaps been more communicative. They may communicate better, perhaps, than the State does. It will be interesting to see what happens over the next few years, because Greece is one of the few countries in Europe that actually did devote almost 2% of its RRF to culture and various types of cultural projects[8] and investments with an impact on the cultural sphere, even if once more there is a focus on heritage. So, there could be a significant, by Greek standards, amount of money coming through the public sector for either infrastructure or training or digital projects, including new infrastructure in museums, for example, cultural routes, and so on. If things go well, and it's not a given that they will because it's complicated and the timeframe is short, I think there will definitely be quite a few ways in which the public sector will have an important input over the next few years.

OLGA: Can you see a model of State support which would do away with the need for private foundations?

CHRISTOS: No, because it would be an impoverishment of society if all cultural decisions were taken by the State. I think there's the need for niche interests and innovative ideas that the State, by definition, cannot necessarily develop. So I can imagine a lot that could be done by the State, especially going back to something I said earlier at that sort of incubation level, at the city level, the town level that could be done a lot better perhaps. But no, I can't imagine that it would be good to do away with private, non-profit input to the arts, into culture generally.

OLGA: How has Onassis Stegi changed cultural policy?

CHRISTOS: Well, it has to a degree. I'm not sure exactly how it has changed policy *per se*, but I definitely think that having an institution that really promotes contemporary work, did shift the spotlight onto an area that perhaps was less privileged in the past. We played a role certainly in also supporting elements of the artistic community to enable them to shape what today's cultural sector looks like. So in that sense, it wasn't exactly policy, but the opportunities we've given have definitely had an impact on who's doing what – so in that sense, it's not policy, but what is happening on the ground. I would say also, but I don't think this has had an influence on policy necessarily, that our tendency to be relatively outspoken and to connect cultural action with things that sort of border on the political, certainly has transformed the way people think about this idea, what the legitimate area of cultural involvement is today. But it's probably easier for people outside the organization to see these things than from within.

OLGA: How do you see the involvement of private foundations at a micro level in cultural life? So for example through funding small and regional initiatives, rather than being active in big urban centres.

CHRISTOS: Again, I unfortunately don't have the data about it. I think there is a tendency to invest in large projects in Athens because that's most visible and that's also where a lot of the creative community is, but I believe it is very significant for private non-profits to work regionally. And ideally in some kind of strategic collaboration also with the regions themselves and through being part of regional strategies. For example, through the smart specialization strategies that are designed to help regions through the collaboration of private and public organizations, and develop local regional strategies, of which culture and tourism are usually a part. That is another issue to be discussed: it would be significant to work regionally, but at the same time to somehow disconnect culture from tourism. I mean, culture is not just about developing good tourism products. One has to have a much broader understanding of the relationship between culture and the creative economy. And I think that at a regional level there's a lot to be done and that private institutions have a greater flexibility and capacity to innovate, than a sort of heavier State. So that kind of synergy I think on a regional level would be super important. I'm afraid I don't know the degree to which that's happening in practice.

OLGA: There have been initiatives by private foundations intervening with projects in public spaces, some of which have drawn much criticism. How do you view that?

CHRISTOS: I think the foundations' activities in the public space obviously need to be regulated by those who manage the public space. One needs to take each case on its own merit. Often it can be a public institution that invites a foundation or several foundations to do something in the public space. That's one case. Another is when you do an artistic intervention in the public space. I very much believe in the value of producing contemporary work in the public space. I think it creates opportunities for people who might otherwise not see something to be surprised and perhaps intrigued by what's happening. But there's no doubt that the bottom line is that public space has to be regulated by the public sector and that whoever is doing this needs to weigh the pros and cons of allowing a particular project to go ahead.

I think the private sector, generally speaking, also participates in the creation of the public space, right? I mean, to the buildings that are created, through the advertising, the technologies that are installed, and so on. So there's not such a complete division between who regulates what in the public space. And commercial interests often have as much of an impact on the public space as public strategy does, so it's a complex issue. That having been said, I believe in the value of art in the public space and contemporary work in the public space, as long as there are mechanisms for approval and regulation.

Notes

1 For more on Onassis Stegi, see www.onassis.org/onassis-stegi.
2 This is the European Cultural Foundation survey (European Foundation Centre, 2019). The data mentioned here is on page 3 of the report.
3 Corporate social responsibility.
4 There are different views on the starting point of the financial crisis in Greece. For some, the official date is 2010 when the country entered a bailout programme with financial assistance from the International Monetary Fund, the European Union, and the European Central Bank. However, significant problems had already started earlier than that. For more on the financial crisis impact on the Greek cultural sector, see Kolokytha (2022).
5 The Museum of the Basil and Elise Goulandris Foundation in Athens, which opened in 2019. For more, see https://goulandris.gr/en/.
6 This is the NEON Foundation. https://neon.org.gr/en/.
7 See https://starts.eu/what-we-do/residences/repairing-the-present/.
8 According to Culture Action Europe data (Culture Action Europe, 2021, p. 24), Greece has devoted 1.06% of its RRF budget, that is €610 million, to culture, with an additional €306 million to tourism. However, data by Bruegel from June 2022 demonstrate that this percentage categorized per NACE codes is 1.99% for arts, entertainment and recreation (see Figure 5, here www.bruegel.org/dataset/european-union-countries-recovery-and-resilience-plans, accessed 19 November 2022).

References

Culture Action Europe. (2021). Culture in the EU's National Recovery and Resilience Plans. https://cultureactioneurope.org/files/2021/11/NRRPs_analysed_digital.pdf.

European Foundation Centre. (2019). Arts and Culture at the Core of Philanthropy. https://philea. issuelab.org/resource/arts-and-culture-at-the-core-of-philanthropy.html.

Kolokytha, O. (2022). Crisis as change: New paradigms in cultural policy. The case of Greece. In C. Mathieu and V. Visanich (Eds), *Accomplishing Cultural Policy in Europe: Financing, Governance and Responsiveness* (pp. 71–86). Routledge.

Artistic Directors and Cultural Leadership

Helen Marriage, Director of Artichoke and Former Creative Director of Galway 2020 European Capital of Culture: In Conversation (UK)

Steven Hadley

Chapter 4

DOI: 10.4324/9781003390725-4

Helen Marriage is Director of Artichoke and was Creative Director of Galway 2020 European Capital of Culture, until April 2020 when Artichoke's involvement ceased due to the outbreak of COVID-19. Artichoke works with artists to reimagine public spaces, aiming to appeal to the widest possible audience and has created some of the most celebrated outdoor art in recent times, including the Lumiere light festivals, The Sultan's Elephant, Antony Gormley's One & Other Fourth Plinth commission and PROCESSIONS, a mass participation artwork celebrating 100 years since some women won the right to vote in the UK. Helen's previous work includes a seven-year period as Director of the Salisbury Festival. She created the first Arts & Events programme for Olympia & York, the developers of Canary Wharf in London, was an Associate Director of the London International Festival of Theatre (LIFT) and managed a variety of independent artists at Artsadmin in the early 1980s. In 2012, she was awarded a Loeb Fellowship at Harvard Graduate School of Design, a prestigious fellowship awarded to individuals working in urban design and planning. Her appointment was an acknowledgement of the impact Artichoke has made on the way mass public art events are negotiated and staged. She was awarded an MBE for services to the arts in the New Year's Honours list in 2016.

This conversation took place online on 28 May 2020.

STEVEN: I'd like to begin by asking you, which sector do you work in?

HELEN: I don't really work in a sector. I think there's a sector that doesn't have a definition, and in my mind, it's called non-aligned. And that is people who work on the margin. I don't think in art form silos; I never really have. And I don't think Artichoke sits happily in anybody else's art form.

STEVEN: I'm interested to interrogate whether you see yourself inside or outside or nonaligned with the establishment that exists within the arts sector, or the creative industries?

HELEN: Me personally, or the company?

STEVEN: Both, I suppose. If they're different, I'll take two answers.

HELEN: Well, I sit on the board of the Arts Council, London, as an individual, so am I in the establishment? I suppose that you might say yes to that. But this interview is not me as ACE London council member. These are my own opinions. Does Artichoke work within an established framework? Really not, and never has. So, if you look at the subsidised position, the Arts Council contribute 10% of our annual income. And we're not earning money from anyone from tickets, or anything like that. We're raising our own money to do the stuff that we do. And while the Arts Council support is very welcome, they don't have a majority stake in the company or anything like that. I've never minded because I think being marginal or maverick is quite a strong position. For me, our work is about creating opportunities for artists to make things that are on a scale that they've never imagined possible. And putting that work in a context that allows it to speak to the broadest possible audience. And I don't think there's an Arts Council category for that.

STEVEN: Where does that way of working and that philosophy situate you in terms of "the great and the good" that you're co-mingling with? Because there is a history in the English subsidised cultural sector – and I think we'll probably dance around these ideas – that being popular and being excellent are frequently seen to be in tension with each other?

HELEN: I get what you're saying. The things that we do are rarely reviewed in the media. I think they think that so-called "spectacle" can't be serious. So, art critics either find the work problematic or don't consider it even. But I suppose the distinction is that Artichoke engages – I hope, we engage – on an emotional level. There is profundity to what we do, and there is depth, and there is thinking, and there is lots that behind the scenes of the four-day moment or the 20-minute moment or whatever it is, that people are gaining from that project. But the surface is very emotional. There's an emotional engagement which you see and hear from people. Currently, the prevailing critical discourse is around cerebral engagement. I don't want to be part of that particularly.

STEVEN: I'm just going to pick up briefly on this word, spectacle, and your dislike for it, because I had a question about whether you traced an intellectual history to your work. What is it about the word, "spectacle", that you don't like?

HELEN: I think it's become debased, or at least, as you're alluding to, it implies some sort of surface, momentary, transitory moment of enjoyment. I think there's a sense that it's not serious, whereas I think that the work that we do, notwithstanding its emotional impact, is deeply serious and very political. And I think that the remaking of public space is a political act, and Artichoke has been engaged in that since its very first outing with *The Sultan's Elephant* in 2006.

Just the conflict around accessing those spaces, those particular routes in London. It took seven years to negotiate so it obviously wasn't an incidental thing. You were messing with people's assumptions and perception of what "the Ceremonial Route" was to be used for, and that definitely wasn't a theatre show with a giant elephant in the middle of it. So, the challenge to accepted assumptions and traditions is part of what we do. And that's always conflictual because you're trying to transform – and in that transformation of physical space, you're also transforming what people think. And that's an intensely political thing to do.

STEVEN: If there was a unifying philosophy, for want of a better word, to Artichoke's work, which there seems to be, does it then make sense to ask who the work is for?

HELEN: That question is asked and we ask ourselves all the time. And the easy answer is everyone. I think that the barriers to accessing our work are never financial because almost everything we do is free. I think they're perceptual and territorial, if you like. I can do as much of the closing of roads, and the creating free access zones, and all of that kind of stuff I like, but if the messaging isn't getting through, you still won't succeed in getting that broad audience that we crave. So right back in the early days, we always said that Artichoke's work was a marriage of production, exceptionally high production values, and a really clever, well-thought out communication strategy.

GALWAY AND EUROPEAN CAPITALS OF CULTURE

Galway (Ireland) and Rijeka (Croatia) are the 2020 European Capitals of Culture (ECoC). In January 2019 Helen was appointed Creative Director of Galway 2020. Due to the impact of COVID-19, the contract between Galway 2020 and Artichoke ended in April 2020, shortly before this interview took place.

STEVEN: When you took the Galway job, what kind of understanding did you have of how ECoCs functioned?

HELEN: Partial.

STEVEN: You're just going to give me one-word answers now, aren't you [laughter]?

HELEN: Well, you asked. I mean, I've worked on loads. I worked on Liverpool. I worked on Glasgow. I had been on the outside of them coming in. I didn't have a sufficient understanding of the European political dimension that surrounds them. But you have to remember I came in right at the end. I mean, I wasn't part of the setting up or anything like that.

STEVEN: Were you conscious of the history, of the fate of so many of those ECOC artistic directors that came before you?

HELEN: Yes.

STEVEN: And how did you feel about that?

HELEN: I was always up for a challenge.

STEVEN: Why does that happen so frequently? The departure of artistic directors?

HELEN: That isn't the correct question, I think. Why is the framework within which an ECoC happens so dysfunctional, is the question. The departure of an artistic director is often just a symptom of what else is happening.

STEVEN: Have we got to the point where the balancing between all of the political imperatives and the economic necessities of an ECoC have started to outweigh the artistic content and the value of it?

HELEN: I disagree. I think that it's entirely possible to do everything for everybody. I mean, I would say this, wouldn't I? But I think that Galway's programme, had it been able to be delivered, and if I had been able to be there a bit earlier, could have done everything that everyone in Europe and Ireland wanted, and still have served the interests of artists and the audiences, which was always my primary objective. I think you just have to be very clever about what you're doing and how you're doing it, in order to deliver. I mean, the great benefit of doing a European Capital of Culture programme is you have a year, and a year is a long time to fill with programme. And within that timeframe, you can do loads of different things, so you don't have to be doing one thing at any one time. So, you can deliver your bed/nights and tourism benefits and all of that kind of stuff when you can, but you can also do very grounded, grassroots work throughout that time with communities where you can. You can create platforms for artists. And I think you just need to be very savvy and you need to be not interested in only one aspect of it. You have to be interested in all of it serving a bigger purpose.

So, if you take *Lumiere* as an example, when you look at *Lumiere* Durham, it's a huge success for the region, and that's not only culturally, that's in terms of reaching the audiences and publics who are undiscovered by other arts organisations, maybe. But the economic return on the council's investment is over 1,000% what with the benefit to the local tourism industry but also in car-parking, food, beverage etc. So what the ECoCs do on a big scale is what I'm doing every day of my working life, which is delivering for audiences, but also to stakeholders. It's challenging, and the scale of it is a challenge, but I think that the difficulty is that people, boards, and executive teams are often appointed to run an ECoC who don't have that experience of delivering across that scale of activity. And therefore, they're reinventing the wheel slightly because they're trying to get to the endpoint, and not really experienced in working with multiple stakeholders and interest groups, and all of that kind of stuff. Whereas, actually, for us, we've had 15 years of it. If you look at *The Sultan's Elephant* where we cut our teeth on that sort of thing, and that was practically back in the day when you sent messages by fax. I mean, it's a really long time ago. So, an ECoC, with its complicated matrix of stakeholders and desires and outcomes, it's not rare for us. It's just new, often, for the city that's trying to do it.

STEVEN: Is there inevitably a spectrum of belief around the extent to which the arts should feel compelled to deliver those sort of benefits as part of their role?

HELEN: I don't think there's any compulsion required. I think it just does. If it works, it just does. I suppose my thing is there shouldn't be targets but there should be measurement. You know that that stuff will happen, and you know that you will reach lots of people and create inward investment. Setting a target is a bit pointless because you can't know the answer till you've got the answer. But you should definitely measure what's been achieved.

STEVEN: Do you have any thoughts on the politics around evaluation of large-scale events and which methods would you advocate for from your own experience? It's clear from having met you and talked to you, and watched your TED video and so on, you're a brilliant rhetorician. You're a brilliant advocate for what you do. But you're presumably also very cognisant of the fact that the rhetoric has to have an evidence base to go with it?

HELEN: Well, you say that, but it's interesting. When we did *The Sultan's Elephant* and there were a million people on the streets, two things happened in relation to the establishment. One of which was that the DCMS in the UK/Arts Council England declared that the audience didn't count in terms of audience figures generated that year, because there was no transaction between us and them. And therefore, in those days, 2006, a million people (which wasn't our number, that was the BBC's number), were statistically irrelevant. So, I think today policy has changed somewhat in terms of valuing people who are attending free events. And the other thing was that the HMRC[1] decided, for VAT purposes, that we were non-business, although we'd spent a million and a half quid doing the event. Again, there was no transaction between us and the public. So, we went into a huge battle with the tax people about – I think – it was about £80,000 or something that we felt they owed us a refund on our taxable activities. And they came back saying we were non-business and therefore couldn't make that claim. And we tried to get Arts Council England to take that on as an issue for non-building-based, free-to-experience activities, which they sort of vaguely did but didn't really do anything.

So, we're used to having this argument: the numbers are a problem, aren't they? I mean, in that people only value numbers. I remember being at a seminar in America hosted by the Ford Foundation. And there was a whole conversation about quantitative evaluation. And I just got a bit irritated, so I said, "Okay. Let's do a quick survey. How many people in this room have ever been in love?" There's like 30 people in the room who couldn't admit to not having been in love, so they all put their hands up. And I said, "And we could go on. We could say how many times did that love affair turn into a permanent relationship? And how many children were born out of that love

Steven Hadley

affair? And for how many people was it a one-night stand? And how many were homosexual? And how many were–" we could do a whole bunch of numbers. And then I said, "But none of that tells you what it feels like". And that, for me, is the thing. You have to have the numbers because other people want you to have the numbers. And I can quote any metric that you need in relation to any of our events, but none of that tells you what it feels like. None of that tells you. Those are the things that matter to me. They don't matter to a statistician.

STEVEN: Let me put your question back to you then. How do you capture that?

HELEN: Well, when I was doing this thing, someone said, "Helen, the plural of anecdote is not data". But I think it is. And that is backed up by testimony. I think Ben's [Walmsley[2]] got a case – it's hard to do what he's doing because we've come to believe that numbers are true and that stories aren't true. But I think stories are true.

You ask about evaluation. The truth is, it's like editing a film. Evaluation is all to do with the brief, isn't it, and how you design the questions. And what questions you're asking, and what questions you're not asking. So, we help the independent evaluators cover the territory that we'd like to see measured. And for us part of that is not about money. It's feelings. So, I can tell you that something like 96% of people in Durham who answer the survey say, "This made me happy," or they say, "This is good for this city," or, "I feel proud". It's still evaluation – you can generate numbers from the qualitative if you include them in your evaluation. I can tell you those numbers. I can tell you that interestingly, this year at *Lumiere* in 2019, we had fewer people there because the weather was shit, or who knows why? But let's say because the weather was shit. We were down from 240,000 to about 165,000. So you could say that's a terrible drop, and in the future, we'll have a terrible time. But the satisfaction rating was 20% higher. The problem is that those who evaluate have made an industry out of the way that they evaluate, and that is bought into by lots of the stakeholders. And that means that other methods of evaluation are less valued.

STEVEN: Is each ECOC unique or is there a longer narrative about capitals of culture at play?

HELEN: I think each one has to be unique in the way that it articulates something about the place where it is. But I think you could look at that long history as Beatriz [Garcia[3]] has done and others and see a way of working that to a lesser or greater extent is about creating cultural infrastructure whether that's buildings or whether that's organisations and individuals. I think the usefulness of the capital of culture is the spotlight or searchlight it points at a particular place and the place's ability to respond to that. And that, again, is like the question of pride and profile and all of that stuff that goes with that label. But then I think each one's different – there's no way that Galway could be the same as Lille. They're different places, different politics. They have different things to say, I think, each one but with a wider narrative that is about, not so much regeneration necessarily, but a sense of renewal and articulation about the place itself.

STEVEN: Can I ask you about approaches to diversity, perhaps in relation to Galway?

HELEN: That's a really important question, I think. 25% of the population of Galway City is non-Irish. That's a quarter of the population of the city. Even out in the county, there are pockets of other ethnicities. So the town of Gort, for instance, in the 80s, somebody built a meatpacking factory and then discovered that the Brazilians were better at meatpacking than the locals. So Gort became known as Yellow Town because the whole high street was Brazilian. And although in the economic recession of 2008 some people left, by that time there was intermarriage and all of that kind of stuff. So there is real cultural diversity in that city and in that surrounding area. I think I found when I got there that the Bid Book[4] programme didn't particularly reflect that.

If you look at the three Bid Book programme themes, there's lots about *language* and *landscape* and very little about *migration*. And migration in an Irish sense, seemed to me to be interpreted exclusively as emigration, the loss of land and home. But if you look at the published programme, you'll see I absolutely did integrate BAME projects and communities into the programme, in the short time I had to make that happen.

STEVEN: You have made a career out of testing public realms, particularly within UK cities that have not taken in such large-scale cultural activity before. What has been different in Galway up to February 2020? What has been common to your most difficult experiences in previous cities?

HELEN: Well, I think what happened in Galway was the whole project collapsed, not just my lovely outdoor events programme. I think the hard thing for me, and the way I work in relation to large-scale events, is that it's painstaking work and it takes a long time. And you have to really get to know the people that you're working with, who are the gatekeepers to the land of permission. And in Galway, I was only in there a very short time, and I wasn't native. And therefore, I needed another year to win the trust of those people. That would have made it easier. So, is it harder? No. It's the same hard. It's always hard. Was Galway harder than anywhere? Nowhere was harder than Liverpool. I mean, really, nowhere was harder than Liverpool. But in Galway, there was the added complication of being foreign and therefore, in a sense, it's more challenging to read the song beneath the words. People are saying things, and in London or Liverpool or Durham or wherever we worked, we sort of know what's being said or not said. But in Galway, it's different.

STEVEN: Do you think that will shape how you approach your future work?

HELEN: No. I mean, the question about Galway is should we have done it, given the short time frame and the state it was in when we arrived? But I'm absolutely confident that we would have pulled it off, and it would have been a very spectacular ECoC programme. I'm very proud of the programme as it stands. The external, prevailing circumstances meant that that wasn't possible. I think you just had to look at the programme launch. I don't know if you were in Galway for that day?

STEVEN: I was, yes.

HELEN: So you were in Eyre Square, and you could feel it, couldn't you? Everything that we've talked about at the beginning of this interview. That's anticipation, amazement, inspiration. That sense of wanting to have been there for the moment. All of that stuff, that's the hallmark of what we do at Artichoke and that's what we were doing with Galway.

STEVEN: Should we ask who these things should be for? Is it not about serving the needs of people who were already super-served with their cultural consumption, but the people who wouldn't normally attend?

HELEN: See, I disagree with you because I think they're both important. Because I think that those who don't normally attend are really important, and those are the people that you fight to get there, but you and people like you are equally important because of your sense of entitlement and the fact that you think you've seen everything. And I bet you, you've never seen anything like that [laughter].

STEVEN: True. You're correct. Yes.

HELEN: So, that sense, the sort of smug, (not that you're smug), but the educated arts-going literati people, they're also my target. Because I want them to understand that there's a world out there that they don't know about, and that they can – I mean, the whole thing is about sharing, isn't it? It's about standing shoulder to shoulder with people that you would never normally spend time with and realising a common humanity and a common sense of marvel. Marvelling at what the imagination of an artist can do to a very familiar place. And you share that. It isn't for anybody in particular. So when everyone says, "Who's your audience?" and we say, "For everybody," we really mean it. Really mean it. And it's to knock the complacency out of the arts audience and it's to introduce a new experience to people who would normally go to the hurling or sit in front of the telly, or something. And my whole passion is always about 'live'. It's about the live moment; about being there. Which is why this whole push currently, COVID-inspired, to shove everything online I'm finding quite difficult. Because there will be a return. A need to return to the live experience.

STEVEN: Absolutely. I'm going to have to edit this, so I don't come across as a member of the arts-going literati now [laughter].

HELEN: I didn't say you were. You just implied you were, and I took you up on it.

STEVEN: Well, it was actually an interesting moment because having been to several Artichoke events over some years ...

HELEN: Oh, you're a fan? Would you describe yourself as a fan?

STEVEN: Well, what's interesting is that breadth of perspective. Because I'm stood there at the launch having seen your work in different countries, different places in time. Having that kind of knowledge infrastructure of why I'm stood there or why that event's happening with people who wouldn't know Helen Marriage if you ran over them in your car. So, to have those different things come together in one moment and be able to be a broad church if you like, for all of it, is the rationale?

HELEN: I really care. I mean, it's what I really am passionate about. I love working with artists, however difficult, and they are, because of what they can do. But I really love the audience. I love being able to give people a present that changes their life. It does. I don't care what anyone says. But that sense that you've embedded a memory in people. When we were in Derry and we did *Lumiere* and it was such a fight around what sites we could use, and what was safe, and what wasn't safe, and what "after dark" would mean so that people could move safely from one territory to another.

Everyone was very nervous about all of it. And the authorities wouldn't close the roads, and it was all very complicated. But then suddenly there was a moment when the Peace Bridge, which is usually very underused obviously, was suddenly heaving with people. We had to close it and pulse people across because so many people wanted to cross at the same time – and one of my Board members was walking across behind a grandmother, her daughter and her grandchildren, and he heard her say, "I'm just so glad that your childhood is so different from mine". Well, if that don't make you cry … [laughter].

ART AND CREATIVITY

Following the recent publication of Arts Council England's (2020) Let's Create strategy, with its focus on creativity and (an apparent) move toward more culturally democratic ideas of everyday participation, there has been much debate in the English policy sector around the potential impact of these ideas.

STEVEN: I'm just going to quote you back at yourself for a moment[5]: "I believe that artists are the prophets of the future. They see a world people like me can't see. So it's always worth creating a platform and opportunity for them to express themselves". I think a lot of what you said today and a lot of what you've said previously – I'll let you put your own description on it, but there's a privileging of the artist. It's an artist with a capital 'A'. It's an artist that somehow is in touch with things that us mere mortals are not. I wonder, do you – first of all, do you accept that?

HELEN: I think they are different. I don't know about privileging but they're certainly seeing things.

STEVEN: I don't necessarily disagree with you. I mean, I think it is a specifically Romantic conception you have?

HELEN: I think that's a classification hang-up. I mean, it's just a truth. It's not saying anything other than – I'm sure a scientist – I don't know – looks at some bit of engineering or a skin disease or something and goes "Aha!" – I mean, I don't know how a scientist genetically engineers a cure for leukaemia, but they have, and that's a kind of visionary thing.

STEVEN: So it's not privileging the artist above other professions. It's saying–

HELEN: It's about brain patterning – I have an autistic nephew who has taught himself Chinese and is fluent in Chinese. He's a linguist. It's a talent. It's a skill. Artists have another particular skill, and their skill is to tell us stories about ourselves.

STEVEN: So "Everyone an Artist"? Discuss.

HELEN: No. Absolutely not. I think everyone is creative. I'm super creative. I can knit. I can knit without a pattern. I can make beautiful things, but I'm not an artist. My knitting doesn't tell you anything or reveal anything about life or truths or – so the whole 64 Million Artists business is not something that I particularly subscribe to. They got me to make a video for their website and I think I'm probably the only person who says, "I disagree".

STEVEN: And you're on the London Area Council, so presumably you are aware of the direction of travel towards cultural democracy within the Arts Council?

HELEN: Yes. The whole *Let's Create*[6] thing is absolutely driven by a desire to explore the idea of creativity in everybody in the country. And I think creativity is absolutely great. Go for it. But they're not artists. Just as they're not architects. I mean, I wouldn't want my house to be built by somebody down the road who fancied building a house.

STEVEN: You were at the London Area Council meeting in September 2018 when Simon Mellor[7] – I don't know whether he was reassuring Alex Beard[8] or just the room in general when he said–

HELEN: Were you there?

STEVEN: Was I there? As if. [laughter]

HELEN: So how do you know?

STEVEN: Well, it's in the minutes.

HELEN: Oh, okay.

STEVEN: So I'll quote you the minutes: "It's important to be clear that the Royal Opera House is as important as *Creative People and Places*". Being–

HELEN: What's the question?

STEVEN: Being the cultural policy nerd that I am, I think future historians are going to see that as a seminal moment in the English arts sector. It strikes me as frankly amazing that a senior director of the Arts Council should have to even utter that sentence. And 10 years ago, it would have been unimaginable, partly because *Creative People and Places*[9] didn't exist 10 years ago [laughter].

HELEN: As I was about to point out. Yeah.

STEVEN: I just wondered if you have had anything – whether you have any thoughts on that?

HELEN: Well, I think it's true, is the truth. I think the Opera House is as important as *Creative People and Places*. Is your question, why is it necessary to say that?

STEVEN: Yeah. So I mean, obviously, if you turn the sentence around – if you say *Creative People and Places* is as important as the Royal Opera House.

HELEN: That's what you would expect, isn't it?

STEVEN: It's obvious. That's what one might call a recalibration of the scales, isn't it?

HELEN: But I think that you have to take what has happened in the context of the ROCC Report[10] and the whole rebalancing agenda and the idea of creating a balanced portfolio. And the Opera House has always been held up as the home of the London elite, a place where huge amounts of money are spent on the stage and also by a certain section of the public on the tickets, etc., etc., etc. So it's always been a sort of Aunt Sally [an easy target] for those who feel that the London metropolitan elite is something to be attacked in the name of a broader kind of democracy. I think the Opera House is extraordinary. It employs 1,000 people, most of whom are artists of one kind or another whether these are armourers or wig makers or the orchestra or the chorus or the technicians. And they're producing work of the highest quality. I mean, really extraordinary stuff. And I defend them completely. I think that they could probably do more, but they do already do tons to encourage greater access and education and outreach and all of that kind of stuff to reach those undiscovered people that we're trying to get to as well.

There are limitations, financial limitations, in running a building of that size and scale, and the capacity is the biggest limitation. If opera could be performed at Wembley, if that was a culturally satisfying way of doing opera then it wouldn't feel like an elite sport because 40,000 people would get to see it as opposed to – I don't know what capacity is – 2,000 or something. So the economics of it don't work because it's an expensive art form with a limited capacity to reach people and therefore the balance between ticketing income and the numbers of people who can get to it are skewed – it's a weighted balance. I don't know. If Spurs perform to let's say 40,000 people – I don't know what the capacity of White Hart Lane is or whatever. 40,000 people and the tickets there are, what, 100 quid?

STEVEN: No idea.

HELEN: Something. But you can see immediately that if you're doing £100 times 40,000 you've got a huge amount of money generated from box office to pay the very expensive costs of putting on a football match, most of which are going into the players. Most of those costs are going to players, and still, it requires subsidy from the owner. Manchester United still needs to be bailed out by the American owners etc. So the economics of opera are problematic, and the issue is how can we fund it in such a way and generate interest in such a way that it is not an exclusive moneyed activity? So in the old days when Raymond Gubbay[11] used to do the giant operas in Wembley Arena, I mean, they were fantastic [laughter], and I think demonstrated that there was an appetite to see the stuff. It was just hard to make the economics work. But more important are the 1,000 people, all of whom are probably about to be thrown out of work due to COVID, and that level of skill that is very particular. We should really fight for it to be retained, the wig makers and the armourers and all of those people. It's a very particular thing that you lose at your peril, because you won't be able to remake it.

STEVEN: How would you feel, were Darren Henley to put his foot on the throttle in a post-COVID environment, with a view to the Arts Council delivering rather than articulating a culturally democratic approach which resulted in significant de-funding of national institutions like the Royal Opera House?

[silence]

HELEN: I think it would be a mistake.

STEVEN: I'm going to pride myself and sleep soundly this evening on the thought I managed to ask you a question that resulted in you pausing before you answered [laughter].

HELEN: It's hard. The Arts Council now describes itself as a development agency, which is a new thing. That's not a model that I've grown up with. I'm old. I've been around a long time. It's not what I think – it's not, historically, what they've done. And I am old-fashioned enough to believe – call it romantic if you like – that the best ideas, the new ideas spring from artists, not administrators.

STEVEN: Aside from whether the Arts Council are actually able to deliver on the signalling that's come out of the *Lets Create* work, is the question of how they can reconcile that ongoing desire for excellence and subsidising the leisure pursuits of a small elite via large sums of public money. I mean, it doesn't …

HELEN: "of a small *tax-paying* elite", I think you should add [laughter].

STEVEN: Is it that you feel your ideas that you've talked about there, in terms of your age and tradition and so on – is there a sense at which you think your ideas have become old-fashioned, in some way?

HELEN: Just constant. Imagine a different world. You say they get too much money. What do the Royal Opera House get? 15 million? 20 million? What do they get?

STEVEN: I think it's 24, wasn't it, last year?

HELEN: Okay. So imagine a world where they get 24 million, and the Southbank gets whatever it gets. But Dance UK gets 24 million, and I get 24 million, and everyone else gets proportions of that, would you care, then? Because I would argue that the problem is a political problem in the underfunding of the subsidy given to the Arts Council to make investments in new, diverse, whatever they want to do. But the balance is historic. And the funding overall is ridiculously small. So, the reliance on lottery was never what was ever intended. Call me old-fashioned. But when the Arts Council grant is less than 1% of the National Health Service overspend, and the Arts Council is heading into doing art in mental health, art in hospitals, filling gaps that the Health Service itself isn't funding or can't fund, whatever. I think the proportions might be wrong but the cake is not big enough to make those proportions bigger. I can spend 24 million quid a year easily and I would produce lovely and fabulous things that millions of people would see. But that doesn't make illegitimate the fact that the Opera House is spending it on something that is very particular, that is a jewel. I think it is a very special extraordinary art form.

In the end, it's the music. In the end, it takes you somewhere that you would never go in your normal life. So when the Three Tenors were around and when *Nessun Dorma* was the lead song of the 1990 football World Cup in Italy, and all of those moments we remember. It's not an elite art form. It's just the means of production. And if you're going to do it at that level and quality in such a small space which is a space that is hand-built for that art form, it becomes economically problematic. But the problem is not how much they're getting, it's how little everyone else is getting.

STEVEN: Let me ask you about politics, because I want to ask you whether you see yourself as a political beast in all of these debates?

HELEN: Yeah. Of course.

STEVEN: And how do you reconcile wanting to maintain and indeed increase funding for the Royal Opera House – where's your politics of everyone an artist just to revisit that?

HELEN: I think everyone creative, not everyone an artist. I think it's different, and I think access is hugely important.

I think the problem with the opposition to the Opera House is – forgive me, but it's based on envy. It's not the art form anyone hates, it's the audience. That's why I asked you if you'd ever been and you say you went once. And then six weeks later, you're

Steven Hadley

listening to the music that you'd heard there and you're crying. I mean, we wouldn't be having this conversation if you hadn't had that experience and been moved by something that you were fiercely critical of. But its power to move you was real. It's real. It does do stuff. People would say, "Well, I've never been because I can't afford it", and that's a real problem. People need to be enabled to appreciate it as an art form, not as an enemy.

STEVEN: I feel we've come full circle because you talked so eloquently about personal subjective experience at Artichoke projects, of which I have had many myself. This is where the whole issue around cultural value and cultural democracy becomes so important because it's a dangerous place to go to say, "You have this cultural experience of crying at the opera, that's valid and legitimate and I endorse that. But you have this cultural experience of a CPP project and that's illegitimate and I don't ..."

HELEN: I didn't say it was illegitimate, I said that the amount of investment didn't necessarily produce work of quality.

STEVEN: It's not intended to though is it? I think the essence of the approach of cultural democracy is that the value is determined by the people who are experiencing it, not the people who are delivering it.

HELEN: But is it enough? What I try and do with our work is that if we're working in an unlikely setting with people who are easy to ignore, and don't usually get involved in cultural activity, that just working with them isn't enough. It has to be great. It has to be great. It has to be an experience that they go, "This changed me". Not, "I knitted a doily". *It has to be fantastic.*

To me the issue is about investing in community. It's about making it a million times better than it could be if an artist weren't there. And that's part of the problem. The whole cultural democracy argument that says "don't you tell me what's good, I'll do what I want, and that's good enough". I've never believed that the production of art and artistic experience is ordinary. People always say when we're doing a new piece, "Have you consulted the community to see what they want?" And the answer is always 'no'. Because what they want is generally what they can already imagine. And what I want is to do something that introduces that audience to stuff that they could never imagine. But when they see it, they know that it's what they've always wanted.

STEVEN: I don't know how apocryphal it is, there's a Henry Ford quote about developing the first car where he says "If I'd asked my customers what they wanted, they'd have said a faster horse".

HELEN: I mean, I'm with Henry. It's a profession. That's why I make the distinction between creative and artist. Everyone is creative, they can knit, or cook, or paint a picture, or play the violin. I can play the violin but I'm not a musician. I've learnt to play the violin. I think it's sad about the Arts Council direction of travel which you will have seen from the minutes that were in *Arts Professional*.[12] The whole argument about the word "art" originally not being included in the Arts Council strategy. And that, for me, is a mistake. It's a special thing. They're the only people in the country who have that word in their title.

STEVEN: This debate has been rumbling through the Arts Council from the 70s to the present day.

HELEN: But it's circular. It'll change.

STEVEN: It is circular. I think the difficulty is they have tied themselves in knots with *Let's Create,* in an attempt to do the impossible, which is to have an approach that embraces cultural democracy while simultaneously maintaining excellence. Is it the equivalent of having a strategy that promotes multiculturalism and apartheid?

HELEN: Excellence is not antithetical to cultural democracy. Excellence is an adjective that describes everything that they should be doing. It's not a separate thing. The Opera House is not the only thing that's excellent. I mean, we started by you talking about our work and whether it was valued by the arts establishment. Even if not, you can't deny that it's – in terms of production values, in terms of the way it looks, the way it behaves, the logistics around it, it's excellent. It is. Because I wouldn't let it be anything else. But the two are not antithetical. Excellence is just an adjective and is something that one should strive for. That doesn't mean work created in the context of cultural democracy can't be excellent.

STEVEN: There's a passage in the *Let's Create* strategy that explicitly says that ACE no longer believe in a scale of values and will no longer advocate for one art form or one experience as having more value than any other. The implications of saying that in the strategy effectively creates a kind of flat terrain and a flat horizon. Where not only can you not advocate for one art form being better or of more value or higher up the hierarchy than another, but you can't advocate for an experience being more – or less – excellent than another. But I feel that your guiding star is much more focused on there being an external, almost objective notion of what is excellent, that you want to navigate toward?

HELEN: It feels like it's subjective, but there is an attainable objectivity around knowing when something is fabulous. I mean it is just fabulous when it is. You know when you've fallen in love. You just know. And that's an emotional thing always. I think assuming that levels of investment equate to excellence is wrong. I think that different art forms require different investment or have historically required different investment because of the means of production that is required to get to that state of excellence.

So, an orchestra – what the hell will happen to orchestras post-COVID? I have no idea. You have 80 or 90 hugely well-trained professional people and a repertoire that is so old-fashioned that only a certain tiny fraction of people wants to listen to it. And anyway, they could listen to it in much higher quality on their CD player at home or streaming it, whatever. But that doesn't mean that you don't need to be present – I listen to the Bach Double Violin Concerto and I cry every single time. It's the most beautiful thing you can imagine. And to lose our ability to produce that level of beauty I think would be a tragic thing. And I say all this as a person in the arts operating at a certain level that is, and has always been, massively committed to those broad audiences. Almost nothing we do, do you pay for. Anybody can come. We do all the outreach to get people to come who would never normally be there. But that doesn't blind me to the fact that there are art forms, particular other art forms that need other conditions in which to flourish and play to different audiences and interests. And I don't think one makes either illegitimate.

STEVEN: It would be wrong of me not to return to COVID. Do you have any feelings about where you think we might end up and what your sense of this "back to normal" or a "new normal" is?

HELEN: I think that there are organisations that probably won't survive and for the individuals who are invested in those, that's obviously tragic. I can't see an easy way for building-based organisations that have fixed auditoria and fixed ways of working to reopen quickly. I think that the economics of playing to a 25% house, which is what social distancing suggests, and not letting anyone use the loos or the bar is going to make opening problematic, in the commercial theatre world anyway.

I'm fascinated by, but not interested particularly in, the rush to online. I think that that whole "we can do it just as well online" is not true with lots of art forms. And I think that the need to be visible online is a need to be present and to be seen to be still operating, as well as to keep people occupied and to provide entertainment. But it just isn't the same to watch a live stream out of the National Theatre as it is to be in that space. And I am, as ever, a huge advocate of the live experience. I think that post-COVID the need for live experiences and the need to congregate in whatever way that's possible will become more important. Because actually what everyone is feeling at the moment is the loss of that. And the screen, although hugely useful, is a means of dissemination rather than a real experience, I think. You can't smell it.

I think that financially the challenge will come when both statutory authorities, trusts and foundations, and corporates decide that their priorities lie elsewhere than the arts. I think then that would be a challenge for us because we raise so much money from all of those sources to do what we do. But I think there are real opportunities if the money can be found. If you gave me the Opera House's 24 million quid, I could show you some amazing stuff [laughter].

STEVEN: I think that is the nub, isn't it? Because you can make any number of arguments about other sectors and low levels of funding and so on, but when you're forced – and I think this is where the Arts Council have to reconcile philosophy and pragmatism, is when you're in a zero-sum game where your pot isn't going to get any bigger, and you just have to choose to spend what you have, then–

HELEN: But that's the failure. That's the failure. I mean – what do they get, the Arts Council? 407 million or something.[13] That's the failure. You double it. You keep the Opera House on the funding that it's on. You carve up the rest differently. You don't have this binary tension between elite and community or excellence and creative or whatever. It all disappears. The failure is not lack of balance. The failure is lack of investment. And doubling it, particularly in the current circumstances, is peanuts. So that's the real argument. The real argument is about successive Arts Councils and historic Ministerial inability to get the Treasury to cough up. So, carving up an increasingly small cake is going to bring all of those tensions. But it isn't inevitable. They talk about balanced portfolio. That's an Arts Council expression. You could rebalance the portfolio without doing harm to anything that already exists. It just needs more money.

STEVEN: They've been talking about that for decades. That's the thing about the ROCC Report, and the *Hard Facts to Swallow* report. That was based on the title of a report from the 1980s.[14]

HELEN: In my lifetime, we've moved from, "We do not fund amateurs," to "Everyone is an Artist". And I am consistent in my view, which is everyone isn't an artist, but everyone is creative and that you need to support the making of work in whatever context that needs. Whether that's a solo artist working in their studio, who needs a way to show that work or whether that's an orchestra or an opera house or whether it's me. It just needs to be properly invested in and not to be seen in competition with each other. It's all part of the same thing. But because the cake has more or less stayed the same, shrunk even, the priorities are changing according to the political perception of what is important. The arms-length principle is being abandoned. So, the Arts Council no longer make policy separate from government, and they sway in the political wind. But the real failure is the failure of successive Arts Ministers not to get the funding doubled, in my view. If I were Jennie Lee, if I were Arts Minister, that would be the deal "I'll take this brief. Give me twice the money for the Arts Council". End of conversation.

STEVEN: I'm glad you managed to get Jennie Lee in at the end. That pleases me [laughter].

HELEN: Well, I mean, look what she did. I mean, have we ever had anybody since her who was so great? – Chris Smith, I suppose, Ed Vaizey a bit, but none of them persuaded the Treasury that it was a worthwhile investment. Even now, in the era where Rishi Sunak is dealing out money hand over fist, as far as I'm aware, the Arts Council is spending its reserves. I don't think the Arts Council is benefiting from additional funds and in this situation that's extraordinary.

STEVEN: Yeah. I agree completely.

HELEN: There you go.

STEVEN: Thank you. Thank you enormously.

This interview took place before the Government announcement of a £1.57bn grant to the arts and creative industries. The text has been edited for length.

ACKNOWLEDGEMENTS

With special thanks to Ben Walmsley, Beatriz Garcia, Steve Green, Pat Collins, Kim-Marie Spence and many others for question suggestions and to Anna Vinegrad for help with planning and coordination.

Notes

1 HMRC is Her Majesty's Revenue and Customs is a non-ministerial department of the UK Government responsible for the collection of taxes.

2 Prof Ben Walmsley is Director of the Centre for Cultural Value (https://ahc.leeds.ac.uk/centre-cultural-value-1).

3 Dr Beatriz Garcia is the Director of Impacts 18 | European Capital of Culture Research Programme and a member of the European Capital of Culture Selection Committee.

4 The "bid book" is the document submitted by a candidate city in response to a call from the European Commission, setting out the city's objectives, programme, etc. Galway 2020's bid book, *Making Waves*, can be accessed from: https://galway2020.ie/wp-content/uploads/ 2016/07/G2020-Bid-web.pdf.

5 The Journal (2020) *Official Galway 2020 Opening Ceremony Cancelled Due to Weather Warnings.* Accessed from www.thejournal.ie/galway-2020-capital-of-culture-helen-marriage-interview-4997214-Feb2020/.

6 Arts Council England's Strategy for 2020 –2030 accessible from www.artscouncil.org.uk/letscreate.

7 Simon Mellor is Deputy Chief Executive, Arts & Culture at Arts Council England (www.artscouncil.org.uk/users/simon-mellor).

8 Alex Beard CBE is Chief Executive of the Royal Opera House (www.roh.org.uk/people/alex-beard).

9 www.creativepeopleplaces.org.uk/.

10 *Rebalancing Our Cultural Capital*, a report addressing the balance of arts funding between London and the rest of England, can be accessed from www.gpsculture.co.uk/rocc.php.

11 www.raymondgubbay.co.uk/about-us.

12 www.artsprofessional.co.uk/news/fears-within-ace-over-dumbing-down-art.

13 For details of Arts Council England funding allocations see: www.artscouncil.org.uk/
    about-us/how-we-invest-public-money.

14 *A Hard Fact to Swallow* (1982) by the Policy Studies Institute found Arts Council
    England expenditure in London in 1980–1981 to be £3.37 per head of population (php)
    as against £0.66 php in the rest of England.

Post-Capitalism and Cultural Leadership

Milena Dragićević Šešić, UNESCO Chair in Cultural Policy and Management: In Conversation (Serbia)

Višnja Kisić and Goran Tomka

Chapter 5

DOI: 10.4324/9781003390725-5

Dr. Milena Dragićević Šešić, prof. emerita, is former Rector of University of Arts, Belgrade, founder of the UNESCO Chair in Interculturalism, Art Management and Mediation, and Professor of Cultural Policy & Management, Cultural Studies, Media Studies. She was awarded the Commandeur dans l'Ordre des Palmes Academiques (French Ministry of Education) in 2002, the ENCATC Fellowship Laureate (2019) and the University of Arts Laureate in 2004 and 2019. She has worked as an expert for UNESCO, EUNIC, European Cultural Foundation and the Council of Europe.

INTRODUCTION

In today's integrated global capitalism and its neoliberal cosmovision, contemporary cultural policies have increasingly been mirroring this dominant way of global governing. We see discourses and practices of economic impact measurements within cultural policies; precarity and austerity measures in the cultural sector which go hand in hand with the push for profit-friendly creative industries; privatisation of public resources and increased commodification of cultural experiences. All this has normalised capitalist logic within dominant public policies, making it hard to stretch the imagination beyond it. Numerous voices within cultural policy research have spoken against these directions (Banks, 2010; Belfiore, 2020; Lee, 2014; McGuigan, 2005). Today, there is more and more literature on post-capitalism, and there is increasingly a sense, after the pandemic, that capitalism is experiencing its limitations and frontiers. So, more and more thinking is invested in post-capitalist futures. However, cultural policy today hasn't been actively dealing with post-capitalist imaginings and it is hard to see practical advancements away from its "business as usual". The challenge of exploring substantial alternatives, other visions and different ways of governing culture beyond capitalist logic remains to be grasped. In this conversation with Milena Dragićević Šešić, we discuss the tenets of capitalist cultural policies today and wonder about alternatives to them – about possibilities for different, post-capitalist futures for cultural policies and ideas that are maybe on the margins today.

This text is a compilation of four conversations that took place in person in August and September 2020 and online in April 2021. Interviews were edited for length and clarity.

A CRITIQUE OF CAPITALIST CULTURAL POLICY

VIŠNJA & GORAN: As a cultural policy researcher, educator and expert, you have been educated and worked in the context of socialist Yugoslavia, a country that has been openly socialist and has been experimenting with cultural policies in this direction. At the same time, you have followed many counter-cultural initiatives across the world, many of which are also anti-capitalist. But what is also interesting is that you have witnessed the process of transformation of socialist cultural policies after the breakdown of the Socialist Federative Republic of Yugoslavia and the Soviet Bloc, a process that has been marketed as democratisation and liberalisation of cultural policies, but could also be described as a shift towards capitalist cultural policies. This process did involve interventions from international and intergovernmental bodies, in terms of know-how sharing, experts and consultants as well as funding in the cultural field. Looking back at it, what would you say were the traits of such transformation?

MILENA: Well, cultural policies have changed dramatically even within the Western, capitalist world. With the arrival of neoliberalism, or late capitalism, so many things have changed even in France or the UK. But, as I was living in Yugoslavia, which was pushed into a rapid transition, processes that lasted maybe decades in the West, happened overnight here, so they were easy to spot. I would highlight two immediate pressures on cultural policy-making within all the post-socialist countries in Central and Eastern Europe. First is *competitiveness* as the crucial value of the capitalist system which has been introduced within each country but also in-between countries. So, *competitiveness* motivates ministries and countries to present internationally their cultural policies much better than they really are. The introduction of competitiveness in the cultural sector had immediate repercussions in the theatre field, publishing field and many other areas that had been organised completely differently in socialist countries.

The other element of capitalist logic in policy-making is a *pressure of project logic.* Socialist actors, cultural organisations and institutions had learned to plan in a long-term manner and their programmes and their activities had a certain security in a long-term financing period. They did not have to rush from project to project to survive. On the other hand, this pressure of project logic was accepted by the part of the cultural community as a potential agent of change. We thought that it would bring desired change and serve as an antidote to the routine work of institutions who were just recycling their annual programmes over and over again. Because, unfortunately, permanent activities, like permanent exhibitions or yearly festivals, were not evaluated. That was a weak point in socialist policy. So, we hoped that the project logic pressure would finally replace the political apparatus (nomenklatura), by young, motivated artists and cultural workers. However, in fact, we got terribly tired, exploited, over-exploited as artists and cultural operators. We became a cultural precariat as a social class.

VIŠNJA & GORAN: Are there any good illustrative examples of this shift to a competitive short-term project logic?

MILENA: In socialist countries, there were theatres with ensembles, even studio-theatres. The system that was offered after the 2000s was asking for theatres without ensembles, where each actor is going to be in a permanent competitive position, going from audition to audition, to get another engagement. This was not only an element of direct capitalist logic where everything is about fighting, and only the most competitive are going to survive. This was one of the practices which was totally decontextualised – it was not part of our cultural context. Here, theatre with ensemble[1] was not a part of socialist logic but of artistic and cultural logic and tradition. When the famous theatre director Bojan Stupica was invited to become artistic director of Atelje 212 Theatre in the 1960s (this was the first and the only theatre without a permanent ensemble in Belgrade, Serbia and Yugoslavia), he said that he would accept that position, if the operational director (Mira Trailovic), succeeded in persuading local authorities to give 20 salaries for 20 actors that are going to form the permanent ensemble. He basically thought that theatre work is worthwhile artistically only if they are able to create common shared values in one artistic ensemble together.

So, he was not making this suggestion on the basis of so-called "socialist cultural policy" that will guarantee jobs and salaries to artists, he was speaking about the necessity of having a permanently paid ensemble to be free to experiment, to research within artistic practice and not to just create performance after performance in the shortest possible time, where every time the actor will be in another group of artists with another theatre director. Consequently, he knew that there would be no time and no possibility for the creation of artworks which have a real public value.

VIŠNJA & GORAN: Competitiveness and the productivist pressure of project logic have brought much more insecurity and precarity for the cultural sector. But these are not the only traits of capitalist cultural policy-making. What would you suggest are some other important tenets of capitalist logic in cultural policy which you see today across the globe?

MILENA: Well, a lot has been written about the processes of commodification of culture and arts as a mechanism of capitalist logic. I would say that the copyright system is a perfect illustration of that because of the extent that it detaches the artist from their own artistic work. Just as an example of that, in 2004, I was participating in Minneapolis in public debates about the future of public art in Minneapolis, where several working-class neighbourhoods were supposed to be torn down. They had been built in the 60s, with murals and mosaics done by local artists at that time. All of those artists were present at that moment in the Minneapolis debate, and they absolutely thought that the destruction of their artworks is something that has to happen, that they don't have any rights over them, as they were paid in the 60s for those mosaics. Now, the owner, the city or a corporation, has all rights to tear it down and make new buildings. Those artists didn't understand my comments about their moral rights, that they should demand conservation of murals and mosaics or their placements in other locations or at the same location, but in the new context of the new urban policies. They really thought that by selling their copyrights they just can have a photo of their former artistic work and nothing more than that.

And this example of course, very much points out another element of capitalist logic in cultural policy and the cultural field today, which is the process of privatisation of public resources, that puts into question the ownership of the instruments and tools of production and participation in the artistic process. That is the reason why many generations of cultural workers had lobbied for public spaces, so that not everything is in private ownership. Today, we are witnessing the huge privatisation of public spaces and resources. Of course, in some areas of art, such as novel writing, the tools of production might be very easy to gather. But in many other fields, ownership of the technical resources for production – ownership of spaces for production such as film studios or theatres, the theatre equipment – might be crucial elements which prevent artists and cultural workers from being able to work.

I witnessed the tragic situation of a group of artists in India, because the lack of public spaces for both rehearsals and for presentations is extremely visible there. Sometimes it seems to me that in India they really celebrate a kind of a cruel capitalism as a model of behaviour in a society. The successful survive and become multimillionaires. In Mumbai now, the rich move around only with helicopters – living and working in buildings with heliodromes – thus, that they do not participate in city life, which is tough and hectic. And on the other side, you have millions, in fact, you have a population of a billion living on the edge of survival. How many theatres should exist for that many audiences? How many public spaces for representations, for rehearsals? No one thought about it. In capitalism, if you are an artist, you have to be an entrepreneur at the same time. You are responsible for everything. Making research about theatres in India, I have found the most entrepreneurial, resourceful and skilful groups.

So, where do they rehearse? One of them, Katkatha theatre, on the roof. Luckily, most of the time Delhi is relatively dry, but during monsoon season, they have no possibility to work. Jana Natya Manch (Janam) theatre for 15 years had rehearsed on streets, in the parks, in private houses. It was due to the solidarity action of mostly colleagues, friends of the Indian left, that they succeeded to have a studio house devoted to Safdar Hashmi (Studio Safdar). And this place is serving not only Janam theatre but all who like to present something, to discuss, to make exhibitions, etc. So, this is the model of responsible civil society that has empathy and solidarity, offers its space and acts as a substitute to the public sector because there is no real public sector in the arts.

Many of these private, but open places are owned by sons, daughters or wives of big Bollywood actors that have earned money. And then they built theatres in honour of their grandparents who used to be travelling actors, travelling artists. These few auditoriums, one in Mumbai (Prithvi), one in Bangalore (Ranga Shankara), are the rare theatre spaces that one artistic collective can decently rent. When I say decently rent, it means to share profit from the tickets. Most auditoriums and theatre halls that are privately owned are rented for the same price no matter whether you are a theatre troupe or a company that would like to rent the space for some celebration. Can you reach this rent by selling the tickets? Usually not. Because theatre tickets are extremely cheap in India – some states, such as Bengal, even have a limit on the price, of 50 rupees. If the ticket costs more, you have to pay tax to the state and it becomes absolutely impossible to cover expenses as a small theatre group. So, the capitalist way of production, distribution and consumption is severely preventing any kind of socially responsible art to be developed, any kind of experimental art, any form that is demanding lots of resources, investments, time and professionalisation.

VIŠNJA & GORAN: This example shows quite well how difficult it might be to have the basic access to resources and instruments for production even if you are a professional artist, a professional ensemble. Which makes it extremely difficult to practise certain arts as an amateur. Even if contemporary cultural policy pays attention to audience development and cultural participation, it does so in a way that is highly mediated via professionals, in a way that predominantly puts non-professionals in the role of consumers. As we know, things used to be different?

MILENA: Yes, capitalism is asking for professionalisation, you have to be very professional "to count". But many artists, writers for example, are not "professionals" in the sense that they make a living out of writing, because even the best of them can't. In most of the countries, with smaller markets, if they're not writing in English, they can't make a living out of it. But the very logic of capitalism asks for the total division between professionals and amateurs. It is disqualifying amateurs as those who do things in their spare time, again, as non-productive. In the 60s, within the counter-cultural movement, especially theatres of intervention and social action, this distinction was much more blurred. Even big theatres wanted to integrate those who they recognised to have interest, energy, talents and skills into their work. Those amateurs could contribute a lot to the research, to the problem that they want to make performance about, but then finally, also, to the performance itself. On the other hand, the logic of cultural policy-making in late capitalism demands that this distinction has to be absolutely clear. Who has the right to be supported by the state? The one who is a professional, a member of an association, formal collective or institution.

Here of course, I am not talking about the surge of support for volunteer work and commitment to safeguard heritage and to socially engaged arts, across the UK for example, which often acts at the expense of shrinking the funding for professional paid work in culture. There is a distinction between amateurism and volunteering. Amateurism as a part of "workers culture" was an important element of cultural policies in welfare France in the 60s and 70s, and a highly relevant topic in Yugoslavia. That topic has totally disappeared with late capitalism. Cultural operators are expected to rely on volunteers in order to reduce expenses, even for the highly professional and skilful tasks. So, workers are abandoned in the cultural sense. Nowadays, no one talks about the culture of the workers, while the term organisational culture has been taken from the business management and cannot even function properly in the field of culture because it is confusing and contradictory. Finally, "organisational culture" has often been shaped to allow greater exploitation or greater utilisation of someone's work.

In the 70s when Yugoslavia tried to introduce Western European working hours, from 9 to 17 h (in Yugoslavia we worked from 7 to 15 h), this was faced with such resistance. We were so much against that, because this way your work uses you in the period of the day when you are the most productive. That does not allow for part-time study, specialisation, dedication to more serious hobbies, such as amateur theatre. You cannot have a city amateur theatre with people of different professions and generations if you work from 9 to 17 h. This is something which cultural management today does not pay any attention towards, and it used to. In Germany, you even had the term "leisure engineer" – a person who organises activities in spare time, because the assumption was that people would have more and more spare time. My professor Dumazedier wrote a few books in the 60s, one of which is "Towards the civilisation of leisure" (Dumazedier, 1962). It leads us towards a future in which four hours of a day would be occupied by work through which you earn your living, while the rest would be reserved for time with the family, hobbies, activities, leisure and mental improvement. Today, his books are rarely mentioned, and we see not the decrease but increase in working times and burnouts.

CAPITALIST FRAMES OF ANALYSIS IN CULTURAL POLICY

VIŠNJA & GORAN: Contemporary cultural policies have been criticised for their economisation and the adoption of analytical and evaluation tools that are quantitative and monetary. Do you see that as another kind of late capitalist pressure on the cultural sector?

MILENA: My latest example of this kind of pressure on cultural experts comes from the evaluation of a festival on the river Niger, in Mali, that I am doing at this very moment, for a foundation from Holland. I thought, and that's my understanding of the impact of the festival, that we have to look at the impact of this festival on pan-African cultural processes; on cultural processes that would reintegrate the state of Mali, which was severely disintegrated in 2012; that we have to look at the contribution to artistic developments that this festival is assisting; to social cohesion and to social integration of the communities, etc. I proposed a lot of parameters of evaluation, and following those I made a lot of analysis options to prove how impactful the festival had been for capacity building, for raising self confidence among cultural operators, for contributing to the creation of an authentic entrepreneurial logic in the cultural sector, African logic called *Maya entrepreneurship*, etc. And for me, that was enough argumentation to show the importance and impact of the festival.

However, my evaluation was returned saying: "we appreciate the report, but our Board wants to have numbers: numbers of audiences, numbers of countries, numbers of participants, numbers of how the network has enlarged". Basically, numbers and numbers. This is what I call capitalist logic. I responded that much more important is the creation of the ICAM network[2] with eight members, then the creation of the KIA network[3] of 24 members, and that one is still more important on the field than, for example, ARTERIAL network[4] of more than 100 members. Numbers are not really showing the impact, the extent, the reasoning of the network. So, why, and how have I tried to prove that? It's not about 100 contacts with cultural organisations throughout Africa that are going to easily make change but finding eight partners that are capable of spreading the idea of *Maya entrepreneurship.* They are eight partners that can create capacity building programmes and training centres for artists in eight countries of Western Africa, to raise their capacities of survival in this not very favourable world. This is really the outcome, which is beyond quantification. It's only eight. But those eight are extremely important.

VIŠNJA & GORAN: What you are mentioning here as an experience, very much relates to the analytical frameworks that we choose to use as cultural workers, cultural policy researchers and makers. And of course, these frameworks act to reconfigure and limit how we understand arts and culture within broader society. As a professor, researcher and expert you have been criticising the adoption of the "value chain" as an analytical framework, and have promoted a "socio-cultural cycle" as an alternative that reflects diverse aspects of cultural fields within society.

MILENA: Well, I never wanted to use the word value-chain, and its frame of analysis, which has been taken from business discourse and business vocabulary, and introduced in the artistic sector, not only in creative or cultural industries such as the music industry, cinematography or publishing but in all areas of art. That framework excludes many crucial aspects of the cultural sphere. It excludes education, memory preservation, organisational memory development and so on. It excludes mediation unless it is part of the distribution and marketing.

So, it's limited to three processes: production, distribution, and consumption. And this logic is in fact reducing every artistic field, and that's absolutely typical capitalistic logic, that stimulates investments in production, eventually in distribution, if the consumption can cover the cost. And that's the circle. So, there are no investments in education, someone else has to do it. No investments in conservation, digital memory or any physical memory for the safeguarding of contemporary art. No investments in mediation, in understanding of the art, unless it is connected with "paying" consumption. Thus, the value-chain will consider festivals as money making, profitable businesses, not as mediating processes, not as cultural communication platforms.

This is why in my teaching, writing and expert work, I have been using the framework of the socio-cultural cycle[5] which includes the whole cycle of one cultural field, from education, mediation, safeguarding, all that is beyond the capitalist logic of profit. One whole art field can be developed through self-organisation as strategy and tactic, to use de Certeau's term (De Certeau, 1984). In the socio-cultural cycle of contemporary dance, small dance companies in the Balkan region created not only their artistic collectives and productions but their own festivals, manifestations, education and know-how exchange through those manifestations, through numerous mediation processes aiming to audience development. Thus, knowing they are responsible for the whole field because of the lack of public policies, they were crucial in thinking about cultural policy, developing their own policies and practices.

INSPIRATIONS FOR POST-CAPITALIST CULTURAL POLICIES

VIŠNJA & GORAN: Based on your very diverse and rich experience, what do you think will be some crucial contours, crucial points and crucial anchorings for future post-capitalist cultural policy? First of all, what has been an inspiration for you and where could one look for inspiration?

MILENA: There are few authors like Aaron Schuster (2012) and Franco Bifo Berardi (2009) that I find inspiring regarding the ideas for an anti-capitalist or post-capitalist world. They are discussing the thesis that laziness is a part of postmodern ethics, different from protestant labour ethics in which artists have often been criticised for not participating in it, because they are not working non-stop. Schuster's text, "It is very difficult to do nothing. Notes on laziness", might be very significant, as well as the words of Franco Bifo Berardi about the "Soul at work – from alienation to autonomy", where he is speaking about *strike* as a main form of workers' struggle that implicates the refusal of the command of capital as the organiser of production. That is a way to say "no" in a certain moment of the process. The refusal to complete the work. Kind of an economic blockade of the working process. And many artist and artistic researchers are experimenting with these tactics and strategies, that should provoke capitalist cultural policies.

Another powerful tactic against capitalist cultural policies is *boycott*. For example, it was used by the contemporary dance scene in Zagreb. The city decided to hand over management of the Zagreb Dance Centre, a new cultural policy initiative and a new venue for the dance scene, to the Zagreb Youth Theatre. So, not to create a new institution with the help of the dance scene that had been advocating for it for years but to establish it as a department of an existing city institution. As a response, dancers boycotted it and introduced here, again, a self-organised method of work and struggle, called *Plenum*. The Plenum of Zagreb dance scene was a decision-making form that was key in demonstrating to the public and decision makers the possibilities of autonomy and self-government. In fact, it succeeded in engaging the wider community in its debates. Wider community, the cultural community, joined the process, hearing what things dancers are doing in Plenum. Why did they organise themselves in the Plenum and why did they boycott city policies? All other arts in Croatia have their autonomous public spaces and institutions. Theatres are more or less autonomous, museums professionally autonomous. But to open a dance centre within Zagreb Youth Theatre, under its patronage, not as an autonomous dance group that's going to have its own space, that was seen as a top-down repression that is also often an integral part of the capitalist cultural system. If you are not capable of earning money to be your own boss, then the state, ministry of culture or the city powers, think they have all the rights to govern over you. This combination of state and market control is something that is not debated openly.

VIŠNJA & GORAN: You mentioned art interventions and artistic research as a source of inspiration, and in your research, you have been documenting and analysing these acts of dissent and counter-cultural practices. Are there any inspiring examples that come to mind when discussing anti-productivism, boycott or the position of artists in late capitalism?

MILENA: There are many art works that are dealing with these issues, and these are often much more inspiring than the academic literature. I will never forget an art intervention which is in a way a part of the anti-productivity movement. Dalija Acin, choreographer and dancer from Belgrade, got less than 500 euros for a new production from our Ministry of Culture. So, with this, she organised a "reading performance" in which she presented a scenario of a future dance piece. The 50% of audience entered, sat and read the scenario, while 50% of the audience that bought tickets watched how this other part of the audience is reading. Then, these two parts of the audience exchange places. This was a very powerful performative moment, but it was also a cultural policy statement. Do not offend us with such misery grants! We are not going to produce art. We are going to produce a statement!

Another paradigmatic project dealing with work and art, which targeted the heart of the capitalist worldview, was called "Chez Anne" (Anne's Bar). An audience was invited to come exactly at 11 pm to one of the most popular clubs. Anna, who is a dancer and choreographer, was serving audiences in the form of dances. Choreography was in a way bar-tended. The project was announced and conceptualised as dealing with performativity of any labour, including service labour. But then, it raised another issue about artistic labour. In what ways artistic labour is hidden in these forms of labour that everyone considers very banal, like bartending.

So, a decision not to produce any more artwork is a practice of dissent. This resistance to productivity, this homage to the right to laziness is part of this reconsideration in the artistic world through artistic process. And this is something that cultural policy

Višnja Kisić and Goran Tomka

really has yet to consider. Time for artistic reflection, for artistic, often invisible, research!

Also, Bojana Kunst (2015) has an important text about art and labour, on consumption, laziness and less work, where she's questioning art as a paradigm of labour. If art becomes only praxis, only labour, it loses *poiesis*, and something is wrong in this kind of capitalist society. On the other side, if we are fighting as artists, then art becomes political activity. Again, it's losing out. So, there is no space for the arts in late capitalism, because there is no space for play. Instead, an exploitative system is forcing artists into self-precarisation and eradicating of the boundaries between work and free time.

VIŠNJA & GORAN: What cultural policy mechanism could support this anti-productivist logic and the processes of exploration and non-production?

MILENA: Well, French cultural policy is a rare cultural policy system which recognises this. Since 1946 it considered periods in-between contracts of artists – *contrat de travail intermittent* – as legitimate to be supported by the Ministry who covers artist retirement, health and social security taxes. But today, this right is in question even in France, because you are artists only if you produce. If you do not produce, you are not working. This is something that the future post-capitalist cultural policy will have to consider. Periods of non-producing are not periods of non-work, those are periods of research and reflection that are an integral part of artistic work. And that is much better elaborated in artistic work as such, than in theory of art or in labour-laws and labour-theories.

BEYOND CAPITALISM: NEW DIRECTIONS FOR CULTURAL POLICY

VIŠNJA & GORAN: So, if you would envisage a post-capitalist cultural policy today, what would be its most important contours in your opinion?

MILENA: I have to say that since the beginning of this millennium, and concretely in 2005, I have been trying to introduce the notion of *shared cultural policy* in one of our big world gatherings of cultural policy experts and analysis organised by the Cultural Link, Zagreb and IMO Institute of

International Relations. But this concept of shared policies never really was accepted by scholars and researchers, because one alternative concept was introduced – that of *participative cultural policy-making and participative decision-making* in cultural policies. I see here a strong resistance of the so-called "democratic" cultural policy system, which is in fact capitalist, to really change. Instead, it tries to integrate some democratic demands in order to survive and continue its own growth. At first sight, there is no huge difference in those two concepts. But in reality, in practice, there is. Participative cultural policy-making just means enabling the voices of others to be heard. But it never says that at the end, consensus has to be achieved, and that common, joined, shared platforms should be developed. Capitalist society is competitive, consequently, the process of cultural policy-making is going to be made participative, but competitive. You will have to fight for your idea, first, to be heard, and then to be accepted and approved.

That is the reason that I thought that it would be better to speak about *shared* cultural policies. Because that would mean that we have discussed in a participative manner, but that we have agreed upon something. When everyone knows what we are implementing, it's shared, we can defend it – all of us – because we have agreed upon something that we are going to share. That includes those that are on the top side of the cultural policy-making as well as those that are on the bottom – citizens, groups of citizens, collectives, artistic collectives, etc.

VIŠNJA & GORAN: That not only relates to the decision-making process but also the tools and instruments of production, to the very question of the ownership of resources.

MILENA: Of course. I would definitely go back to the ownership of resources. We need to rethink it because it is the core of the capitalist system. That is the reason why some theoreticians in cultural policy and management are lobbying for so-called *public service institutions*. But not only those created in civil society, such as Stanica, an NGO from Belgrade, that itself doesn't have many resources but is trying to offer a lot of services to contemporary dance ensembles. That needs to be done on a much bigger scale, by public service institutions in all art fields.

Višnja Kisić and Goran Tomka

State film studios in socialist Yugoslavia had been this kind of service institution, on a big scale. In fact, they were very open and progressive – even Yugoslav dissident movies were produced with the help of state film studios. They had annual budgets decided by artistic boards so they could experiment. Unlike them, private film companies had to ask for sponsorship, usually from large state companies, so they were much more cautious. In contrast, in capitalism, film studios are dictated by producers and the capitalist logic of earning. Take the so-called *final cut*. We have earned what we could with the final cut of the movie *Apocalypse Now* by Coppola. Can we earn once again? Twenty years later we are going to launch a *director's cut*, which we, as producers, previously prevented and censored. Now, we are launching it on the market, to earn once again with this altered product. This is showing that, in capitalism, producers are not in the service of the arts. Instead, they are imposing rules of the game and while doing so, they are following the logic of the capital. They have to be sure that the money they invest is going to be paid back. Not that the work of art is the best possible, because this best possible might be relevant for a small number of audiences. This would have to change.

VIŠNJA & GORAN: Could you elaborate more on what would be the main operating principles of a service institution?

MILENA: It means institution that is having numerous "service" functions, helping artistic research, innovative productions, like, IRCAM in France within Beaubourg. It has top-level technical equipment, it has a budget to invite artists in residence every year, to use this equipment and to create without obligation, like some other public art residences (e.g. Schloss Solitude). As an artist-in residence, you don't even have an obligation to finish or to present your product; but if you would like to, then, the art residence will do everything possible to make this presentation happen.

So, the concept of the cultural institution has to change, to be more open and to be in service to all. To all artists, and even more broadly, to the public. What does it mean? For example, Student City Cultural Centre at New Belgrade, during the golden era of self-governance in Yugoslavia, regularly discussed the yearly programme with students who were residents in the Student City.

And then, at the end of the year, they discussed the annual report and evaluated it together. That means to reach out, not on a one-off basis but at the strategic and structural level. Sadly, cultural institutions have turned away from such practices.

VIŠNJA & GORAN: You mention self-organising and self-governance as a kind of historical alternative to competitiveness, as well as to privatisation of resources. That legacy is still an inspiration for some new transformative cultural initiatives, but not on a state cultural policy level.

MILENA: Yes, such practice has moved to the independent scene, to civil society. Currently, in Serbia, we have an important civil society experiment in the independent cultural centre "Magacin". They have an open calendar, which functions on the "first come, first served" principle. Whoever signs into a time slot and for the place, they can use it – no hierarchy. Also, you can count on the solidarity of other members, to ask for help, to use their resources, including the Karkatag Workshop that is on Fridays offered for public use to everyone without charge (artist or not an artist). It is a metal and wood workshop, and you might do there whatever you need. That develops trust and collaboration. These experiments in the independent scene are showing to what extent these kinds of operations are necessary. I think this only shows how badly we need public service institutions. Right now, we do not have such practice in any public institution.

VIŠNJA & GORAN: In what ways do you see that such change – of shared cultural policies with shared decision-making, resources and processes of creation – can be brought within the public institutional system?

MILENA: Within cultural policy another change would have to happen. We need to see more delegated cultural policy instruments, ones that would delegate power to all public cultural institutions to share their space, technical, even human resources. Not to exploit them in order to commercialise them, not at all but to make them available for collaborative projects, to raise additional value for their own programming. Also, to gain more benefits from this collaboration with others – different knowledge, different experiences, artistic input, inspiration.

That would help artists a lot too. These long-term, strategic collaborations of public institutions with NGOs or artistic collectives, could be seen as a form of employment. It could be a multi-year contract with a group of artists for certain collaborative projects. It would be fantastic to imagine every city museum to have an artist-in-residence every year, and to have the Museum of Contemporary Art of Serbia to have not only foreign but also domestic artists in residence. These kinds of hybrid organisational formats are very rare, because our cultural policy is stimulating clear divisions. If you are a museum, you are a museum, and then you might do exactly what is defined or what was defined one hundred years ago, when the museum was founded.

Cultural policy should give more freedom for reconstructing, for re-imagining institutions in the public sector. These strong and open institutions could then function as an alternative to the arts market. Otherwise, we have in the public sector very, to use the term by my colleague Dragan Klaic, "scleroticised" institutions that are just doing what is their routine.

VIŠNJA & GORAN: What about cultural policy support for individual artists and non-institutional actors? Principles and criteria of selection have always been a troublesome point of cultural policies. What could be a post-capitalist logic in this area?

MILENA: The core issue is, to what extent public cultural policy should ignore capitalist markets as a value ranking mechanism. Capitalist logic is creating distortions in cultural life. It can be seen in visual arts, with examples of overly paid artists such as Damien Hirst or Jeff Koons, on the one hand, and huge precarity among the majority of artists on the other side. All of them could live yearly on one honorarium given to Jeff Koons. Many artists in France could live out of the money he received from Versailles for exhibiting his work there.

Instead of that logic of supporting big names that are valued by the arts market, post-capitalist cultural policies should be able to value what markets are not capable of. For example, departing from result-based criteria completely, not purchasing art works but rather funding the processes of artistic work. I am absolutely against the domination of the product-logic in arts and culture.

Even when teaching arts marketing, I'm not using this logic of the marketing mix that starts with the product. No artistic process is something that should be communicated and shared. That might also be interesting for audiences, not only products. Sometimes, without a final product, the process might be an important contribution to artistic and cultural development.

SOLIDARITY AS A CULTURAL POLICY PRINCIPLE

VIŠNJA & GORAN: Numerous ideas and practices that you have mentioned in these conversations revolve around solidarity in one way or another. Do you see solidarity working as a kind of wider principle, a logic much wider than sporadic acts of kindness?

MILENA: Solidarity is something that cultural policy should take from feminist politics. Solidarity could act as the very principle of public funding. Right now, the logic of public funding ends with supporting the one who is the most competitive, and potentially successful. Nothing about solidarity! A logic of solidarity would work in a totally opposite direction. Supporting those that are weakest, that have the least chances to gather some funds on the market, because of the lack of audience interest for such a form or because of their highly experimental work that is not comprehensible to most audiences. This question of the basic logic of public funding is never debated in cultural policy. We need to provoke these debates.

We need more mechanisms of mutual support, mechanisms of self-organisation, of solidarity. We are seeing some of those mechanisms in bottom-up policies in the Balkans, and throughout the world. We can find these elements of mutual help, but absolutely not as much as it is needed, not on the scale needed. As a result, Palestinian artists are still in a very difficult situation without help from any side; Kurdish artists are absolutely ignored (no one even dares to call it Kurdistan or Kurdish territory, but "free territory", not to offend Turkey or Syria). It means that the international cultural scene is complicit in those massive injustices.

VIŠNJA & GORAN: In such context, what would be your message for cultural workers and cultural policy professionals across the globe?

MILENA: Today it's not very sexy to be leftist, to support minorities. That is something that we have to re-institute again, specifically in cultural policy. However, not only through sharing know-how, because giving know-how can be a form of colonisation. We need to do it through support for local knowledge to be developed, or subaltern knowledge to be acknowledged.

In December 1999, in Sarajevo, we had the first Balkan gathering after the wars, supported by Nordic countries mostly. And my colleague, a theatre director from Sarajevo, Dubravko Bibanović, stood up very angry because everything they were offering was based on their workshops (how to work with children in theatre, how to deliver artistic workshops, etc.) He stood up and said something like: "Listen, guys, I'm fed up with this kind of help. You come, you do a workshop and you go. And we stay where we are without any help for our productions, our artistic research". We need to understand this act in its context – in those years, many people came and left. They were making their careers, making their names being in Sarajevo, but in fact, there was no substantial help through which life can really develop. And now, this kind of angriness exists throughout the world, in countries that are on the receiving side of so-called "development aid".

The cultural world needs a lot of help. Cultural operators throughout the world need to know that someone cares about them. That is the reason why we need to have public institutions, not to care only about heritage but to care about people, both about those who create – artists, and about those that are going to enjoy this – audiences. And that is the reason why cultural policy should be based on the *ethics of care and solidarity.*

Notes

1   In Serbia still, most public theatres have large numbers of permanently employed actors, dancers, choreographers (National Theatre in Belgrade close to 1,000 employees), many of whom are not actually acting in plays or dancing but still, receiving full salary. All of them are called theatre ensemble.

2   Kôrè Institut of Arts and Crafts (L'Institut Kôrè des Arts et Métiers – IKAM) is a network which promotes Maaya cultural entrepreneurship in Africa, with members from Mali, Togo, Burkina Faso, Mauritania and Congo. For more details see: https://ikamsegou. com/en/home/.

3   KYA is a network of cultural operators in Mali, created in 2010 by four cultural managers, which today has 24 members. For more details see: www.facebook.com/res eau.kya/.

4   Arterial network is a network of African cultural operators. For more details see: www. arterialnetwork.org/.

5   For more on the tool of socio-cultural cycle, Serbian speaking readers should see Dragićević Šešić & Stojković (2011).

References

Banks, M. (2010). Craft labour and creative industries. *International Journal of Cultural Policy*, 16*(3)*, 305–321. https://doi.org/10.1080/10286630903055885.

Belfiore, E. (2020). Whose cultural value? Representation, power and creative industries. *International Journal of Cultural Policy*, 26(3), 383–397. https://doi.org/10.1080/10286 632.2018. 1495713.

Berardi, F.B. (2009). Soul at Work: From Alienation to Autonomy. Semiotext(e).

De Certeau, M. (1984). The Practice of Everyday Life. University of California Press.

Dragicevic Sesic, M. and Stojkovic, B. (2011). CULTURE: Management, Animation, Marketing (6th ed.). CLIO.

Dumazedier, J. (1962). Vers une civilisation du loisir? Seuil.

Kunst, B. (2015). Artist at Work: Proximity of Art and Capitalism. Zero Books.

Lee, H.K. (2016). Politics of the 'creative industries' discourse and its variants. *International Journal of Cultural Policy*, 22(3), 438–455. https://doi.org/10.1080/10286632.2014.991783.

McGuigan, J. (2005). Neo-liberalism, culture and policy. *International Journal of Cultural Policy*, 11 (3), 229–241. https://doi.org/10.1080/10286630500411168.

Schuster, A. (2012). It is very difficult to do nothing: Notes on laziness. *Metropolis M*, 2. Available online (accessed 15.12.2020): www.academia.edu/3413933/It_is_Very_Difficult_ to_Do_Nothing_Notes_on_Laziness.

Media Policy and Cultural Leadership

James Hickey, European Film Academy: In Conversation (Ireland)

Maria O'Brien

Chapter 6

James Hickey is a film and screen content producer and former Chief Executive of Fís Éireann/ Screen Ireland (Irish Film Board) from 2011 to 2019. He has worked as a media and entertainment lawyer and is a former partner of law firm, Matheson. He currently is a member of the European Film Academy, a consultant for the European Producers Club, a member of the boards of Irish Music Rights Organisation (IMRO), the Lir National Academy of Dramatic

DOI: 10.4324/9781003390725-6

Arts at Trinity College Dublin, Ardán (Galway Film Resource Centre) and Screen Producers Ireland.

THE SIGNIFICANCE OF LAW AND POLICY TO CULTURAL AND CREATIVES INDUSTRIES DISCOURSE

MARIA: To preface our discussion, while the Irish audiovisual industries are a small player on the world stage, producing a relatively small number of what we might define as "Irish" films each year, they are a big player on the film policy stage, given Ireland's central position in the global audiovisual production ecology as an English-language territory and active provider of generous tax reliefs to encourage national and international film production. This puts Ireland, and Irish policymakers, in an interesting position; as a place where attempts to negotiate through the complex landscape of production and consumption are faced with the dominance of Hollywood and increasingly the various streaming services.

For me, there are three distinct but very interrelated areas to our discussion.

- Significance of law in fostering audiovisual field: from state supports to copyright
- The national and the global in audiovisual industries and the related concept of cultural value
- Disruption to the industry by the rise of the streaming services

Before addressing these in particular, can we think about the bigger picture? What is the relationship between the cultural industries and the policymakers? What is the role of the policy advocate? We can see the significance of policy in the cultural sphere, and, for me, the necessity of making visible the politics that are involved in framing policy is a really important role of policy advocates.

JAMES: There is a very limited recognition in Ireland as well as elsewhere of the significance and long-term implications of the role of legislation and regulation in the audio-visual industries. Particularly in Ireland, it can be difficult to get policymakers and industry partners to engage in the nuanced detail of such issues as the drafting and implementation of significant legislation.

For example, the European Union's most recent audiovisual legislation, the Revised Audiovisual Media Services Directive (2018) (AVMSD) is one of the most significant regulatory changes across the EU which will have world-wide implications.[1] Implementation of the AVMSD in Ireland is an interesting example of how there is insufficient engagement by stakeholders in some of the nuanced details of, for example, "European and national works" quotas and levy production funds and investment obligations to increase the supply of those works, and the clear impact this will have on future funding of screen content in Ireland. I have a concern that people who understand how legislation works are in short supply on the ground in terms of actually trying to develop policy through legislation going into the future. We now need to think about how both the AVMSD and the EU Copyright Directive are being implemented in Ireland. And I do believe that getting people to focus on this, particularly through organizations like Screen Producers Ireland, Animation Ireland, the Guilds and IBEC (Irish Business & Employers Federation), will be significant in terms of the policy outcomes.

THE SIGNIFICANCE OF A NATIONAL CINEMA IN A GLOBALISED ENVIRONMENT

MARIA: Let's put this into Irish context. The Irish film industry is a global player, with some fantastic productions and people, such as *Room*, *Brooklyn*, and *Wolfwalkers*. How and why do we define a national cinema and a national film industry?

JAMES: The question of what is or is not an Irish film is hugely contentious. Because as an English-speaking territory we can't revert to a language-based definition. I think we have to base it on Irish creative talent, telling their own stories. These stories must be stories that Irish people, by which I mean people who are living and working in Ireland and Irish people living abroad, want to create and audiences want to see and hear. So we need to keep our definitions really broad.

For me it's been a huge concern that the focus has been on the content of the film on the screen. There has been an erroneous perception, in my view, that if it looks as though it tells an Irish story then it's an Irish film. And, by contrast, if it doesn't tell what looks like an Irish story, it's not an Irish film.

I am old enough to remember people debating about the concept of a "national cinema" in the 1980s. It's funny, because to people like me, I am thinking, is that question still relevant anymore? I didn't get involved in all the arguments. Now, in a sense, I regret it. Because it might have been of some value to do so. On the other hand, it's very difficult for somebody who is the Chief Executive of a state agency to speak out on these matters. There is a challenge of being forthright on the one hand, and on the other hand, trying to act as a state agency in a responsible fashion, dealing with government Departments for funding and having to deal with what you need to do in order for the state agency to continue to function and survive.

A prescriptive approach to what constitutes an Irish film concerns me considerably, but in my role as head of Screen Ireland I was reluctant to get involved in contentious debates about the definition of an Irish film. Instead, I supported and followed IFB/Screen Ireland policy of supporting Irish creative talent telling the stories they wanted to tell, regardless of content.

Let me ask the question, would you regard the Beckett play *Waiting for Godot* as part of Irish culture? The two lead characters, Vladimir and Estragon, have Russian names. The work was written in French as well as English. But it was written by an Irishman who happened to be living in Paris. The question is, is that Irish culture? If you sat through *Waiting for Godot*, you would not know overtly that it was written by an Irishman, but it is part of the canon of Irish culture.

MARIA: I want to come back to thinking about the Irish audiovisual industries and about Ireland's position as a global hub for audiovisual production. Is Ireland only seen as a place for runaway production to avail of our generous tax reliefs?

JAMES: It is important to ensure that there is sufficient infrastructure in Ireland to support an indigenous audiovisual industry. We also need to talk about diversity in the Irish audio visual sector including employment diversity, sustainability of employment given the project-to-project nature of the work, and the problems these issues create for a small country like Ireland. The trouble is that unless you create a level of industrial activity, in relation to film, TV and animation production, you don't have the economies of scale within the infrastructure to be able to employ at least a significant number of people on an ongoing basis. This has consequent problems for diversity and sustainability. Therefore, if you remove yourself from supporting the level of activity created by significant inward production, you then create a problem for indigenous production, because you're then going to have to import much of the creative talent and technical skills. So there is a symbiotic relationship between inward production in terms of creating an infrastructure, which is necessary for indigenous production to prosper. If, however, you were to ask me the question about whether the *balance* between inward production and indigenous production is correct, I'd say it needs to be re-established in favour of indigenous production.

And to return to the point made previously, one of the ways of doing that is through the implementation of the EU AVMS Directive which includes the introduction of investment obligations and levies on the audiovisual media service providers.[2] The international audiovisual media service providers have a significant audience in Ireland, and most do not have editorial activities based in Ireland in the first place. Most don't really contribute to indigenous production. And bearing in mind, my view of indigenous production is works created by Irish creative talent (as broadly defined), rather than simply Irish subject matters. Because the difficulty you face is that if you require the large international media service providers to make an Irish story, then that's a very easy thing to create outside Ireland, as well as in Ireland. And unless you focus the investment that these organisations are asked to contribute back into the Irish creative economy on works created by Irish creative talent, you are losing the creation of that talent infrastructure, which you need, as well as the industrial infrastructure that you need. And that's the challenge, how to balance both making sure that you're getting Irish creative talent, strongly developed and based in Ireland, and the industrial infrastructure to go with it as well.

MARIA: I agree with you that there's an imbalance between the supports for indigenous and inward film productions. What other barriers to the development of an indigenous industry in Ireland do you see at the moment?

JAMES: One significant barrier to both inward and indigenous productions is the lack of audiovisual studio space, that is the lack of physical infrastructure that you need one way or the other. Another barrier is the limited availability of funding for the development of indigenous content, in other words, supporting Irish creative talent, to develop their work. And this is why it's so important that any new fund that's created is focusing on Irish creative talents, rather than on the overt content of the work. And you come back to the definition of what constitutes Irish culture. To me, the "cultural dividend",[3] that is the return on investment by the State in the audiovisual industries, is not simply seeing Irish stories on screen, the cultural dividend is Irish creative talent, honing their talents and creativity and creating the work, with the stories they want to tell. And whether the Irish creative talent living and working in Ireland is somebody whose parents happened to come from Poland, or Nigeria, or whether they happen to come from Connemara, and are Irish speaking, or whatever, wherever they come from. They all need to be recognized as part of Irish creative talent, telling their stories for Irish and world audiences.

THE AUDIOVISUAL INDUSTRIES IN EUROPE: PROBLEMS AND OPPORTUNITIES

MARIA: There's a lot of discourse around the European audiovisual sector, the necessary protections to preserve European works in opposition to what is seen as the Hollywood "other". Your work with the European Producers Club involves you in discussions around how to best support the European audiovisual industries. For example, the question on what constitutes a European audiovisual work for the purposes of the exhibition quotas is a really important element of current EU policy. There have been controversial suggestions that the UK will be dropped from the definition of what constitutes European Works under the audiovisual media services directive, for example in the context of the thirty per cent video on demand quota for European works. I'd like to hear your thoughts on this.

JAMES: First, in fairness to the EU, the definition of "European works" is much wider than just simply works produced within the EU. It also includes other jurisdictions within Europe, including both Russia and the Ukraine as well as the UK after Brexit. The reaction to the problem about works from the UK at a European level is that this needs to be investigated. Some people consider that we can't allow for a dominant English-speaking culture, when the whole point of European audiovisual policy for 50 years and more has been to make sure that there's a diversity of voices on smaller screens for television, as well as cinemas. The truth is that in terms of cinema, US cinema still dominates the markets in Europe. The EU has decided, in my view quite rightly, that it has to protect the diversity of language. And the only way you can do that is intervening in the market. Because, otherwise, the screens will be dominated by English language content, much of it from the USA. However, if UK works were excluded from the definition of European works, it still doesn't mean UK works will not appear on VOD services in Europe like Netflix. There will be plenty of room for UK works. There is already plenty of room taken up by works originating from the United States on European-based VOD platforms.

So the challenge is that because the UK mostly makes works in English, which is to its advantage for distribution on a worldwide basis, they make up a significant part of any quotas for European works throughout the EU. And the question is whether this is fulfilling the policy objectives of the EU in this sector? European audiovisual cultural policy is faced with the huge challenge of the multiplicity of languages within the EU. Europe has the most complicated language diversity of any of the large agglomerations of countries in the world. This presents huge challenges, particularly for smaller countries and lesser-used languages.

MARIA: And can we consider this as a challenge or as an opportunity for Ireland?

JAMES: From an Irish perspective this is a difficult topic. And the British reaction to the leaked proposal to change the definition of "European works" was quite exercised.[4] I accept this is very difficult for us in Ireland because we're as close to the United Kingdom as we are to the rest of Europe. This is like friends squabbling in your presence. There must be some way of working this out and that's the real challenge. But there are genuine concerns that the large amount of English language content is not really supporting the diversity of voices in Europe.

HOW CAN WE ASCERTAIN THE CULTURAL VALUE OF THE AUDIOVISUAL INDUSTRIES?

MARIA: So far, we have really discussed the film industry as an industry. However, the audiovisual industries have an important cultural role. You have mentioned the value of the audiovisual industries. Is there a way to quantify this cultural value?

JAMES: This obviously raises the difficulty of evaluating something as unmathematical as culture. In some ways, thinking of what we can term the "cultural impact" might be a better phrase for it rather than "cultural dividend". But the point about it is that I think you can measure it narratively, because the whole thing about the impact of culture is that it is about telling stories. But how do you explain the value of telling stories? The problem in the past was that we have focused on the economic impact. To put it in context, when the country was in such economic difficulties, the only real way in which you get the message across to policymakers was in terms of economic impact because the country needed to rebuild itself. That is no longer the case. And while that was a virtuous thing in the past, we now have to move forward in relation to establishing a cultural as well as economic value for audiovisual production. I struggle to see how you can give a mathematical result for how cultural impact can be calibrated. But there must be a way of giving a narrative impact to that story, and to recognising the value of diversity in the voices telling stories in Ireland. But how do you explain that? And then how do you explain it when you need, you know, a cast and crew of 300 people to tell that story and you need to pay them because they all have livelihoods they need to earn?

MARIA: For me, one interesting way to look at these questions is to think about how we measure the immeasurable. It's coming back to thinking about what questions we are asking of policies for the audiovisual industries? Particularly for example the over-emphasis within policy discourse on the economic value of tax incentives for the audiovisual industries.

JAMES: The over-emphasis on the economic value of tax incentives was to help the policymakers who needed that argument at that time. And in fairness to the policymakers, we were trying to give them the arguments to justify the supports for the industry. The economic situation in Ireland was so bad that you had to prove your case economically because otherwise you were not going to be listened to. The real difficulty that we have identified is the fact that the value of culture is not fully understood and then articulated in Ireland, particularly by policymakers and stakeholders. And this ranges across, whether it's the Oireachtas or the Arts Council, whether it's the Department of Culture or Screen Ireland, whether it's the BAI or RTÉ.[5] One of the things I found most difficult recently has been the consultations by the Future of Media Commission.[6] The Commission has spent most of its time discussing the importance of news and current affairs on Public Service Media (PSM). The bankruptcy of that narrow view of public service media, to me, is shocking.

Because PSM is also about Irish people telling stories themselves. It is about TV drama and animation for children. Local soap operas are an equally vital part of PSM, as vital as a news and current affairs service. I am staggered by the lack of discussion in the context of the Future of Media Commission of the importance of TV drama, in particular, and animation storytelling, because that so disregards fictional storytelling and creativity, in terms of what should be included in PSM. At least when the British Broadcasting Corporation and Ofcom talk about the role of PSM, they put drama up there as a huge part of what PSM encompasses. In Ireland, we're not talking about it in that way. And that is a huge problem. What we don't seem to value in our culture, which is ironic, is storytelling.

MARIA: Given Ireland's reputation as a land of storytellers, that's a strange omission. These discussions also point to a dissonance in our definitions of media. Certain policy bodies are overly focused on media within the context of news and current affairs and neglect the cultural aspects of media.

JAMES: And the problem is the politicians that are dealing with all this. The politicians in Ireland seem to live in a bubble of news and current affairs. I would say that one of the significant addictions of the country, apart from alcohol and drugs, at least when it comes to our politicians, is news and current affairs. And, when it comes to policy formation, this is focussed on instead of storytelling.

MARIA: To expand upon this point, do you think there's a lack of respect for film as a form of culture and an overemphasis in Ireland on policies towards news and current affairs?

JAMES: Absolutely. And the complete irony of all this is that huge numbers of Irish people are subscribing to Netflix as a service. Netflix does not supply as we know, news and current affairs. What it supplies is mostly drama, whether it's feature films or TV drama series, and Irish audiences are avid consumers. They don't ever seem to wonder about whether any of their own stories should be told. And the difficulty is the occasional success that we then have, like *Normal People*,[7] which is mostly funded from outside Ireland anyway. We must tell our own stories. And yet, there's no discussion about whether there's a pipeline of production for those stories and how they will be funded. It's quite extraordinary that for the most part, a dialogue about that is not going on, in the context of the Future of Media Commission, as well as in the debates about the new Online Safety and Media Regulation Bill.[8] And the difficulty about all of that is that we are as a country, in my view, in danger of losing that concept of cultural value. Because we just don't value it. And we're back to this discussion about how you value it. Most people in our main public service broadcaster, RTE, do not come from drama backgrounds, and therefore don't fully relate to it as part of our cultural production.

THE ROLE OF COPYRIGHT AND INTELLECTUAL PROPERTY IN THE CREATIVE INDUSTRIES

MARIA: We are both lawyers by training and are acutely aware of the significance of the intersections of law and culture. For me, the importance of copyright and IP are underplayed, or perhaps underestimated in policy discourses around the cultural and creative industries broadly, so not only in the audiovisual industries but the music industries also.

JAMES: The other gap in the creative industries discourse in Ireland is a question of how this cultural value is protected and monetised. We do not have any real debate about the importance of copyright for creators. And this comes back to discussions of intellectual property and the importance of it in the context of rewarding creativity. The technology policy proposition has been that copyright is regarded as a barrier to innovation. This, to me, is one of the great lies because copyright is designed to support innovation. It is not a barrier to innovation. The leading question in Ireland's recent review of copyright regulation (2014) was whether copyright is a barrier to innovation?[9] The short answer is that it is the wrong question. It betrays an ignorance about how important creativity is and how it is protected and rewarded.

Copyright is designed to protect literary, dramatic, musical, artistic works, films, television programmes. Ireland needs to have a better understanding of the importance of copyright policy in supporting creativity. But policymakers have struggled with the impact of copyright law. For example, implementation of the Copyright Directive is not being interrogated by legislators, but is being implemented by Statutory Instrument, signed by the Minister, without fully engaged stakeholder consultation. The Copyright Directive recognises the value of creativity. Articles 17–22 of the Directive are designed specifically to rebalance the relationship between authors and performers on the one hand, and online media services on the other hand, so that the authors and performers are properly remunerated for their work. However, the lack of understanding of the importance of copyright to the creative industries is a real problem in Ireland.

There is a dissonance between the importance of the software industries and the role of copyright in that context, and the lack of critical thinking on copyright in the arts and creative industries. The most extraordinary thing about this is that Ireland owns more copyright per capita than any other country in the world because the multinational software industries are based here. It's extraordinary that most of that is protected in terms of intellectual property by copyright law. And we have recently changed copyright law,[10] fundamentally, for the first time in 20 years, and we didn't take the opportunity of even discussing what draft legislation should look like.

That's certainly going to have wide implications for much more than the audiovisual industry. This is the biggest single change that will take place in Irish copyright law in recent memory and a draft of the legislation was not made available for discussion in Ireland. This is in contrast with other EU jurisdictions where the legislation was and is being interrogated by the relevant parliaments.

One of the significant questions is, "what do Irish people own arising from their creative work?". The importance of the value of intellectual property in music, and the cultural dividend of investment in the music industry includes the ownership of intellectual property arising from it. For example, *Riverdance* delivered in terms of wealth creation because the intellectual property was retained here in Ireland.[11] So one of the cultural dividends, if we're going to use that phrase, is the intellectual property that's created and owned in Ireland. And it's one which I'm not sure is being fully factored into policy discussions.

TAX INCENTIVES AND NATIONAL CULTURE

MARIA: Linked to the above points, I want to shift to think about the notion of digital games. During your time at Screen Ireland you were actively in favour of extending film tax incentive policies to the digital games industry, a policy which has finally come to fruition with the introduction of a digital games tax relief in Ireland.[12] Do you see the digital games industry as part of Ireland's creative industries?

JAMES: First of all, my understanding would be that the proposed support mechanism will be a cultural initiative. And it's important to emphasize that because of European Union state aid laws, the extension of any tax incentive to computer games needs to be framed as a cultural initiative, not a technology initiative.[13] And the irony of it is that the games industry in 2011–2012 attempted to pursue an unsuccessful technology (R&D) solution to investment in the games development sector in Ireland. And the truth is, they should have been pursuing a cultural one. But they didn't see games as a cultural product, which in fairness to them, is a problem of failure of policy in Ireland, and not the industry's fault. Because the truth is that it's hard for people in the technology sector to see culture as important. This is because the technology sector is very much focused on freely available content. The technology sector was always working on the narrative that copyright is a barrier to innovation and since the technology sector has strong policy influence, these narratives were particularly strong in the policy discourse. And whereas

Maria O'Brien

in fact, the dial has now hopefully moved back in the EU to a recognition of the value of creative content and a recognition that the value of all those things which relate to copyright relate to creativity. In my view, that's what we should be focusing on. I mean, games to me, comprise creativity and storytelling and are an amazing creative form. This is interactive storytelling, which is extraordinary and wonderful. I'm not a person who plays computer games, but I think the concept is absolutely wonderful that people would, in a sense, retell stories for themselves, because of the interactivity with the story of the game.

Unfortunately, the dialogue in Irish media on this has been very limited, and surprisingly, unfocused on the importance of storytelling.

MARIA: From my perspective, the policy and academic discourse in Ireland often focuses on how film is either a cultural force or an industry rather than seeing these concepts as mutually constitutive. In particular, the debates on the value of our tax incentive, Section 481, rarely address the cultural value of big-budget productions.

JAMES: A good example is to consider how we define culture within the context of the cultural test for qualifying for tax incentives in Ireland. It is designed to make sure that most projects qualify. For example, certain films in the *"Star Wars"* franchise qualified for both the Irish cultural test and the UK cultural test because filming took place on location in Ireland and the UK. And then the irony of that cultural test story was that from one perspective, *Star Wars* used a culturally significant location in Ireland, Skellig Michael, thus ending up being an "Irish story". But the story is framed as a Jedi origin story, so these concepts don't really quite gel! Again, it is with both regret and relief that, in my position as CEO of Screen Ireland at the time, I didn't get involved in the public cultural and environmental arguments about whether the use of Skellig Michael by the makers of *Star Wars* was a good or a bad idea. The problem I felt was that the argument was polarized. Some people thought it was a disgrace that this wonderful monastic site could possibly be used for this fantasy sci-fi story. And then on the other hand, you place a story about a wonderful Irish cultural monument into a worldwide context where millions of viewers across the world see this strange island off the coast of Ireland and wonder who lived there and why?

MARIA: It's interesting to think about what the recent sale of two major studios in Ireland (Ardmore and Troy Studios) to a US-based consortium means for the Irish industry, and also the future of filmmaking in Ireland?[14]

JAMES: I have the same feeling as I do about the enormous level of funding for production brought to Europe by the US-owned streaming services. The investment is very welcome but it needs to contribute to a fostering of creativity and diversity of European works, with rewards for that creativity in terms of the ongoing ownership of rights and a share of downstream revenues staying in Europe. Regulation is needed to achieve that and while there is great legislative work done in France and more recently in Italy, regulation needs to be extended across the whole of Europe to achieve this.

MARIA: The references to tourism are particularly interesting in the attempts to reflect both cultural and economic value in the audiovisual industries. However, how can we identify cultural value in the audiovisual industries?

JAMES: We do need to think about the cultural value, because value is a word that has a non-economic sense to it, as well. And we need to think about the economic and cultural impact of tourism. But we need to also look at intellectual property impact. And ultimately, that cultural impact is about telling your own stories using technology. And it has to be material which audiences want to respond to. I mean, *Normal People* was a great example of a very clear story which people worldwide responded to. And the intellectual property behind that, Ireland owns that IP [intellectual property] for the next 70 years. It's hugely important as part of that cultural impact.

DISRUPTION TO THE INDUSTRY BY THE STREAMING SERVICES

MARIA: You have been very influential at an EU policy level. How does the proposed Code of Practice by the European Producers Club aim to protect independent producers in the face of challenges brought about by the rise of streaming services?[15]

JAMES: The proposed EPC Code of Fair Practice says that in respect of fiscal incentives and subsidies, which support European or national works, they need to be recognized in terms of the value they provide and that value should accrue to the independent producers who should be producing those works for the international streaming services. The Code is an extraordinarily strong statement of independent producers needing to be placed at the heart of the ecosystem of European audiovisual content. The intention would be that regulation would provide that an independent producer needs to be brought on board. This would apply to all European works, and to national works, qualifying for quotas, as well as those receiving subsidies and being produced under investment obligations. The value that's been put into these works by European taxpayers, needs to be recognized. For example, Netflix has to spend at least 20 per cent of its turnover in France, on French works.[16] And they're defined in a particular way, including a significant percentages (75 per cent to 66 per cent) which have to be independently produced.

The French legislation crucially recognises the importance of IP (intellectual property) rights. For example, it says that the rights granted to Netflix are limited to a year for a cinema feature film, and three years from the end of the last season for TV series. And all other rights remain with the independent producer. And that's a very straightforward solution.

Can you imagine if every European country had an obligation on VOD services to invest 20 per cent of their turnover into indigenous cultural works? That would increase the amount of money available for storytelling and production enormously at no cost to the Irish tax-payer. It would be a most extraordinary thing that could happen.

In Ireland, we are discussing the introduction of a Levy Production Fund, imposed on audiovisual media services including non-European streamers which I believe should be administered by Screen Ireland rather than the new Media Commission, which is effectively the successor to the Broadcasting Authority of Ireland (BAI). There's a reasonable degree of unity amongst the industry about trying to make sure that any new levy Production Fund is not a repeat of the narrowly factual and entertainment focused BAI Sound & Vision Fund, but that it would provide development as well as production funding in a flexible manner, particularly for the more expensive TV drama and animation.

MARIA: This links very much to what I want to ask you about next, which is the European Producers Club (EPC) and the proposed Code of Fair Practice regarding the streamers. How can content creators, as widely defined, retain some rights in intellectual property? The rise of the digital in the audiovisual industries has complicated the notion of retention of property rights.

JAMES: It's worth putting the EPC Code of Fair Practice in dealings with streamers in context. Under Articles 18 to 22 of the EU's Copyright in the Digital Single Market Directive (Copyright Directive) authors and performers are already entitled to transparency and accountability and to fair and proportionate remuneration. There are complicated questions to consider. If authors and performers are entitled to these rights under the Copyright Directive, why wouldn't the production companies which deliver the works to the streaming services not be entitled to the same rights as well? One of the curiosities is the extent to which rights have been granted to authors and performers under the Copyright Directive, which have not been granted to production companies of the works.

Individual rights are recognised, but the production company which puts all the work together and delivers the work to the streaming services isn't accorded the same rights. Independent producers should be entitled to retain rights, to fair and proportionate remuneration depending on the success of the work and to transparency and accountability. The European Producers Club's proposed Code of Practice holds that the intellectual property on works developed by independent producers should still be retained by those independent producers, even when fully commissioned by the streaming services. That's something which is really important to the future development of independent production in Europe.

MARIA: Finally, a general question. What is the future for the Irish audiovisual industries?

JAMES: That's a hard one.

There's so much going on in this question because of the convergence of technologies and the content they deliver. We are circling back to the importance of the policymakers, who, I know for the most part are well meaning. It's a complex industry, however. Industry is even the wrong word, because it doesn't necessarily capture all the cultural value we've been discussing.

It's a complex ecosystem which includes television broadcasting, film exhibition, streaming services, even YouTube. There's a lot of work to be done in influencing policy, a lot of people to be listened to, to get things right for the industry and for future proofing. The groves of academia should be talking about these things. And yet, it's very difficult because the media and cultural sector of the country doesn't debate these issues in public. I see it as a mission for me, which I could spend the rest of my life pursuing, which could be in my view of value and importance. And it gives me a sense of a job to do.

I have also worked with the music industry extensively. In my work on the board of IMRO, much of the talk is about music and audiovisual production. Music in audiovisual production is the other main activity, alongside live music performance. This is where I get exercised about Irish politics and the lack of discussion of significant issues. We can contrast this to recent work in the Houses of Parliament in the UK, which did a huge review of the music business. The MPs were well briefed by all sides. However, in Ireland, there is a lack of discussion at a policy and political level about this, as well.

The question always comes back to how we (citizens and policymakers) value cultural creation? It should be the underpinning of a lot of these discussions. It should shape issues like whether there should be Arts Council funding for popular music as well as classical music creation. Can you make a living from being an artist? Whether you're a musician, whether you're a filmmaker, whether you're an actor, whether you're a makeup artist? Is it a viable career? In addition, the challenges of working on a project-by-project basis and of the gig economy are a big issue. It is sometimes easier for example for people with a more privileged background, to be able to survive the challenges of the industry, and this raises issues of equality and diversity. But all this needs a clear focus of policy and funding, and there is much work yet to be done.

Notes

1   The Audiovisual Media Services Directive (Directive (EU) 2018/1808 of the European Parliament and of the Council of 14 November 2018 amending Directive 2010/13/EU on the coordination of certain provisions laid down by law, regulation or administrative action in Member States concerning the provision of audiovisual media services (Audiovisual Media Services Directive) in view of changing market realities) is available at EUR-Lex. https://eur-lex. europa.eu/eli/dir/2018/1808/oj.

2   The audiovisual screening landscape globally has changed significantly in the last few decades, with the rise of on-demand screening platforms. The EU Audiovisual Media Services Directive (AVMSD) attempts to increase the visibility of European works through the provision of rules for investment obligations and levies on on-demand platforms under Article 13. To summarise, Article 13(1) AVMSD sets a 30 per cent share of European works and a prominence obligation with regard to those works. Article 13(2) provides that member states may also require AVMS providers to contribute financially to the production of European works, including via direct investment in content and contribution to national funds. For further information, see Cabrera Blazquez F.J., Cappello M., Talavera Milla J., Valais S., *Investing in European works: the obligations on VOD providers*, IRIS Plus, European Audiovisual Observatory, Strasbourg, May 2022.

3   The Irish Department of Finance's Cost Benefit Analysis of Section 481 in 2018, the audiovisual tax incentive, referred to the unquantified Irish cultural impact emanating from Section 481 as a form of cultural dividend. There have been various attempts in the past to quantify the value of Section 481 in terms of looking for a quantifiable return on the tax foregone to the Irish state through the operation of Section 481. The recognition by the Department of Finance that there are cultural benefits to the tax incentive is important. This is further evidenced by the commissioning of a report by Screen Ireland on the cultural value of Section 481 to be published in late 2022/23. Department of Finance. (2018). *Report on Tax Expenditures. Incorporating outcomes of certain tax expenditure & tax related reviews completed since October 2017.* Tax Policy Division.

4   There was a controversial proposal to exclude UK content as European under the quota requirements in the AVMSD which requires that at least 30 per cent of titles on video on demand (VOD) platforms such as Netflix. The reason for such a proposal, as reported in The Guardian was to avoid the disproportionate presence of UK content within the European VOD quota. www.theguardian.com/world/2021/jun/21/eu-prepares-cut-amount-british-tv-film-shown-brexit. For now, UK audiovisual works count as European.

5   The Oireachtas is the national parliament of Ireland. The Arts Council refers to the Arts Council of Ireland, the Irish government agency for developing the arts. The BAI refers to the Broadcasting Authority of Ireland and RTE refers to Raidio Teilifis Eireann, the Irish national broadcaster. The Future of Media Commission was tasked with considering the future of print, broadcast and online media in Ireland, established in 2020 and reported in 2022.

6   The Future of Media Commission was established by the Irish government in September 2020 and tasked with developing recommendations on public service media provision in Ireland. The report was published in July 2022. www.gov.ie/en/publication/ccae8-report-of-the-future-of-media-commission/.

7   *Normal People*, directed by Lenny Abrahamson and Hettie Macdonald, Element Pictures, British Broadcasting Company, Hulu Originals, 2020 based on the novel *Normal People* (2018) by Sally Rooney. The release of the TV series *Normal People* during the COVID-19 pandemic attracted national and international acclaim. Abrahamson is an internationally recognised Irish film director who also directed feature films including *Adam & Paul* (2004), *Room* (2015) and *The Little Stranger* (2018).

8   At the time of writing the Online Safety and Media Regulation Bill 2022 is before the Irish Assembly, Dail Eireann Fifth stage. www.oireachtas.ie/en/bills/bill/2022/6/.

9   The *Modernising Copyright* report was published in 2013 and was compiled by the Copyright Review Committee comprising Dr Eoin O'Dell of Trinity College (Chair), Professor Steve Hedley of University College Cork and Ms Patricia McGovern of DFMG Solicitors.

10 Copyright law in Ireland is governed under the Copyright and Related Rights Act 2000 and the Copyright and Other Intellectual Property Law Provisions Act 2019 and the 2021 regulations. The transposition of the Directive on Copyright in the Digital Single Market into EU law by way of the EU (Copyright and Related Rights in the Digital Single Market) Regulations 2021 came into effect on 12 November 2021.

11 Riverdance is a traditional Irish dance performance which originated as a seven-minute dance performance first performed on 30 April 1994 during the Eurovision Song Contest hosted in Dublin. It has expanded to a global phenomenon which has been performed worldwide and has led to the production of significant intellectual property including live performances, recordings and animated film.

12 The Irish government first proposed consideration of a digital games tax credit (DGTC) in October 2020. The tax credit has recently (October 2022) been approved by the European Commission and legislation has been introduced in Ireland (November 2022). Full details of the nature and conditions of the credit have not been finalised.

13 Any fiscal aids offered by a government to entities operating within their own jurisdiction are prohibited under Article 107 of the Treaties of the Functioning of the European Union unless they come within a number of exemptions. Aids to film and games industries tend to apply to come with Article 107(3)(d) TFEU as measures to promote culture. Ireland is in the process of introducing a tax incentive for digital games.

14 Ardmore Studios in Wicklow and Troy Studios in Limerick were sold to Hackman Capital Partners and Square Mile Capital Management as reported in Variety on 13 August 2021. https:// variety.com/2021/film/news/ardmore-troy-studios-hackman-capital-partners-1235041597/].

15 Founded in 1993 and with 130 members, the European Producers Club is an association of independent film and TV drama producers from all over Europe. It has developed a Code of Fair practice for Video on Demand services when commissioning new works from independent producers including fair and proportionate remuneration, producers contribution and right to participate in future derivative works. www.europe anproducersclub.org/ our-code-of-fair-practices.

16 Decree No. 2021-793 of June 22, 2021 relating to on-demand audiovisual media services. www.legifrance.gouv.fr/jorf/id/JORFTEXT000043688681.

Museums, Decolonisation and Cultural Leadership

Esme Ward, Director of Manchester Museum: In Conversation (UK)

Roaa Ali

Chapter 7

Esme Ward is the Director of Manchester Museum and has been leading the 'hello future' £15 million capital project to transform the Museum. Re-opened in 2023, the Manchester Museum includes a brand-new South Asia Gallery, Lee Kai Hung Chinese Culture Gallery and Belonging Gallery as well as an Exhibition Hall and more inclusive visitor facilities and spaces.

DOI: 10.4324/9781003390725-7

This interview is part of a project led by Professor Bridget Byrne and Dr Roaa Ali at the Centre on Dynamics of Ethnicity (CoDE), University of Manchester. We have been exploring how institutional practices in cultural institutions can reproduce and mitigate ethnic inequality, and Manchester Museum has been one of our case studies.

This conversation took place online on 2 September 2021.

DECOLONISATION

ROAA: Stuart Hall[1] questioned what and who are museums for? Whose heritage do they preserve and celebrate? How do you respond to these questions in light of the Black Lives Matter movement and a pandemic that exposed racial inequalities, both within the UK and globally?

ESME: Well, I suppose my initial thought is that is a question posed quite a significant time ago, but which is more relevant than ever. And the "who museums are for" has changed over time. For me, museums are about reflecting and exploring the complexity of the human condition, and a place where we can understand each other. But, of course, we know that in terms of who comes to our museums, who see themselves in our museums, who feel they belong in our museums, that is not the population of the UK – that is not everyone. So, for me, it is the question that should be on every museum workers' lips: who are museums for, what are we here for? The ICOM[2] has been grappling for the last 3 years now with a definition of museums. There is a real sense of a shift in what museums are for beyond this idea of preserving, analysing, interpreting and displaying, to thinking about the difference that they can make.

If we do what we've always done, then we're going to get what we've always got – and the world has changed, it changed before COVID, it changed before Black Lives Matter. All of the inequalities were there, but they have been bought into such sharp relief, not least inequalities around race. It's now so central to the work of an institution like a museum – it has to be part of the conversation. The question is what we do about that, and how we make that move. This is about really opening up your museum, asking who works in your museum, examining the way we talk about people in museums – I'll be honest, I think it's grim and dehumanising.

I struggle with the language of audiences, target audiences!
That is an appalling way to talk about people. So, actually for me,
there's a real shift happening that is about us understanding the
care and the concerns of the people in our wider communities. All
museums want to be more relevant and more inclusive, but do we
understand what that means. I think there is a crisis going on in
museums, because I think we have fundamentally failed to engage
wholeheartedly with the cares and concerns of the people who
are on our doorstep, the citizens, and the communities. And I think
until we do that and we respond with urgency – and it's not just
a program over there, but a whole museum response, we have a
long way to go.

It's the museum thinking in public, having conversations with
people, opening up whether that looks like co-production, greater
collaboration, working across sectors, bringing lived experience
to the heart of your museum and grappling with actually what
that means. That means you might stop doing some of the things
you've done before because you have always done them for
the same people. That's at the heart of how we have to move
forwards. Museums have always reflected preoccupations and
values of their time. How are we going to do that today? The
reality is museums have changed, but they have not changed that
much, still.

So, it's an understanding of what your museum is for and then, if
you want it to be for more diverse people, then on whose terms?
I'll be honest, I have this real frustration with museums, and I had
a moment in my career where I realised that what existed was
a veneer of inclusion. I find that phrase helpful because I think
museums are very comfortable with a veneer of inclusion. So, it
can all look incredibly inclusive, you can have wonderful inclusive
programmes, but actually, in terms of the systemic changes we
need to make, it still isn't happening. We have to find ways for that
to be the case, and the only way I think we're going to ensure that
those changes happen is if we have people who are impacted
directly at the heart of these decision-making processes in our
institutions.

ROAA: Thank you. I'd like to follow up with a question related to
what you said. I'm intrigued by your use of the word "crisis" and
I see that in the context of the colonial legacy of the museum and

how it's dealing with the contemporary moment of decolonisation. So, could what you said about bringing the lived experience into the museum space be, perhaps, in conflict with the ideals behind museum establishment? Within this context, what do you see as the role of museums in general, and Manchester Museum particularly, in this current moment of history where debates of decolonisation are both urgently called for in a broader discourse for equality and social justice, and contested in "culture wars" rhetoric? So, if we confront the crisis and the colonial legacy of the museum with this moment now of both "decolonisation" and "cultural wars", what is the role of the museum? What is Manchester Museum's role in those debates at this moment?

ESME: In terms of Manchester Museum, our mission hasn't changed and it is really clear: it's to build understanding between cultures and build a more sustainable world, and I think that could never be more relevant. But, I suppose underpinning all of that – and I think this does speak directly to this moment – I think museums have a real kind of power and I think they can be almost an empathy machine able to build empathy and understanding. I think they are among the few predominantly free civic spaces where you bring generations together and encourage conversations among them. So, for me, it's about how we build empathy and understanding through more inclusive stories, through broader narratives, through grappling with different perspectives. They help us understand the society we're living in, where it's come from, and also what we want to make for the future.

People may think museums are just about the past, but through the way you care for the past, you are staking a claim on what matters for the future, you are. I want to convey very clearly just how much museums are implicated in imperialism and how embedded that is within our disciplines and knowledge. A significant part of our work is exploring and challenging our assumptions, including divisions between nature and culture, chronological displays, etc. (all Manchester Museum's new galleries for example will challenge those hierarchies and divides).

At this moment, I think museums have to step up to the plate and open up these conversations, and also be clear about what they stand for, not what they stand against, not what they're reacting to. Manchester Museum will always have this broader educational mission to build understanding and empathy and consider what society we want for our collective futures. To become the kind of museum your city needs it to be, you must be open and engage with what's going on in your city, with what the impacts are across different communities, and that's how you enable your organisation to be more porous, perhaps, and then you can respond to that. That requires a level of agility and response that is a challenge for our museums. But for somewhere like Manchester, with the breadth of collections, it is a huge opportunity for us to support conversations and create, whether that's particular collections, exhibitions, displays or whatever it might be that encourages the kind of conversations that people want to have and need to have for the future.

How we show a greater commitment to healing and care and build a new ethics of care is critical to this work. That includes work on governance, distributing and supporting emerging leadership and resources – above and beyond, more inclusive recruitment. Decolonisation is a whole museum project and I've been reflecting on how we might make room (and current structures and work don't create safe space) for emotion, spirituality, protest, challenge and new possibilities … it's one of the reasons why I'm so excited about the Belonging Gallery, not least its imagining of different inclusive futures – it will be the first gallery you visit and sets the tone for your entire museum visit (this gallery didn't exist in inherited plans and has only emerged in the last 12 months).

ROAA: I'd like to probe you a little bit further, if I may, because you mentioned that museums can be, and are, civic spaces open for all—

ESME: Well, they're open for all if you know about them, and if you have overcome a whole host of barriers. I'm not being delusional and thinking "Oh well, they're open for all, so why don't we get more visitors?" There is serious work to do. Take threshold anxiety, that sense of "why on earth would I come to this museum, it has no relevance to my life", all of that is at the heart of the work we're doing at the moment to understand how this museum can genuinely be useful and inclusive. The reality is we've done that for years in museums, but not with everyone. I mean, if you take it from a perspective of the collections: of course, museums are about collections, but museums are also about people! Yet, to be honest, the people most intimately connected to our collections, which are often people in countries of origin from source communities or diaspora communities, are the ones who are least connected to those collections. They are the ones who are often least engaged with.

ROAA: Why is that?

ESME: There are a whole host of reasons and that's everything from lack of curiosity around engaging them, concern around if they become more engaged with them, what demands they might make. The fact that they are often so distant from these collections has to do with the way they encounter them: the loss, the trauma and the way that these collections may be displayed, I think that there has been a lack of care around working with those people to ensure that these collections are displayed, and those connections are made. We have so much work to do around how we create the conditions that mean the museum can feel like a safe space for those communities. There's that thing about museums being safe spaces for dangerous ideas, well I'm sorry, but safe for whom? There are a lot of people for whom somewhere like Manchester Museum is not a safe space, actually – it's a traumatic space.

ROAA: And is that because of the acquisition of the collection and the way that those collections are stored, and sometimes curated?

ESME: The acquisition is a key part – to make an acknowledgement of that acquisition, there is so much in what museums don't say. It can be the way that those collections are used or not used, or how they can be turned into a product for your shop. It can be the way that those museums have failed to draw upon the expertise and knowledge that exist within communities to develop an understanding of those collections. Part of this for me is the presentation of those collections – there's a lack of transparency. So, all of those are part of this and a whole host of other issues around inequalities that are part of the story and completely interconnected.

We need to put significant time and effort into understanding how we might work with people in a way that isn't essentially replicating what's happened before, i.e. extracting the lived experience and the knowledge we need to do this or that for our institutional ends. I've been reflecting a lot on how a lot of museum work is still quite transactional, and a real challenge for us is to figure out what it means to work more relationally; how do you do that? How do you build these relationships not for this project or this bit of funding, but for the longer term? How do you do this so it's genuinely enduring, so it builds and it grows and starts to change your organisation?

For me, the work we're doing around building the South Asia Gallery is such a good example, and where that might go is changing all the time. It's a really interesting example of how you might start somewhere, but the minute you start working with people and building the relationships, it changes you fundamentally – it changes your processes and your practice and it starts to change your policy. It means that we have members of staff at the museum who weren't there before, and we have posts that initially were project-based and now are permanent because when the doors open on a new gallery, it doesn't stop there; it just starts. We have decision-making processes that are changing in terms of who is making the decisions here, how do we avoid moving back as in "Oh well, thanks very much, we've got everything we need from you, you've co-curated the space and now we'll just go back to default and the museum takes over here".

If we're going to do this work and we're going to be much more open and are serious about creating a sense of belonging, we have to understand what the needs and concerns are of individuals, and then create the conditions for that belonging. That might be anything from some bricks-and-mortar changes – for example, we're working with a whole host of people on our new prayer room – or creating a particular space and thinking about who programs that, or how you distribute your funding beyond the museum to those partners you work with.

ROAA: You raise important issues and questions. I want to go back to the idea of decolonisation and the fact that even though museums are civic spaces and can be open, we know that some communities are either made to feel excluded from that space, or they don't feel they belong. That also has to do with how

Roaa Ali

museums collect and curate the past in a selective way. So, within this frame of museum practices and legacy, can decolonisation happen? My second question comes from the problematic "transactional" relationship you mentioned between the museum and communities, which in a way commodifies communities. I'm wondering what funding bodies like the Arts Council, National Lottery Heritage Fund and policymakers can do to first acknowledge that this is a problem, and then make changes to address that? How can we shift this "transactional relationship" through policy and funding strategies?

ESME: So, first question is really interesting and, as you said, there's an inherent tension between a commitment to decolonising your museum and then essentially a curatorial practice and individuals and whether they are best placed to do that and open to do that. How to navigate that? If I'm really honest, I don't know. I've been reflecting on what's happened to curatorship at Manchester Museum in the last couple of years, and it is shifting quite a lot. We now have a curator for our South Asia Gallery, Nusrat Ahmed, who started as a member of the South Asia Gallery Collective,[3] so her background is community organising rather than museums. She has a fantastic range of skills in terms of creating the conditions for collaboration and being very open to that, but also an absolute commitment to bringing new narratives to the fore. In a short time, she went from being a member of the Collective to being what's called a "Community Producer" and then we realised very quickly that this notion of community producer is a bit weird because she was the curator of the gallery, so she now has a permanent role as the curator of the South Asia Gallery. Nusrat is building her knowledge and expertise about those collections, working with colleagues at the British Museum and with the collective, and they are building the knowledge together. I think this is a really interesting moment I'm observing in my museum regarding a different kind of knowledge generation.

That's one example and I've got another two to show this further. We now have a new role – "Curator of Indigenous Perspectives" – which has essentially emerged out of all of the work that we've done with partners in Australia. It's absolutely at the heart of decolonising the museum and has a very clear focus on indigenising the museum. Dr Alexandra P. Alberta was appointed to that role and is working with everyone in Manchester Museum, but particularly the curators to support them, to challenge and shift their practice. So, we're thinking about the wider shift, shift of processes as much as a shift of how we work with people and support them, not least the way that we record information about all of our collections and challenge the narratives around that. Alex is working with a whole host of colleagues but leading a new gallery development which will open along with the rest of the museum, in mid-February 2023. It will explore the notion of belonging, the emotional realities of belonging, looking at where collections are from, where they belong, but then also thinking about future notions of belonging.

My final example is that we recruited a new Curator of Living Cultures. More immediately we've been thinking about the way we work internationally, which is again still quite transactional. The way museums work internationally can be through touring exhibitions or research projects, and so we started thinking about what it would look like if we did this a bit differently. What would those relationships with source communities in museums in other countries look like? Thus we were very clear we wanted to have the opportunity to recruit internationally for that role, to allow for the possibility that we would recruit someone with a very clear commitment to decolonising the museum who wasn't coming from a coloniser perspective. We appointed Dr Njabulo Chipangura, and he is bringing a perspective of having worked in South African and Zimbabwean museums. These examples show that we're thinking about what the future of curation is, how we have a real commitment to inclusive narratives, to working with people, and what are the shifts we need to make. I genuinely think we are learning as we go along. The thing I love about museums is that they are a collective endeavour. So, we're creating the conditions for listening to all of those different perspectives. The skill set needed for curators is, I think, shifting quite radically. I believe the future is collaborative, but you need to be able to work collaboratively with others, be attentive to other perspectives, bring those to the fore, honour and acknowledge those, and consider which stories you'll choose. You will always be selective, that's what curation is, so the question then is how you focus on bringing those other narratives to the fore.

ROAA: I want to probe further and ask: How have these decolonisation debates changed decisions about what should be in a collection, for example? And whose voice and agency are represented in the collection? I am also interested in shifting the narrative about what a curator is. As I intimately know the South Asia Gallery because of the research[4] we have done there, I'm interested in how progress from a "member of the Collective" to a "Community Producer" to a "Curator" has happened? In terms of recruitment, I think this is transformative, as it also unsettles hegemonic expectations and ideas of what a curator is, as a custodian of knowledge and expertise that is, in a way, exclusive to racialised communities. So, could you situate that within the bigger question of the actual impact of decolonisation on the thinking and practices of museums?

ESME: I've been thinking a lot about this and that notion of this being exclusive to racialised communities is a significant point. There are lots of examples in the museum where we recruit someone who may not be the most experienced candidate and what we do is support them in that role. Why would this be any different? So, for me, this is about our intention.

If we meet somebody and we feel they align with the values of the museum, they have a wholehearted commitment to being the kind of museum we envision to be with people and they need some additional support in whatever area that may be, I think we must support them. And to be frank, I think it's lazy if we don't. So, if we want to change, and I think we need to change, we have to work at it. At the moment we're recruiting an Environmental Action Manager, and while it will be important that they have a relationship with the environmental sector, they may come from an activist background and have never worked in an institution or a museum. But we can support them with that, we know the museum bit! It goes back to wanting that enduring relationship and where you choose that investment to go, which links to your question about funders actually – particularly with the permanent role, we're in this for the long term. I don't know if I've answered your question?

ROAA: You have, thank you, and it's a way of also re-questioning what skills are needed and valued, and what skills are devalued or not even on the radar in museum recruitment. I think it's really important if the sector wants to go forward to question who an ideal candidate is, is there a preconceived idea of what they look like and what skill set they have, and think deeply about our ideas of the "ideal candidate".

ESME: That's one of the things we're interrogating. If you look at what we would want for certain roles now, it is different. For example, why would you need to have a degree for certain roles? There are a whole host of other forms of experience and relationships somebody may hold that may be far more useful, and we can support people to study for university. For me, this is us thinking long and hard about who works in the museum and what they bring, and what are we valuing. We're a university museum, we have all sorts of researchers, access to expertise, you name it – actually what's a hugely valuable skill for us moving forwards is people who can really work with that and others and bring all of that together.

ROAA: Could this decolonising momentum translate into policy? If yes, then how? How can we address the wider museum sector? How can policy relate to, and have a current relationship with, what's happening socially and politically?

ESME: This is a really interesting question and I think one of the things that are challenging with this question is a sense that the museum sector is a coherent or cohesive sector. One of the things I love about the museum sector is its diversity, not least in terms of governance – whether independent museums, DCMS-funded government museums, regional museums, university museums, council museums. There isn't a kind of sector policy above and beyond. We have the Museum Association Ethics. But even with Arts Council England, they do not fund every museum – they are the sector development body for museums, but only for England. We are a very fragmented sector. So, I think this becomes a question about influence as much as about policy and the ability to influence the policies, whether that's within a city council or in my context, within the university.

So, if you just look at the work around recruitment, for example. We're going to be doing significant recruitment in the next year, with over 30 roles as we reopen. That is an enormous opportunity to do this work. The university has a new Head of EDI – it won't surprise you to know that I am pushing for the museum to be seen as almost like an R&D for the university itself, as a place that is grappling with this and trying new processes to make sure that we have the most inclusive museum workforce we possibly can. So, that's me then trying to engage and influence, have those conversations and do it with the university.

ROAA: So, influence by practice?

ESME: Exactly and influence actually by the vision of where it will go and where it will take us, and that's where the policy does come in. So, the Arts Council's "Let's Create" strategy focuses on relevance and inclusion, as an investment principle, then every organisation should be grappling with the things we're talking about here. The other part of this for me is that funders are essential to all of this, and I am hugely thankful. If you take something like the Indigenising Manchester Museum work I've mentioned, it's funded by the John Ellerman Foundation, who availed funding to support curatorial expertise and new thinking about what curation might be, with the idea that that work will then influence the organisation as a whole.

We must be able to draw on funders like that, that funders are clear on what they stand for, and that we're allowed to try things that don't work. If you gave me a magic wand, what I'd love is to be thinking about funding generationally. The 2-year, 3-year projects are part of the problem here. That's why as soon as possible we prioritised and invested in a permanent curator for the South Asia Gallery. It is important for so many reasons, not least for us to think about how we do the work for the long term: you build the relationship, you don't just sort out the bricks and mortar and move on.

ROAA: And what do you think about the politicisation of the museum sector in light of the former UK Culture Minister Oliver Dowden threatening funding cuts to those cultural institutions which remove controversial objects from display[5]?

ESME: You know if I'm … I think… I think it was and is interesting. Because we've been having this really lively conversation and you've asked that question and immediately I'm so mindful of my words. And, that matters, and actually, just for the record, I'd like you to reflect that. Because that sums up, in part – and there are many other impacts – but that sums up part of the impact of this. So, I think it is not surprising, it is inevitable. I think it is exhausting. I think it is beyond unhelpful. And I, I think it means that we focus on the wrong things.

The sense of threat and fear. I'll be frank – me as a white woman, if I am feeling that in a role like mine with all the power and privilege it brings, how are so many of our partners in a whole range of organisations and communities going to feel? I have conversations with them … what impact is this having? So, mostly I find it deeply upsetting and I am so mindful of the language I use. I am tired of the op-eds back and forth, not least from people in my sector. The positioning of who are the "good guys" and "bad guys" is beyond unhelpful. The language of war is used all the time – there are "battles"; its "culture wars"; it's all about taking a position. It detracts from the work. So, if anything, what it makes me do is double down and focus on what matters, which is the work.

ROAA: I think it is important to record how it made you feel, and the threat and fear it created. Acknowledging these feelings in the context of the privileged position you have highlighted the precarious and vulnerable positionality that people who have been racialised might be experiencing in the climate of "culture wars". And it makes me wonder: what is our relationship with culture and the history we are writing. Should we be fearful to even ask this question? So, thank you for raising this, it is really important.

ESME: The only thing I want to add is that I don't want there to be a sense of "therefore, we aren't doing anything", because the doubling down is important to me. When we repatriated collections to Australia at the end of 2019,[6] I wrote an open letter[7] to the museum sector reflecting on my, and colleagues', experiences and sense of how much of this work had been wrongly framed. The things I kept hearing people saying about repatriation and then my direct experience of it, and certainly my conversations with indigenous leaders and others, just felt like they were poles apart. And I wanted to find a way to articulate this mismatch, this separation.

I wouldn't, I don't think, write that open letter now. In part that's because actually, I'm quite bored of hearing from museum directors. I know you and I are having this conversation and I understand why that is, but increasingly in all of my work, I'm not doing so many keynotes. When I do, I try and do them in partnership. Recently Nusrat and I did one together. I do think there's something about really understanding when my voice is not helpful or does not move things forward. Instead, I could use my position to make sure other voices are heard, as part of my commitment to moving things forward.

ROAA: I'm pleased that you picked up on the issue of looking always for leaders as the source of all knowledge and decision making. Because, even coming to you with the invitation to do this interview, I questioned the ethos of *Cultural Trends* focusing so much on leaders in this specific call. You lead and influence and have massive knowledge and it is amazing to have that conversation with you, but does that make other cultural workers in your institution of any less value?

ESME: I completely agree and I accepted because I didn't want to be rude to you, but the same thing went through my head. Because recently, there have been a whole host of things I've just said "no" to, or "yes, but me and this person". Because this for me is absolutely about a very narrow understanding of what leadership looks like. I've been reflecting on this moment as the time to break with some of our traditions, and who exactly is the subject/focus of the in-conversation. I did a tweet a while ago where we had we had a leak as a result of heavy rain asking "Are there any leaders in museums not stressing about the rain" or something similar. It was really interesting because what people read into that was "museum directors", which isn't really what I meant. I mean I was one, but actually, I'd been talking with our conservators and building operations team – they are museum leaders. So, I got a lot of people saying they weren't museum leaders, but they were stressing about this, and I got back and said "yeah, you're a museum leader". We still have this seductive old-fashioned notion of leadership.

ROAA: I think it is fruitful to re-examine the idea of leadership, and whose voice is included and excluded here.

ESME: Yes absolutely. At Manchester Museum, we don't have a leadership team as such, but a more distributed model. We have a Social Justice Group composed of staff from across the museum, and the co-chairs will be part of the new strategic team at the museum. They will be supported as co-chairs, but they are one of five key decision-makers, myself included, and they will be directly influencing and involved in the decision-making around investments, policies, you name it. If you run museums, you are thinking a lot about what leadership in your institution looks like and yet sometimes, certainly in terms of media, I think there's still quite a lazy, or kind of a default of what leadership looks like. It's why I was so delighted when Zak and Sarah became Co-Directors at Birmingham Museums Trust,[8] which for me felt like a real moment, but I haven't seen that followed yet.

ANTI-RACISM RATHER THAN DIVERSITY?

ROAA: Since the adoption of the Creative Case for Diversity in 2011, Arts Council England has argued for more diversity in the sector and attempted to address the issue with project-based funds and required diversity figures to be embedded into a reporting system. Conversely, Sara Ahmed[9] argues for "uncertainty" around the term "diversity" contending that the question of race (and racism) often recedes when diversity comes into view. In this context, can a museum be actively anti-racist through current diversity policies and initiatives? How can this be mitigated?

ESME: This sits at the heart of the birth of the Social Justice Group in the museum. Interestingly, they collectively had a conversation and were very clear that they wanted it to be "Social Justice", not "Anti-racist" group, so there are maybe some parallels there. However, we – and I say we, because it is across all levels of the museum, although I wasn't involved in these conversations – had a very clear commitment to anti-racist training, not diversity training, and being very conscious of that difference. In terms of whether museums can be actively anti-racist, obviously I would bloody hope so, and if you're not, what are you doing?! I think it is crucial to understand the impact of the contributions you can make beyond your walls. What's your understanding of that anti-racist work you are participating in – is it in the context of broader anti-racist work within your area or city, or is it is solely for your ends as an institution to tick the box, for whatever funding it might be?

I suppose the current diversity policies and initiatives – despite all of the projects, the campaigns, the funding – none of this is systemic and that's the problem. It doesn't seem like rocket science to me, and this is why I am excited about what I'll be doing with the University of Manchester over the next year because we've got to do things that make an enduring change, not for the "when I happen to be running the museum", but for the future – they've got to be embedded. At the moment, if we give our figures, as indeed we do around the diversity of the museum staff on board, and we haven't made any shifts to be more diverse, then what's the implication of that, what's the accountability? The lack of accountability, urgency and transparency is critical for individual institutions like mine to address. We've been identifying a funding pot solely devoted to support training and anti-racist work – that is an important thing to do. It's our commitment within the context of the museum to be clear and accountable. It has got to happen across the piece – it's public money, going back to the fact that museums are about people. I look at the Social Justice Group and the knowledge, commitment and values driving a group like that – they are clear and committed to anti-racist work. But if we don't create the systems and the processes that support that work, it's just dependent on individuals who care.

ROAA: So, to summarise, you identified the problem of diversity becoming a tick-boxing exercise that in a way dilutes racism, or how it addresses racism in a way that dilutes the issue; and the problem of project-based, short-term investment that does not have sustained legacy moving forward.

ESME: The other bit is thinking about "how you do this work". Sorry, I'm going full circle back to the questions: to what extent is your museum engaged with the work that is making a difference in this area? And I don't mean just in museums, it might be in an educational, charity context, or any sector. To what extent are you open? If you have that clear commitment to be anti-racist, how are you going to do it? Who are you going to work with? How are you going to support and finance it? Thinking of not just the next 3 months when everyone's done the course and it's done, but actually what does that work look like and what difference has it made in 5 or 10 years from now? How does that change your shop, or cafe, or the training you give your staff? I'm so interested in how museums learn to do more of this thinking in public, because actually if we do, we really bring in so much knowledge, expertise, support and challenge. At the moment, we are at the stage where we're sort of bizarrely trying to be solutions-focused, rather than grappling with what would this mean for us to do it wholeheartedly.

ROAA: And it ends up being a trend. It should not be just a trend, a "flavour of the month", or that, for example, the impact of Black Lives Matter should be temporary.

ESME: Yes. Black History month is such a good example. I understand where that came from, but we should think of the "and beyond". We've got to focus more on the beyond.

ROAA: Indeed. On that note, the inclusion of ethnically diverse people in museum spaces without regard for the terms under which they are included is often criticised as a quick fix rather than addressing structural issue of inequality. What is Manchester Museum doing in terms of recruitment, which you mentioned before, but also contract types, and pay structure to ensure this is not the case? You mentioned the diversity reporting for the Arts Council, for example. And we know that those diversity reports quite often don't re fleet accurately on what is happening. So, for example, off a hypothetical 15% of staff that are ethnically diverse, a good percentage of those are in the low-paid service and maintenance kind of category, which does not reflect the creative:

ESME: Or are on fixed contracts, as is likely in museums.

ROAA: Right, and I think that's a real problem. So, on paper, it might look like there is a lot of progress happening, but in actuality, the fixed-term contracts, grading and who's in what roles get conflated in the overall picture, showing a veneer of equality, when in fact inequality is deeply seated in an institution. So, how is Manchester Museum addressing this?

ESME: Yes, I think slowly, if I am really honest.

ROAA: I think acknowledgment is part of the process.

ESME: Part of our work with you[10] to date was to clearly understand, interrogate and have conversations with staff and a whole range of people around exactly these issues. In the sector, we're not going to be doing anything meaningful and productive until we understand the nature of the issue and how deeply embedded it is, and what might be needed to start to make that shift. Over the summer we reopened for a short time because of all the cuts we've had during COVID, we had essentially very short-term contracts for a range of people to come in just for that period, and they were fantastic; brilliant. But that short-termism isn't how I ever want to work again even though there was a distinct reason for doing it. Those 30 new posts that I've mentioned are all permanent and that's important to me. Because the fixed-term contracts, the short-term thinking means that actually, even if you do start to make some changes: you recruit this person and they're at a higher-grade role, or whatever it might be, and the money runs out, they move on. So, thinking about those kinds of permanent roles to me is critical.

We've done the things you would expect, we changed the way we interview. We changed who shortlists, so we have very diverse – that's all areas of the museum – and a wide range of staff represented on both shortlisting and interview panels. We've transformed the way we interview, and I think the people who are appointed show that. But, there has to be more we can do, and we're not there yet.

ROAA: I'd like to open up the conversation more broadly, to how the museum sector in general can move forward in terms of policy to mitigate ethnic inequality?

ESME: I think there are some fundamental core things, so I'm a big fan of things like Fair Jobs,[11] that's starting to call out things that aren't OK in terms of our sector. I think all those initiatives, which are very much kind of ground up, are really important because they make this conversation visible. And I think that conversation with funders around pay levels, and expectations of funders could be setting some very useful context for us. I think, working with your HR team, or whoever it might be, around how you can be more explicit about what you're looking for. I think it is essential to put time and energy into building the relationships with people, communities and organisations that you'd like to recruit and work with. So, you're changing where ads go, and the language we use is so important. What are you doing to have conversations with people and test whether that language resonates? Does it put people off? Is terminology important, when it could be a huge barrier to what you do? All of these things are central.

ROAA: And maybe considering the ethnicity pay gap reporting (similar to the gender pay gap,[12] for example), which is not mandatory yet. Do you think a call to make it mandatory might make that accountability just a bit stronger?

ESME: Absolutely. It all comes down to accountability and understanding that if you haven't delivered essentially, then you need to live with the implications and what you've lost. Concurrent with this, we also need to profile the amazing examples of where this has happened, documenting the huge advantages institutionally, personally and in terms of relationship-building. Because that's a big part of this, as well. It's the right thing to do, but actually, in my case and my role, I want us to be the most inclusive, imaginative and caring museum we can be, because I think that's what Manchester should be asking for from us. And we aren't going to do that if everyone in my museum looks like me. Part of it is also, clearly showing the advantages – that has to be done very carefully and obviously with full consent from everyone, but I think it's just something that I've observed that hasn't been apparent.

ROAA: If I may rephrase, I think what you're saying as well is just to link social justice and social responsibility issues and embed them within institutional practices, the rethinking of institutional organisation, and how these two work together actually to create a representative, inclusive narrative and culture.

ESME: They are completely interlinked and they are co-dependent.

ROAA: To make the museum work better.

ESME: Totally and to make the museum work better with and for the communities. For the future. I think there's a lot of museums that are very comfortable with storytelling and narratives – admittedly very particular narratives that always take precedence. Increasingly, I'm interested in how we show so much of this work rather than solely kind of tell it and re-tell (and who's doing the telling). What we end up doing is crafting a narrative that doesn't reflect some of the experiences of those at the heart of this, certainly in terms of talking about race. I think there's something very interesting in that global majority perspective and how that is absolutely at the heart of what you do. But the way that museums tell the world about their work, including us, doesn't prioritise enough that perspective and that's the perspective I think needs prioritising.

ROAA: This has been very insightful and thought-provoking. Thank you very much for your time and candid perspective.

FUNDING

This work was supported by Economic and Social Research Council.

Notes

1 Stuart Hall (1999). Un-settling "the heritage", re-imagining the post-nation: Whose heritage? *Third Text*, 13:49, 3–13. doi:10.1080/09528829908576818.

2 The International Council of Museums.

3 Manchester Museum employed a process of co-curation with members from the South Asian community, referred to as the collective, to design and curate contents for the new South Asia Gallery.

4 Professor Bridget Byrne and myself at the Centre on Dynamics of Ethnicity (CoDE), University of Manchester, have conducted intensive ethnographical research at Manchester Museum as a case study for a research project exploring how institutional practices in cultural institutions can reproduce and mitigate ethnic inequality (Ali and Byrne, 2022).

5 See www.museumsassociation.org/museums-journal/news/2020/10/dowden-letter-on-contested-heritage-stokes-fears-of-government-interference/.

6 In 2019, Manchester Museum worked with AIATSIS (Australian Institute of Aboriginal and Torres Strait Islanders Studies) to return 43 sacred and ceremonial objects to their communities of origin. See www.museum.manchester.ac.uk/about/repatriation/.

7 See https://museum-id.com/the-tide-of-change-open-letter-from-esme-ward/.

8 Zak Mensah and Sara Wajid were appointed joint CEOs of Birmingham Museums Trust in November 2020. See www.birminghammuseums.org.uk/blog/posts/zak-mensah-and-sara-wajid-appointed-joint-ceos-of-birmingham-museums-trust.

9 See Ahmed, S. (2012). *On Being Included: Racism and Diversity in Institutional Life*. Durham and London: Duke University Press.

10 Referencing the research project mentioned in note 4.

11 See fairmuseumjobs.org.

12 See www.gov.uk/government/collections/gender-pay-gap-reporting.

Reference

Ali, R. and Byrne, B. (2022). The trouble with diversity: The cultural sector and ethnic inequality. *Cultural Sociology*. https://doi.org/10.1177/17499755221114550.

Corporate Engagement and Cultural Leadership

Thomas Girst, Global Head of Cultural Engagement, BMW Group: In Conversation (Germany)

Leticia Labaronne

Chapter 8

DOI: 10.4324/9781003390725-8

Professor Thomas Girst, PhD, studied Art History, American Studies and German Literature at Hamburg University and New York University. Between 1995 and 2003 he was Head of the Art Science Research Laboratory in New York under the directorship of Stephen Jay Gould (Harvard University). Since 2003, he has been the Global Head of Cultural Engagement at the BMW Group while also lecturing at various international universities. In 2016, Girst received the "European Cultural Manager of the Year" award. His books have been translated into numerous languages and most recently include *Art, Literature, and the Japanese American Internment*, *The Duchamp Dictionary*, *BMW Art Cars*, *100 Secrets of the Art World*, and *Alle Zeit der Welt*. His upcoming book, *Cultural Management: A Global Guide*, will be published by Thames & Hudson in 2023.

This interview was conducted online in the summer of 2021 as the pandemic situation seemed to be improving in the wake of the introduction of the vaccine. The text has been edited for length and structure and was modified slightly in March and July 2022.

CORPORATE CULTURAL ENGAGEMENT: A GLOBAL PERSPECTIVE

LETICIA: Can I start by asking, what is "corporate cultural engagement"?

THOMAS: I would define "corporate cultural engagement" as part of "corporate citizenship", the umbrella term under which you also find terminological entities such as "corporate social responsibility". Many also speak of "corporate cultural responsibility". The concept of corporate cultural engagement does not translate into any partnerships in a broad definition of the cultural realm but rather those long-term cooperations that lean more towards social sustainability than towards brandbuilding. The latter is seen in things like hiring an actor or a band to ramp up communications of a launch event, collaborating with an artist on the design of a product, or partnering with a commercial art fair, whereas institutional partnerships, say with museums, opera houses, or theatres define the parameters for the former.

LETICIA: This conversation with you about corporate cultural engagement leads me to ask how such engagement on a global scale could influence both national cultural policy agendas and international trends. Is there such a thing as "cultural policymaking" by corporate actors?

THOMAS: I am not aware of any countries that have rules or laws regulating how much companies should contribute to cultural activities. This means that all corporate endeavours with regard to culture stem from an organisation's own initiative. This is a crucial fact to mention before we dive into this topic.

In that sense, there is no policy as such but there is a notion of right or wrong with regard to corporate cultural engagement once any company decides to become active in this field. Wrong, I would say, is jumping from event to event, not having any strategy in place, not providing any planning security in terms of long-term, sustainable engagement. In other words, we can define sponsorships based not on strategic thinking but solely on the affinities of the CEO or senior management as wrong – mostly because this tends to translate into wanting to decide on artistic content, which is a fundamentally flawed approach whichever way you look at it. A lot of things can be problematic when going down this road because that means the company is only answering the call for cultural engagement reactively. A proactive approach involves having a strategy in place that is based on the shared values of any one business enterprise and engaging in partnerships that are truly meaningful.

Here, it is important to differentiate between sponsorships and partnerships. To me, sponsorship focuses on moving financial resources from A to B and vice versa. These activities can be considered purely a monetary transaction, whereas partnerships are based on interaction. The main distinction between sponsoring and partnerships is the relationship you build. Partners communicate with each other, they look out for each other, they consider the benefits of a long-term commitment building on genuine curiosity about each other and a shared system of beliefs. Ideally the company should offer full artistic freedom; the company's freedom takes the form of the freedom to decide who to collaborate with.

LETICIA: When you refer to the notion of "wrong" regarding corporate cultural engagement and sponsorships that are merely transactional, are you also thinking about situations of "artwashing"? This term tends to be used to describe the instrumentalization of art to distract from negative action and improve the public image of individuals, organisations, or governments.

THOMAS: I have never heard this term but would agree with your assessment. Keep in mind, however, that the art market itself is a 65-billion-dollar market. While I see museums and artists struggling, the arts are by definition a commercial enterprise, like it or not. The term may make sense when we apply it to companies engaging in questionable practices in the arts. After all, the art market is a rather unregulated global marketplace that is particularly prone to money-laundering. Yet, as I see it, it is not as strong as "greenwashing", where higher standards apply and the demarcation of what constitutes true sustainability versus mere window-dressing is more obvious. Having said that, even strategically wrongheaded arts sponsorship may very well directly benefit artists or cultural institutions.

LETICIA: You talked earlier of the practice of hiring an actor or a band to ramp up communications and the notion of right or wrong with regard to corporate cultural engagement. Recently the band Coldplay have been called "useful idiots for greenwashing"[1] after announcing a partnership with Finnish oil company Neste to halve their world tour emissions. Coldplay's tour has been separately criticised for collaborating with BMW, which is providing 40 rechargeable electric vehicle batteries to power the shows. BMW is an influential lobbyist for the German car industry, according to a report by Influence Map. Given that BMW is lobbying to prevent the EU from setting a deadline of 2035 for vehicles to be zero emissions only, have they been able to use Coldplay?

THOMAS: BMW's revenue in 2021 was over 110 billion euros. Our core business is cars. I don't think that simply in terms of scale, anything we may do as part of our cultural engagement could or should be considered "greenwashing" as true sustainability is what happens along the entire value chain when building a car. In the digital age, customers can see right through and cannot be fooled. Any attempt at "greenwashing" would thus be futile and destined to fail. All numbers regarding CO_2 emissions and electrification are on the table for everyone to see and judge.

As for 2035, we are lobbying for an intensive expansion of the charging infrastructure so that electric mobility has a chance to become widespread. At the same time, legislation should be open to embrace alternative emission free technology such as hydrogen and fuel cell batteries while we are making the transfer from the combustion engine – a huge undertaking we are front and centre of. This will take time as we also need to consider the long-term well-being of over 130,000 employees and their families worldwide. When it comes to Coldplay, what is wrong with them approaching us to provide batteries so that they can power their shows with renewable energy? I applaud their efforts!

LETICIA: Going back to the notion of a proactive approach to corporate cultural engagement, when talking about a global player like BMW, it makes sense to focus on the global strategy. However, I assume that your organisation considers national and regional contexts as well. How do corporate global strategies and national or regional cultural policies relate to each other?

THOMAS: I believe that if you are committed to engaging in the arts on behalf of a major international company, you should consider the policymaking aspects of what it is that you are doing. When I am asked to take part in a panel discussion in India, for example, people come up to me ahead of time and tell me that I need to talk about the situation in Germany, where the government provides €12 billion to the cultural sector and private foundations and corporations give approximately €500 million. I am asked to emphasise that in a country like India, with 1.3 billion people, there is basically no infrastructure for culture, so there are virtually no public museums for contemporary art, not even a handful. I am also asked to state how crucial it is that the government does more for culture and that the same goes for affluent companies that want to create a positive, empowering image for themselves while also creating something meaningful in terms of corporate responsibility.

Naturally, the situation is different all over the world. When I speak in Italy, only a few hundred miles south of Germany, I like to use the ice cream with the cherry on top metaphor. I like to say that the ice cream is something that the government should provide. This means that governmental engagement in cities as well as in smaller towns should be a given, especially within a federal republic. In this metaphor, corporate engagement is the cherry on the top of the ice cream. However, I was once told by a distraught member of an audience that the ice cream part of the equation does not really exist in Italy: there is simply not enough government funding going into cultural infrastructure and into cultural projects, so the arts need to rely on corporate or private engagement. Another related issue is what happened in the United States, where cultural institutions are run like businesses because the financing of arts institutions relies for the most part on a board of trustees and their deep pockets. So, when the pandemic hit, many people in the cultural sector suddenly lost their jobs. In my opinion, you will only find an ideal situation regarding non-nationalist governmental commitment to the arts, or at least as close to ideal as we can get, in liberal, democratic countries such as Germany or Switzerland.

LETICIA: I would like to further discuss your metaphor about the relationship between corporate cultural engagement and cultural policymaking, the former ideally being the cherry while the latter is the ice cream. In Germany, where the government provides generous support for the arts, it might be easy to talk about how companies might add value by being the cherry on top of the ice cream. In other places, adding value might be less straightforward. When you talk in India, for example, and call for more public backing for the arts and culture, what happens? Can corporations exert their leverage in a way that fosters better conditions for the arts and cultural sector?

THOMAS: I think you need to lead by example. Richard Florida's assessment of the creative class being an important economic factor in post-industrial societies is important to consider. However, not all societies on this planet are post-industrial. As the remaining non-post-industrial societies continue to develop, certain measures need to be implemented for culture to also be able to blossom and flourish. Behind closed doors, our company does speak to policymakers. Even though BMW's core business is not culture, our company can engage in a non-public dialogue about cultural engagement.

I do believe that it is possible to successfully lead by example not only when the wind is beneath your wings, but also when it is blowing in your face like we have experienced in recent years. Showing your commitment, showing your strength and supporting the arts is something truly aspirational. Talking the talk is important, but walking the walk is essential. Otherwise, things can go wrong, like we see with the critical attitudes towards the Sackler family for example, who many consider to be responsible for the opioid crisis in the United States and so partially responsible for the thousands upon thousands of people addicted and dying because of it. The Sacklers, of course, were one of the biggest patrons in the whole art world over many decades. There are entire buildings and wings of buildings of major museums around the world named after this family. And now, of course, it's interesting to see that it's been artists such as Nan Goldin, much more than the curators or museum directors who rely on this sort of funding, that have been highly critical of this kind of money coming in from companies. It was artists who finally convinced the Met and the Serpentine, the National Portrait Gallery and the Guggenheim to cut ties with this pharmaceutical juggernaut. The Liberate Tate art collective was behind the museum ending more than a quarter-century of money coming in from BP. As a company, you should know what you do. Criticality by artists remains essential and so does thinking of worst-case scenarios before you enter a partnership.

Knowing which way to steer can be achieved primarily by knowing your company's values, by knowing what it is your organisation stands for, and then building on that to create the cultural policy that may also inspire those that are making policy decisions in the public realm.

LETICIA: You already mentioned that you openly discussed the lack of sufficient public funding for the arts in India and in Italy. What is your impression of this dialogue in more restrictive countries?

THOMAS: When it comes to more restrictive countries, globalisation plays an important role, regardless of whether you view globalisation as a positive phenomenon or are critical of it. Aspiring for intercultural dialogue through culture is a meaningful endeavour. However, such an undertaking is nothing new for a company operating on a global scale. Intercultural dialogue is the basis of any successful global company. As the Head of Cultural

Leticia Labaronne

Engagement worldwide, I find myself working in Munich speaking to my Chinese and Asian colleagues in the morning, then to my Russian and African colleagues in the afternoon and at night to North and South America about what they do. I am not interested in telling them what it is that they should do within their own country because they should know best. All I can provide them with are the parameters in which they should get active in the arts. I can assist them with contractual agreements, and I can provide them with our knowledge, network, and know-how based on 50 years of cultural engagement, but they need to be the ones that decide.

Freedom of thought is something that is as central to BMW's core business as it is for the arts. For example, BMW has been working with many artists from mainland China and Hong Kong. Some of them received the BMW Art Journey scholarship; others were commissioned to create a BMW art car. In both instances, they were always free to do what they deemed right. We need to grant absolute creative freedom to our artists on a global scale, no matter where they are, because that creative freedom is crucial also to our engineers and designers as it is what provides the basis for them to design the greatest cars on the planet.

LETICIA: Moving away from the relationship between corporations and creative artistic freedom, what kind of impact do political restrictions have on the arts, especially in countries where artistic expression is restricted? And what does this mean for corporations engaging in these countries?

THOMAS: Dialogue is an important factor. When working with artists and with cultural policymakers in different countries, you need to consider the sensibilities and the sensitivities regarding the coordinates in which these countries operate. Speaking to someone from South Africa as opposed to someone from India, China or the United States is not the same. All these countries are important markets for the BMW Group, and they are also countries in which we have engaged in culture for in some cases half a century.

One example I would like to showcase is our collaboration with Cao Fei, a great Chinese contemporary artist whose show at the UCCA in Beijing ended in May 2021. She is an artist, wife, and mother and has decided to be a resident of Beijing and not work from anywhere else on the planet. In an interview she gave to *The New York Times*, she said that she knows where the red line is, and she decides not to go there. With regard to her artistic creativity, she still finds she has enough room to express herself.

Another example is literature published in East Germany under Communist rule despite the censorship of the time. This environment heightened the artists' sensitivity about getting the word out despite all the forces working against them. I wrote my PhD on "Art Literature and the Japanese American Internment" to find out how art can thrive in unfavourable, even hostile environments. How can art thrive when there is no material to create art, in the face of manipulation, censorship, and propaganda surrounding the arts? I am very hopeful that no matter what situation we find ourselves in, the arts will persevere. The arts are essential for expressing our way of seeing the world, of reflecting upon the world. Regardless of the circumstances, artists will find a way to express themselves and make themselves heard and find the right metaphors no matter how narrow the possibilities may be. However, this does not mean that the arts do not need our support, which is exactly why BMW tries to support the arts on a global scale. This means that our organisation needs to be aware of the coordinates in which we try to make this possible.

SHAPING CULTURAL TRENDS AND POLICY: THE ROLE OF GLOBAL CORPORATIONS

LETICIA: I would like to further explore the role of a global corporation in shaping cultural trends and policy at an international level by discussing your last statement about how successful global corporations know the parameters in which their businesses operate. While the relationship of public cultural institutions with corporate sponsorship is often under scrutiny, what would you say about corporations positively pushing the boundaries of such parameters?

THOMAS: I think if we look at the interplay of the arts and the criticism of businesses being involved in the arts, it is important to keep an open mind and maintain your curiosity while appreciating all parties involved. In this manner, corporations and the arts can achieve great things together. An organisation can decide against a collaboration but be just as mindful about the benefits that they might be missing. By this I mean intangible advantages the organisation could be benefiting from, such as new ideas and perspectives that you either don't know of or that you don't possess. Often this boils down to know-how or questions of network and rapport. You should also take any criticism to heart and reflect upon the things that artists should never give up on even while in the process of collaborating with a company.

For example, in 2012 we were partnering with the Olympics in the United Kingdom. At the same time, there was an event taking place called the Cultural Olympiad. We teamed up with the Institute of Contemporary Art (ICA) to host an exhibition of the BMW Art Cars. The ICA decided that they didn't want to show the art cars in their own museum because they had planned their exhibitions so far in advance – and also, it might have been perceived as selling out to a company – and rightly so! So they thought it might be much more appropriate to present them in an actual parking lot since, after all, that's where cars belong. This idea jumpstarted the whole notion of satellite spaces for the ICA, which has had a huge influence on other cultural institutions as well. BMW does not need to be seen in the traditional museum space. We are far more interested in branching out, breaking out of our comfort zone, reaching new people and new audiences, and engaging with new technologies. Bringing BMW Art Cars to an actual parking lot on six different levels allowed us to achieve something meaningful and special. Plus, the media loved it.

LETICIA: How is this approach applicable in places where the ground infrastructure for the arts is not as developed yet?

THOMAS: The same applies. A good example is the Kochi-Muziris Biennale in India. We teamed up with them for their very first biennial, which nobody thought would get off the ground and actually happen. No one except the visionary organisers and founders. I realised then that when we put our full energy behind a project, especially as a successful international business enterprise that has been around for over 100 years, we also help others to not only see the uncharted territory ahead but to feel that if BMW is involved, it might be worth getting involved too. So, at the very early stages, we often help cultural institutions and cultural projects to get the visibility, the recognition, and the budget that they need to turn great pioneer ideas into a success. Our logo might therefore become a seal of approval showing that visitors may expect a certain quality, even if that quality enables platforms not for something merely affirmative, but rather for something that sets out to do more than simply please the onlooker.

LETICIA: If we look at current discourses in cultural policy, there is a growing emphasis on evaluation, impact analysis and evidence-based policymaking, among other topics. While these issues and the rationality involved have not remained uncontested among scholars and practitioners, the question of accountability of public spending on the arts and culture is valid. However, although companies are not required to legitimize their spending to taxpayers, they do need to create value for their shareholders. How do you go about looking for this value?

THOMAS: Coming back to the example of Germany where a good portion of taxpayers' money goes into culture, I would like to see more thought go into the distribution of these funds. In Germany, you have hundreds of orchestras, thousands of museums, and many other institutions, all of which are underfunded for exhibitions, for getting the right creatives into the right places, and for acquisitions. But policymakers very often arrive at solutions like creating the Humboldt Forum in Berlin, which costs hundreds of millions of euros and with an annual operating budget of €50 million. Another example is the new Museum for Contemporary and Modern Art, again in Berlin, which comes at a price tag of hundreds of millions of euros. In Germany we find ourselves in a federalist system and to be frank, I would much rather see that very system being supported instead of creating something new and centralised over and over again just because it allows you to make an impact as a cultural policy maker for the few years you are in office.

So how do we navigate this situation? Firstly, I would say it's important to not spend your organisation's funds in areas where public funding is being withdrawn. This sets the wrong example, by making it appear as if private companies are filling the gap that is created after the public sector has pulled back. Here, we need to ask ourselves why the public sector is withdrawing funds. The answer is simple: because the taxes are no longer coming in. Why are the taxes no longer coming in? Because the companies have found some clever ways to avoid taxes, just like in the Anglo-American world, or they are making less profit. If companies are making less profit, they will also not be able to provide more budget when the public sector withdraws its funding. This is the mistake being made in this thought process, which I always find curious and which I wanted to correct in this conversation.

LETICIA: From a fundraising perspective, I agree that a decrease of public funding is never a strong case for supporting the arts. So, again, how does BMW go about looking for opportunities to create meaning, to create value?

THOMAS: You need to align your company's cultural commitment with its goals while simultaneously considering transformation. In this case, we are talking about a general sustainable future that will also ensure that your company specifically has a future. Finding meaning within these parameters basically means that it's reliant in terms of: BMW relies on your definition of premium and of luxury. As a luxury and premium car manufacturer we could focus our efforts on only aligning our social or cultural commitment with our target audience's taste. But then we would miss out on the opportunity to partner with great projects that, for example, allow us to collaborate with the opera to open this cultural art form to a wider audience. We believe that the free concerts that are organised in part thanks to BMW – together with great partners such as the Scala in Milan, the London Symphony Orchestra, the Munich Opera, the Berlin Opera, even occasionally the Jazz Festival in Shanghai – allow for a sense of luxury to return to the society we successfully do business in. Ultimately, this initiative has to do with redefining luxury as something accessible. We want to provide people with the luxury of having an experience that on the one hand is brought to you by BMW, and on the other is still independent in the sense that BMW does not intervene between the art and the onlooker, the music and the listener. To be successful in this endeavour is to be a true corporate citizen, as such undertakings relate directly to the attitude and the character of a company.

The greatest definition of "brand" that I have ever heard comes from the 1960s, from John Hegarty, an ad agency executive in New York City: "A brand is a piece of real estate in somebody else's mind". In that sense, our brand should not only be a fantastically designed car and maybe the garage around it, but the brand should also ensure that the piece of real estate has enough room for an opera house, for a gallery, for a museum and so on. I truly believe that this enriches what BMW stands for as a cultural brand. Of course, driving sales is also a part of this thought process alongside considering our company's behaviour in a society. A firm cannot be considered as a corporate citizen if it only focuses on the bling bling, and if it jumps from event to event. Taking your time, it might take years to get noticed. However, engagement is really all about nurturing and cultivating your relationships with cultural institutions and artists. And when your company believes in that, you truly can make a difference in this regard. We consider BMW to be a cultured brand. No strings attached once you understand that we are not doing this for altruistic or philanthropic reasons alone; there are always questions of visibility, image, and reputation as well.

LETICIA: Drawing on your extensive experience working for a major corporation that is globally engaged in the arts, what particular knowledge do you think cultural policymakers could benefit from?

THOMAS: I would say that when it comes to audience development, it is essential to realise that audiences are more diverse, less affluent, and less educated. Without understanding this, these cultural institutions don't have much of a future.

LETICIA: But cultural policymakers and arts organisations alike have been looking into audience development and cultural participation for years. In Switzerland, for example, the topic of cultural participation is a central axis of action for the federal government's cultural policy agenda. There is still a long way to go regarding audience diversity. In your opinion, what knowledge can successful brands offer to diversify the insights on the subject?

THOMAS: Don't look at diversity as a sprint. Look at it as a marathon. The people in charge, such as myself, are trying to right the wrongs of 5,000 years of patriarchy, misanthropy and

Western hegemony, which cannot be undone in an instant. This undertaking is based on your mindset and your openness. I truly believe that working in a global company where representatives from various places such as Asia, Africa, South America, and so on, come together in the same room, is a type of utopia, which cultural institutions limited to one place can only dream of. The famous German poet and philosopher Holderlin ended one of his most important poems with *Komm! ins Offene, Freund:* "Open it up, my friends!" This may require courage for some, which often comes along with some self-recognition.

So, I would also say, let's get off the high horse! Acknowledge that you are not only part of the solution but also part of the problem. Consider what institution you are giving public budget to. Think about that institution as not being *about something,* but *for someone.* This requires a high level of reflection. Finally, you need to scrutinise your cultural organisation as if it were a brand. You need to know your vision and consider both internal and external opinion. Only by making that change in perception can you compete. You might even get ahead in the attention competition. Because whether you like it or not, there is a competition for attention going on. Therefore, consider everything that your company is doing, including in terms of narratives, in terms of storytelling, in terms of key images and in terms of key moving images. This is not an easy endeavour, but I believe in the importance of this little exercise that comes with the business case attached. It's never been easy to get the word out to new audiences and generations that otherwise might not have heard of you.

It's also important to mention that collaborating with the arts is not about watering down what a cultural institution stands for. It's not about reducing the complexity of an opera, of a dance, of a work of art. The focus lies in packaging the arts in a way that might be of interest to others, and not only those that are already involved. In other words, don't only preach to the converts. This is something I would love to tell every policymaker.

POST-PANDEMIC TRENDS AND ALLIANCES

LETICIA: There are two thoughts we have already discussed that I would like to come back to: Firstly, the expectation that when the public sector is withdrawing its funding, companies should close the funding gap; and secondly, that the arts strive even in times of crisis because it leads to a lasting reflection about post-pandemic developments in the arts and culture. A lot of media and scholarly attention has been given to identifying trends such as digitalisation. My question is whether we can talk about global post-pandemic trends?

THOMAS: I believe it was Yuval Noah Harari who said in an essay that either we come out of this pandemic in nationalist isolation or in international solidarity. Arundhati Roy likened the pandemic to a portal through which we can travel with all our grievances and petty fights intact – or dare to build a better future together. Of course, these are both bold statements to make, but it was Chris Dercon, president of dozens of museums across France, who said that the pandemic has turned all our cultural institutions into national institutions because there are no more tourists. Yes, these institutions were closed for most of the pandemic. However, they had to rearrange themselves and consider their more immediate surroundings instead of thinking of themselves within global structures. I don't want to discuss the socialist term solidarity here, but I believe that Harari has a point. I would like to think of alliances instead. And when I think of alliances, I believe that the cultural sector comes out of this situation stronger than before.

Considering the trends you mentioned, digitalisation has been given quite a jumpstart and is definitely here to stay. Interestingly, we had all the technology before, we just weren't using it properly or to this extent. Before the pandemic, the annual fundraising auction for the Pinakothek der Moderne in Munich raised approximately one million euros per year. Now, they are making three million a year because they are hosting their auction online and they are attracting clients from Asia and the United States that bid on their artworks. Taking advantage of this opportunity is fantastic – even for artists, who often are not being paid enough. For most, the freebie culture of social media and the internet have not made things any better. Yet at the same time, you have OnlyFans, as well as platforms like GoFundMe or Patreon, that present whole new models of raising money for artists. So this is something where I think alliances come in, and this also between companies, which should share more of their know-how and of their network with cultural institutions. I'm happy to see all these things slowly developing.

LETICIA: Could you elaborate more on the knowledge that companies possess that artists and cultural organisations can benefit from as they forge new alliances with major corporate players in the years ahead?

THOMAS: Since the eighteenth century, at least in German-speaking countries, anything to do with money – or, God forbid, a business case – has been defined as being in opposition to the arts. The Frankfurt School may have rightly warned against the culture industry, and culture has always been positioned as something that resists the dominance of the market and businesses. Yet I do think, as important as it was and is, that this 200-year-old definition blinded us somewhat to the possibility of creating meaningful coalitions between partners at eye-level. Of course, partnerships about business and the arts are about a monetary transfer, that is a part of it, but it's also about a dance. Do you want to dance the dance? And with whom do you want to dance? And these things take time. And when I talk about dance I'm back to the idea of the relationship, of the partnership between the cultural entity, be that an institution or an artist, and the company or the entity that does the funding. It would be remiss to only look at the budget. There's so much you can learn and take away from a global company. What do they do? What do they excel in? I see so much beauty in innovation, in engineering and in design. You would have to be completely ignorant of all the things that are happening and developing in order to not make use of them as an artist, to delve into what is new and strange as it is unknown. So, if you are curious about your potential partner, ask them. Everybody wants to be asked something. It's the Socratic way of things. Your partner will be able to help you and vice versa. As a company you are often held back by crunching numbers at the end of the day, whereas artists tend to be more liberal in this regard and much more freewheeling. What I'm saying is that what I gather from artists and collaborating closely with them is that their thinking is often one step ahead. Therefore, we need to listen to their voices and try to catch up, not only when it comes to funding the arts, but also when it comes to our core business. Not necessarily to make it even more profitable, but to learn about how to position yourself as a company when it comes to being a desirable brand.

So this is how I think new alliances are giving rise to new trends in post-pandemic times. What do you think, Leticia? I would also love to hear your thoughts, because I think it can be very valuable for our interview to explore this further. So, I would love to ask you right now, Leticia, when we talk about the learnings for post-pandemic times, the cultural institutions and the discourse that you come in contact with and that you spend your time with, what are your takeaways here?

LETICIA: I am rather sceptical about drawing conclusions too quickly about the post-pandemic implications for the arts and cultural sector. But I have observed two emerging trends, which are related to the need for a paradigm change that has been accelerated and made more visible by the pandemic.

I believe that the pandemic has made apparent that the majority of the "projectification" and fragmentation of funding in the cultural sector, inherent to reforms in the context of new public management, is not sustainable. Therefore, I believe that we are not seeing a trend per se, but hopefully a shift to a realisation that funding practices need to be more sustainable if we want to "create meaning". As you mentioned, it is a marathon, not a sprint. Therefore, we should be reconsidering the strong emphasis of funding at the project level, even though in some cases such as extremely innovative endeavours it might make sense.

THOMAS: Yes, I believe this refers not only to cultural institutions and corporations but also to public and private funding bodies. What else do you have in mind?

LETICIA: A last thought worth mentioning is the need for solidarity among the different actors of the arts and in the cultural sector, the need to find a unified voice to lobby for the arts, against the interest of other socially relevant systems, making the traditional silo mentality within and across the art genres as well as between high and lowbrow culture obsolete. What are your thoughts here?

THOMAS: I think that is important. I believe that cultural institutions often cannibalise each other fighting for the same sources of funding. They eye each other constantly and envy one another, particularly when their leaders cannot see past their bloated egos. This makes no sense at all because standing together makes you stronger. That is why collaborations are so important. So many companies are now doing the X between the names, for example Virgil Abloh X Mercedes or Madonna X Nike. These players have recognised the strength of partnering up to create something together. Consider the example of Arthur Jafa, who received the Golden Lion at the Venice Biennial. He is now considered a great contemporary video artist, but before that he was making advertisements. There is so much going on in terms of cross-branding, but also in terms of cross-disciplinary thinking that, again, we would really be making a huge mistake if we did not consider a more holistic approach.

LETICIA: This brings us to the matter of sustainability in arts organisations, an important topic for the sector's survival and for ensuring that the arts remain relevant for future generations. In your opinion, what do we need to do to guarantee this?

THOMAS: We need to consider the notions of being proactive or reactive. Right now, we don't have the luxury of being reactive. We need to act. And while there is something to be said for short-term solutions, especially in times of a global pandemic, we need to factor in the long-term. While everyone always wants to create something entirely new and unheard of, it remains crucial to be open. I think we have defined this as an important denominator in our conversation. However, continuity is what ultimately sustains the cause. Continuity means safety of planning ahead and relying on what you already know. You don't always have to invent everything from scratch. We are all standing on the shoulders of giants. "Every future needs a past", as Odo Marquard once said. We must be aware that the cultural institutions, the cultural genres that we thrive in, have a history of hundreds if not thousands of years. But of course, to move forward, we must look into the rear-view mirror as if we were driving a car. Look back but also keep our hands on the wheel and look into the future and change with the times, because otherwise, we will become irrelevant.

LETICIA: That is a good thought to conclude our conversation with. I like the idea of cultural leaders at the steering wheel of vehicles of change. Thank you very much for your time and your insights, Thomas!

Note

1   www.theguardian.com/environment/2022/may/11/coldplay-labelled-useful-idiotsfor-greenwashing-after-deal-with-oil-company?CMP=Share_iOSApp_Other&fbclid=IwAR2Io Ct2UN7ngshBuvtoo4Hcza6F95lYxh7d03AA9YTUPdfRV9pvhDXa7oQ.

Artists and Cultural Leadership

Array Collective, 2021 Turner Prize Winners: In Conversation (Northern Ireland/ Ireland)

Jane Morrow

Chapter 9

Array Collective are a group of individual artists rooted in Belfast, who join together to create collaborative actions in response to the socio-political issues affecting Northern Ireland. In December 2021, they won the Turner Prize, an annual award made to artists

DOI: 10.4324/9781003390725-9

born, living, or working in the UK, for an outstanding exhibition or public presentation of their work anywhere in the world in the previous year. In 2021, and for the first time, the Turner Prize shortlist[1] consisted entirely of artist collectives, representative of the solidarity and community demonstrated by artists in response to the pandemic. Array Collective are the first winners from Northern Ireland.

This conversation took place in Belfast on 14 September 2022 with Array Collective members Laura O'Connor, Emma Campbell and Alessia Cargnelli.

INTRODUCTION

JANE: You are all individual artists who contribute to Array Collective and you are also researchers. Can you tell me a little about your specific fields of research and how they manifest in your own practices and as part of Array's work?

LAURA: I'm interested in performative femininity, and the narratives around how women should behave in society and in the media. My PhD research focused on how art practice can infiltrate social media and enable a level of subversiveness online, where I used technology and live performance to play around with audience and experience. In recent years, I've been more specifically looking at the treatment of women in Ireland whose bodies are controlled by the state – how women's medical data is stored, tracked, and used – and drawing on my own body data to create sculptural and video pieces. That extends into one of my main roles in Array Collective, which is around creating the films and performing to camera, as well as influencing the theoretical direction around the treatment of women in Ireland under state and church control.

EMMA: I've been involved – as an artist and an activist – in the abortion rights movement in Ireland since around 2010. My research focus is on art activism and how it can be effective or affecting. My practice is mostly photographic, with a little bit of performance, and some public interventions. I'm trying to address what [renowned feminist scholar] Rosalind Pollack Petchesky identified as a gap in visual knowledge and visual spheres in terms of pro-choice imagery, and how we might counter the negative and dangerous depictions of foetal imagery on the pro-life side. It's also about my interest in collective practice because of my activism work, and because a lot of my research has focused on photography collectives. All three of us contribute quite heavily to the admin and organisation of Array, but my theoretical contributions bring in activism directly to the practice of the collective, as well as through highlighting how important art is to movements and how activist communities need artists.

ALESSIA: My research focuses on different types of feminist-informed methodologies, particularly in the context of artists' collectives across different places and times. Within my current PhD research, I'm looking at artists' collectives that were active in the late eighties and early nineties that were mostly women-led and self-organised. They were established to resist the social and political situations at the time, the institutions and predominant culture and stereotypes. I suppose my work in Array – and as an artist living in the city – is a response to issues that affect me and my peers. My practice allows me to experiment in ways that I might not be able to through my research, connecting different places and times, and slogans in my native language with like-minded movements in Ireland from the sixties or the seventies.

PAYING ARTISTS AND STUDIO SUBSIDIES

JANE: To set the scene, my first questions are around studio subsidies and pay for artists. In Northern Ireland, we don't have a specific "paying artists" policy; until March 2022, there was no mention of paying artists in Arts Council policy at all. A crisis within the studio sector has also emerged, through a lack of recognition, value and ongoing disinvestment within the arts infrastructure. Why do you think that is?

EMMA: I think it's a general trend in the UK, Ireland, and Western Europe, but particularly in the North of Ireland. There is a tendency to focus only on issues which are easily co-opted by sectarianism, and therefore other social issues that aren't as easily divided or controlled in that way are abandoned. I just don't think the arts are valued – visual art, in particular – in the same way here as, for example, sports, which are quite heavily funded as they are often seen under the auspices of peacebuilding. The amount of money allocated to sports and peacebuilding is phenomenal in comparison to the amount of money given to support arts and peacebuilding, for instance. So, it's a question of value. Especially where parties like the Democratic Unionist Party (DUP) are very deeply associated with right-wing, conservative outlooks and aren't known for their cultural diversity.

LAURA: I think that idea of what culture is works on two different levels in the North of Ireland, because culture in an "orange" [unionist and politically right] or "green" [nationalist and politically left] sense is so specific. And it's also viewed in this odd, immutable, static way, like it is fixed and can't change and must be represented in these very particular ways. I also think that there's an assumption, around visual arts, that sub-standard will suffice; we get offered the worst buildings, or we're given grants for buildings that last for very limited amounts of time.

ALESSIA: There is also a tendency here towards seeing visual artists as a tool, where we are useful for outreach projects with certain disadvantaged communities for one day. Our work is really used as a tick-box exercise, as something that can magically make change happen. But if you want to use art as a tool for change, it needs to be funded and there must be a legacy.

LAURA: It was the same situation in Derry, around the UK City of Culture [in 2013]. It seemed to be "we'll have a big opening, and we'll have the fireworks and we'll do all the big exhibitions", but then nothing has any legacy, which leaves all the messaging around it feeling like little more than lip service.

EMMA: There's also an overarching problem, globally, since around the 1990s, where there's a kind of managerialism that's seeped into the art world, where all the money that maybe could have gone to artists and to artistic production has been funnelled into managers and curators and PR people. And it has led to the institutionalisation of artists in educational establishments, where they don't have to worry about money, and then they lose sight of what it is to be an artist. The lack of class awareness around artists, alongside the cost of university education and disinvestment in arts education is a more general, widespread issue. Array becoming a collective was one of the ways of trying to deal with that because we're sharing resources. Artists' studios in general are a way of dealing with that. But there is also a lack of understanding about why artists would work together. "Why would you share resources? Why can't we speak to the same person every day? Why can't we have a meeting with all of you, at one o'clock in the afternoon with no notice?" In places like this [NI], with large working-class communities and socioeconomic deprivation, most of us are doing this because we have a compulsion to do it, not because it's a luxurious hobby.

LAURA: Unfortunately, our success [as Array Collective] has validated that. Which is unfortunate, because we're not working in a good studio [building], we don't have good facilities. We each have four jobs and kids and everything else. There was genuinely a moment where [our installation for the Turner Prize exhibition] wasn't going to happen, or that we almost weren't going to be able to finish it because we couldn't get any funding from the Arts Council [of Northern Ireland]. We started by speaking to them directly, but we eventually had to go over their heads to government departments, and we could only get in contact with them because we had experience of lobbying for other reasons. If we hadn't secured that extra funding, we wouldn't have made the show that we did, and we probably wouldn't have had the success that we did.

ALESSIA: What we need to be clear about is that, in Northern Ireland, the only way that artists can exist is through public funding – we don't have the same levels of sponsorship as elsewhere and a commercial art market system doesn't really exist here. There is pretty much one public funder, and it's either them or nothing.

JANE: In your experience as a collective of 11 people, have you ever received adequate remuneration for your work as a group? Do you feel like your individual contributions are understood in terms of paying artists campaigns? Or are you offered less than what would be acceptable fees for individual artists when you're working together?

EMMA: Well, there's a huge variation. It depends on the organisation.

LAURA: Though when you take the Turner Prize as an example – yes, it's great to include collectives! – but any sense of the fees for the individual members of those collectives, or the distribution of those fees, was definitely an afterthought in terms of how much money it would cost for everyone to be involved and to make the work. We had to fight for money for us all to be able to travel to Coventry[2] and to stay there to install the work. In a lot of cases, if we do something, we take a fee and then split it 11 ways.

ALESSIA: I think that, at the start, our reason to work as a collective was to share resources and that's kind of the only way to survive. But now, it's kind of the opposite, where most spaces or institutions are either not equipped or they're not willing to adequately pay to support a collective of 11 people.

EMMA: It doesn't mean the work is 11 times better! [laughs]. When we do talks, for example, we'll get paid for the amount of people who turn up, or we might have to split the talk fee between three people. Occasionally, organisations are good at recognising this – like the British School in Rome, The British Council, and Creative Europe in Ireland. And Arts Council Ireland make you ringfence artist fees into applications for big projects, which doesn't happen here in Northern Ireland. The argument around whether those fees were enough is another matter …

LAURA: I did a calculation for the Turner Prize fees to establish how much we should have been paid for our individual time. I included all the days that we had all worked, and it turned out that we were only paid for two or three days each per week. The difference between what we should have received and what we did receive was a crazy number – it was hundreds of thousands.

JANE: I'd like to return to the topic of studios for a moment, specifically in relation to public funding and broader conversations around cultural value … artists' studios cannot be measured or evaluated by traditional means or how those means are understood – such as ticket sales or audience footfall. Would you agree that studios have a different kind of currency? That their value lies elsewhere, through the provision of space and the communities of artists they enable?

EMMA: I just think that you wouldn't ask the same questions of a karate team. Not that there's something wrong with your question, but that there's something wrong with the outlook here. Like, why is sports considered to offer better intrinsic value than arts? Why is sport reported in the news every night, and the arts aren't? There are whole artistic movements that wouldn't have come about without high levels of public support, like social realism. That was a vital, dynamic and new way of thinking about things – of using film and using photography in a way that spoke to everyday life, and it was precisely because higher-level education was free. People from working-class backgrounds could participate in that education and were subsequently awarded grants by local councils to take on buildings without having to calculate or justify just how many pounds worth of mental health value they contributed to the economy. It prompts bigger questions about the value of the economy versus the value of people's passions or survivability or their quality of life.

LAURA: Isn't the problem that there's this idea that the taxpayer is paying for us to enjoy our hobbies and stay happy?

EMMA: Well, when I mention survivability, I am also thinking of the huge proportion of artists who are neurodiverse and disabled; a much higher proportion than the general population. You could argue that there is discrimination in not funding the arts because you're actively discriminating against types of activities that would diminish a whole demographic, in a way that wouldn't be acceptable for sports funding. On top of that, we as taxpayers also fund weapons, and nuclear power. We fund lots of things that are actively harmful to us personally. So why on earth can't we fund things that are beneficial? We gave £1.5 million to Royal Down Golf Club, one of the richest sports facilities in the whole region. And we can't give £1,000 to an artist, without a ton of checks and balances? It's ridiculous.

ALESSIA: There is still this misunderstanding that art is a sort of hobby, a passion. It's never considered to be work. And the shift in communicating that and the understanding around that really needs to happen.

EMMA: A recent and really good example of why culture is so important is the new Disney live-action film, *The Little Mermaid.* The actress cast as the main character is Black, which has caused a global outpouring around the politics of race, and a discursive gap has been opened. And if art wasn't powerful, then that wouldn't have happened. We have communicated visually for a lot longer than we have had written language.

LAURA: I think society doesn't make the connection between the "stuff" that's on the TV, or on the billboard, or any of the "stuff" – the visual language – that we are surrounded by in our everyday lives. People do not make the connection that the reason that that "stuff" exists is because we go to art college, and we sit in studios all day creating it. It's about acknowledging the creative process. And how do you measure that? Do people really want numbers and measurements for how creative you are, or if you're sitting in your studio all day or how all this work is being made? Because if they can't see the work being done and they can't see the things that you're producing, then they wonder why you are getting the money to do it.

ALESSIA: It comes back again to trust. Artists are not trusted. They need to be constantly monitored to make sure they are being responsible with money and time and space. And of doing their job, because it isn't recognised as such.

EMMA: think it is an ideological challenge for society to recognise that, because we do open up discursive spaces, and challenge discourse and introduce nuance. We are independent thinkers, and to go back to sport again – I promise I don't hate sportspeople! – how much are they really challenging any kind of status quo? But we must understand that this lack of advocacy and understanding is on purpose. It's not an accident. They're trying to make sure that there are no unconstrained artists making public statements willy-nilly.

JANE: To return to the finances that you mentioned, Array consistently appears at the very bottom of the Arts Council's annually funded client list with the lowest level of funding awarded in the entire region. Do you have a sense yet that the incredible recognition that you have received for your work through the Turner Prize will translate, or has been translating, financially into any kind of increased annual funding?

EMMA: Yes and no. We still have to make a case for our existence. We feel like we are possibly getting a bit more, but – realistically – we're still just begging for scraps. We're also part of an ecology of artists' studios and artist-led spaces in Belfast, and we're all treated as if we are all from the same household, with our funding allocated through [that household's] purse strings. If we get funding, then who misses out? Each of the collective members are part of other arts groups too, so even if Array's funding was to increase we feel the impacts of those decisions. There's certainly been no lobbying on our behalf. There's not been anybody stepping in, except yourself and maybe a few others who have actively sought to support us.

LAURA: We're also only able to apply for a certain amount of money each year because the building that we're in hasn't required much. But we were also told not to apply for much because we wouldn't get it. There was also the mentality that we were safe, because we didn't ask for too much. A few years ago, we were being pushed to move into a bigger, super-group studio. For us, both in terms of our identity and our position in the city, we didn't want to do that. Our studio rent had been pretty low for a long time, but we had to fight for it not to be increased. All the bureaucracy that we face now around trying to find a new space is overwhelming. Schemes like those set up by Belfast City Council require business plans in order for us to apply for a grant to possibly get an empty space in the city, space that will then inevitably be redeveloped in a couple of years anyway. Those processes are not designed for studios.

EMMA: There are no employees in Array. So, whoever's leading on these applications and business plans and arranging meetings … that has a cost implication for our capacity and resources. Staff in arts centres and theatres are different – they can collect data on annual turnover and so on to put into business plans. We can't collect that much data for what we do.

ALESSIA: It's a system that is designed to like keep people in a permanently unstable – yet grateful – status. But it results in a constant state of emergency, where nothing is even medium- let alone long-term.

EMMA: It costs us money to constantly be in this cheapest, lowest-common-denominator situation. There's definitely an expectation – from people outside the art world or in property – that when you're Turner Prize winning artists, you could afford a higher level of rent. And, inevitably, we can't.

JANE: Belfast City Council have recently introduced some new support mechanisms on a pilot basis, which some of us have fed into through consultation exercises. How significant do you think it is that a local authority has taken on support for studios?

ALESSIA: Well, I guess we will see if and how these bodies can work together. There is no reason why they can't. Obviously, our studio system really benefits the city and the arts. So, it's a good step, but it's just one step.

EMMA: It was also tiny pots of funding and, whilst we applied for as much as we could, we still only got two thirds of what we applied for.

JANE: Can you outline some of the issues that you face in terms of the precarity of your studio space? Does it confound the expectations from, for example, visiting curators, that you have to operate in such poor conditions?

EMMA: Imagine moving house, then multiply that by 11. We need a big space to work together. We need storage, we need light, we need to be accessible. So those requirements already make it difficult, but we also have a tiny budget from Arts Council. It's a big task and you almost need somebody to work on that on a dedicated basis. At the same time, to prove our worth, we're doing interviews and exhibitions and art projects. And it's not just us that moves, our stuff does too – all of the things that we've made, and all of the things that we need to keep, just in case we need to make more things, and the technology – then it becomes really expensive. It's short-sighted to expect artists to go into properties where the lease is for 9 months and then we need to move again before we acquire tenancy rights. If Array ever do manage to get a building, then what about all the other studio groups and grassroots organisations? We shouldn't be the only ones. Everybody should be entitled to a space to work in. It's not that much to ask.

LAURA: I look at some of the bigger studio groups that are currently moving or have just moved, and they're going into buildings that were previously abandoned by other organisations, and it's just bizarre.

EMMA: It's complete madness. [Studio and project space provider] Platform Arts were rushed out of their building a few years ago, and it's been empty ever since. It's in the middle of a street that really needs an organisation like that. There used to be such a buzz in that area because Platform Arts and organisations like Catalyst Arts and Pollen were all right next to one another.

LAURA: There seems to be an accepted culture around evicting artists and studios and then doing nothing with the space, and it's just accepted. We are constantly apologising to people, curators, who want to see our space. We take time out of our jobs to try to make the place look the best that it can.

EMMA: We know that councils in Northern Ireland have power to seize assets that aren't being properly maintained and they just don't use that power. I just worry that with so many landlords in government, any legislation or policymaking will always have protection of the landlord and not the tenants in mind. You see protected long-term leases in other places. Some of the bigger cities in, for example, Spain, have lifetime leases.

JANE: How significant is a city centre site for your practice and forms of social engagement?

LAURA: I think it's really important for the groups that we work with.

ALESSIA: Exactly. People coming for workshops or before protests can gather here with their placards.

EMMA: And it's also important to be able to participate in Late Night Art[3] to remind people that we exist. I also feel that it's a symptom of a healthy city to have artists in the centre. I think that the Belfast School of Art at Ulster University should have some responsibility in terms of trying to grow a culture of artists in the city centre; a lot of its research reputation for the arts is predicated on that. Many of the people that have come through the art college are still practising as artists in the city, but the university doesn't take much part in supporting the artists' studios outside of the actual university building, even for its PhD or Masters students. There's just a lot of short-sightedness, and it's not just the arts, the city has a housing shortage too, but quite often we seem to be canaries in the coal mine for those broader issues.

ARTIST-LED ACTIVITY

JANE: Obviously you have all been very busy since your Turner Prize win in December 2021. Do you have any sense of a changing tide in how artist-led or studio-led activity is now viewed in Northern Ireland?

EMMA: Personally, I think there was great interest immediately after we won, but my experience in activism tells me that you have to keep on top of people, or they just forget about things. As we've said, we're quite busy and there's no one else who is constantly lobbying publicly for artists, studios and artist-led spaces. That's how campaigns work, through people being forefront in the media constantly communicating what they need. We don't have the time or energy to do that, and nobody else is doing it. I do think showing *The Druithaib's Ball* at the Ulster Museum[4] will help.

LAURA: There is that sense of striking while the iron's hot, because you're a hot topic for a couple of days and you get lots of emails and then it dies down. There are so many artists displaced at the minute. Like [110-member-strong Belfast-based organisation] Vault Art Studios, for example. Given the reach of their work … it just doesn't make any sense that they would not be offered a building immediately. They are facilitating a huge number of opportunities and community events, and with the range of artistic disciplines that they represent, it should be a no-brainer really. And yet, we still need to argue for it constantly. We're just not top of anyone's list of priorities and that has snowballed into a massive issue.

EMMA: When I have my abortion campaigning[5] hat on, what you must do is look around for anything at all that's happening. We often joke that we can turn any subject or any conversation around to be about abortion – that's what a lobbyist or campaigner for artists needs to do. In Northern Ireland, for us to get the support we need, we need to be the most annoying person in any room – that's how campaigning works. You don't leave them alone until you get what you want. It should be the role of the Arts Council of Northern Ireland. It's not, but it should be. They should be on social media every day, changing any cultural messaging into an opportunity to say "here is why and how we should support the arts". But that's not a job that anybody will pay *me* for, because they don't want artists to do that. For five years, I campaigned – for free – for abortion rights here.

JANE: We've discussed how your work is remunerated, but have there been any changes to how it is profiled and – specifically – how it's been encouraged to continue by funders, such as arms-length bodies, local authorities or government? Has that happened yet, and do you expect it to?

EMMA: Array are big in Japan! Last year, we were in two Japanese magazines, including *Vogue!*

JANE: Wow, I didn't know that! *Japanese Vogue* has nothing on *Cultural Trends* though, right? Are there any gallerists queueing up? Have you been offered keys to this, or any, city?

EMMA: I think there's been a big difference in how we've been received and profiled from people outside Northern Ireland, but not necessarily people inside Northern Ireland.

LAURA: We haven't been offered representation or anything, and we certainly haven't been invited to represent Ireland or even Northern Ireland at the Venice Biennale[6] yet!

EMMA: We're regularly invited to give talks, but those who largely ignored us before still aren't scrambling to include us in projects. I think our exhibition at the Ulster Museum will raise awareness of our work and all these issues again.

JANE: Array are currently exhibiting *The Druithaib's Ball* at Galway Arts Centre. The curator of this exhibition, Megs Morley, is also the initiator of The Artist-Led Archive,[7] an artist-led initiative which began in 2006. How significant is it for you to contribute to the artist-led discourse across the island and further afield?

ALESSIA: It's very important to us. The island of Ireland has a very strong and rich history of artist-led activity, which is often overlooked, unrecorded or unrecognised. There will be a publication released next year[8], and it will be amazing for us to be part of that history and contribute to making it more visible both in and outside of the island of Ireland.

LAURA: I've been told that there used to be a lot more North-South artist collaborations in the times prior to the 1998 Good Friday Agreement. In a weird way, opportunities seem to have gotten worse since then. The possibility of forthcoming Shared Island[9] funded projects is encouraging though. It would be good to represent the island more as a whole, in terms of its artist-led activity.

EMMA: There is definitely an issue around posterity and archiving for artist-led groups. It's a queer and feminist issue as well. If our histories aren't properly archived, then they disappear, and people forget about them and about us. Artist and activist groups just don't have the time or resources because they are fighting on other fronts. Hopefully, because Array's installation has been acquired by the Ulster Museum, a lot of the detail for that piece will be recorded properly in a way that we never could.

ALESSIA: When I started researching artists' collectives, I came across so many archive boxes that were basically empty. Artists – and particularly activists – still keep things in their houses because of institutional distrust.

EMMA: Archiving differs according to cultural priorities too – Amsterdam has a really beautiful feminist archive, which is well-staffed in a beautiful building. Whilst the feminist archive in the UK was basically just sitting in an attic for years before it was moved to a basement. Those are ideological decisions.

INTERPRETATIONS OF ARRAY COLLECTIVE'S WORK

JANE: Through your exhibition for the Turner Prize, the profile that you have offered to issues of social injustice in Northern Ireland is unprecedented but not always well understood outside of Northern Ireland. In December 2021, I co-authored an article[10] outlining the England-centric and poorly informed view that many art critics took of *The Druthaib's Ball*. Since then, have you noticed any change or more nuance in critics' interpretations of your work?

LAURA: Some of the interviews we've done recently have zoned in on the drama of that.

EMMA: The majority of articles were generally complimentary. People who are interested in the kind of things we do are the ones who continue to approach us – activist publications, community engaged practitioners … and *Japanese Vogue* [laughs]. We were approached by a *New York Times* journalist a couple of times, but we just ignored him.

LAURA: When critics or journalists focus on that stuff – like how we "built a pub out of card-board" or whatever they think it is – they're just looking for attention. They're just cheap digs that provide headlines.

EMMA: And different critics from the same paper will have vastly different takes on it – like the vastly differing responses from The Guardian's columnists Jonathan Jones and Charlotte Higgins.

ALESSIA: Art historians, or those who write more reflective pieces really get it and that makes a difference to us. They're also more likely to ask for our opinions and quotes, and it's been great to have those conversations.

LAURA: I remember that the *Irish Independent* got in touch and specifically wanted to talk to Stephen [Millar, Array Collective member] because he'd said on the radio that he's both an art therapist and a painter. It was obvious that the reporters for that piece wanted to go a bit deeper into our independent practices and have richer discussions rather than the general kind of tabloid headlines.

EMMA: Stephen and I also did an interview for BBC Northern Ireland, and the cameramen were visibly shocked when they went to our studios. The best way to describe their expressions is … "haunted". They just couldn't believe the facilities and couldn't believe that we were actually working there. Though that interview felt like a fully engaged conversation, we could imagine people at home watching it and wanting to ask the same questions that Mark Carruthers [BBC journalist] did. There has definitely been some local interest in the issues with studios here, but, at the same time, you always have to prove why your work and space is important.

JANE: What has it meant to have your work acquired into the collection of the Ulster Museum? For example, do you feel that it is significant in terms of museological concerns around the queering and decolonising of collections, or of institutional critique?

EMMA: We're very grateful, for sure. But, to reiterate what I said before, we now worry about the work we've made that hasn't been bought and therefore hasn't been archived and stored properly. We worry about things being ruined in our studios. Though the museum haven't actually acquired the entire installation, so not everything that featured in the Turner Prize exhibition is currently in a temperature-controlled environment. I had to go to the studio a few days ago to check if someone had broken in, and I was really panicking but nothing had been disturbed.

LAURA: It's really significant that the museum has invested in such a big visual art piece, and that it will become part of their collection. Hopefully parts of the installation will be displayed in future as part of other exhibitions to keep that dialogue and social engagement alive in the museum.

ALESSIA: We're still in discussion about the way that the piece will be shown and in which spaces we would like it to be shown. We really like the idea that the piece, and the *síbín* [Irish for "pub without permission", the largest element of the installation] specifically, was born out of artist-led culture and not of large institutions. We want there to be scope in how it's shown for audience engagement and responses.

LAURA: I think the beauty of that work is that, in creating a pub environment, it creates a space for conversation. It would also be great if the museum could lend it to other institutions, where different perspectives on those conversations can be encouraged. The issues that it brings up are different in every place.

EMMA: We talked about this a lot as a group. When we think about acquisitions, we are also aware that they might just languish in a room somewhere for ages with no audience. We think that there are multiple parts of the installation that could speak directly to some of the works in the museum's permanent exhibition. In many ways, the installation represents a cultural moment in time, reflecting on one hundred years of partition on the island of Ireland. And that is a really important reason to have it shown in the biggest museum in the region. The museum's audiences aren't necessarily gallery-going audiences, which means that it might be a bit more accessible. Working-class communities are much more likely to visit the Ulster Museum. If I think of my mum, she is happy to go to the museum on a regular basis but gets a bit scared going to art galleries. We want people to feel comfortable there.

ALESSIA: But obviously there are contentious things in there too, for some people, and we want that to be uncomfortable for those who don't recognise us or our rights.

LAURA: We are preparing museum staff – and ourselves – in case there is any sort of public backlash against elements of the exhibition. Given the context of Northern Ireland, that backlash is more likely to happen here than it would anywhere else. Even that is interesting to us.

JANE: Social, spatial, gendered, health and economic injustices (amongst others) faced by people in Northern Ireland are embedded in your work. Can you say something about how your work takes the perspective that the artist is a member of society, affected by these issues, rather than the approach where art is something that artists "do" "at" or "on" communities who need to be "fixed" somehow?

EMMA: Lucy Lippard[11] writes about three different types of activist artists. Firstly, those who support the cause, but none of their artwork is related to the cause. Secondly, there's the activist artist that is brought into activist communities and works alongside them for a short period of time to produce an artifact. Finally, there are the artists who are embedded within the activist community and work from that position. You can be all three, or you can move between them. Array certainly aren't "community-spotting" and deciding to join a herd. The issues in this region around housing rights, queer rights, abortion rights, environmental issues, gentrification, and mental ill-health affect us all directly. There's an authenticity to the causes we support.

LAURA: There are multiple levels to how we both experience these inequalities – in our personal lives and how we work, how we create work in response, and then how they affect people around us, in our communities.

ALESSIA: Another important point to make is that we often also support other peers or bring them along with us. We bring in other artists a lot. Although we are a collective of 11 people, we're also an extended group as well and *The Druithaib's Ball* illustrates that. Equally, not all collective members are studio holders in Array, some of them work in other studios in the city. But the collective is made up of the people who were always at rallies and protests and were always helping to make protest banners.

REPRESENTING NORTHERN IRELAND

JANE: Have you encountered pressure to be representative of artistic practice in Northern Ireland?

ALESSIA: I don't think so. Not least because there are people from Ireland and England, and obviously an Italian in the collective too!

EMMA: I think that, in the media, there's just an assumption that we're all from Belfast, even though we clearly say that we're not.

LAURA: People seem shocked, but actually this is typical of the makeup of artist groups in the North of Ireland. And I think that's really key because of the different perspectives it brings on the laws and policies here. Even the people that are from Northern Ireland have all lived in other countries for significant amounts of time. Nobody has asked us to feature on the front of a tourism leaflet or anything, which is good!

JANE: With such a low level of investment in the arts in Northern Ireland, it is perhaps unsurprising that art or artists from here rarely feature in international showcases. Has there been interest from national or international institutions, collectives or activist groups in working with you?

EMMA: We were featured in a beautiful big, important periodical about art in Germany. And invited to give a talk in the *Centre Culturel Irlandais* in Paris. But with international work, you can see people start to do the mental arithmetic about how much it will cost for 11 flights, so only one or two of us have been involved in those things.

LAURA: I'm intrigued to see what else might happen. It's actually almost exactly a year on from the opening of the Turner Prize exhibition in Coventry [29 September 2021]. I couldn't be there for the install or the opening because I'd just given birth two days before.

EMMA: Before the Turner Prize nomination, a couple of people in the group were very, very close to giving up art or giving up art for the second or third time. It's still hard for us to get our heads around it. Almost as hard as getting all 11 of us in a room together [laughs].

We're still figuring out how we operate, and we need to make sure we operate in healthier ways, because everything has been so quick, and we haven't had time to take breaks.

LAURA: Once the museum exhibition opens, we can make time to figure out what our next move is. I think it will be a case of being part of bigger projects over longer periods of time, rather than taking on lots of small things.

ALESSIA: That will never happen [laughs].

Notes

1 www.tate.org.uk/press/press-releases/turner-prize-shortlist-announced-0.
2 UK City of Culture 2021, which hosted the Turner Prize exhibition and awards ceremony at The Herbert Art Gallery and Museum.
3 www.facebook.com/latenightartbelfast/.
4 www.ulstermuseum.org/whats-on/druithaibs-ball The Ulster Museum has recently acquired this large-scale installation for its collection. The work contains over 80 individual elements, including some made by other Belfast-based artists, and will be on display at the museum from February 2023: www.nationalmuseumsni.org/news/tur ner-prize- acquisition.
5 UK Government to commission abortion services in Northern Ireland, 24 October 2022.
6 Northern Ireland has only been represented by three Venice Biennale showings, in 2005, 2007 and 2009 before funding was withdrawn. As of 2023, the Welsh pavilion is facing a similar fate.
7 www.theartistledarchive.com.
8 *The Artist-led Archive: Sustainable Activism and the Embrace of Flux* will become a publication published by Durty Books Publishing House in 2023.
9 www.gov.ie/en/campaigns/c3417-shared-island/.
10 Hickey and Morrow (2021).
11 Lippard (2013).

References

Hickey, C. and Morrow, J. (2021, December 15). Does the Turner Prize Deserve Better Art? No, but Array Collective Deserves Better Critics … . *Elephant*. https://elephant.art/does-the-tur ner-prize-deserve- better-art-no-but-array-collective-deserves-better-critics-15122021/.

Lippard, L. (2013). Trojan Horses: Activist Art and Power. In *Modernism*. Pearson Education. www.taylorfrancis.com/books/modernism-robin-walz/10.43249781315833125?refId= b92370f2- ad3d-42c7-9957-6b4a1929a65f.

Opera and Cultural Leadership

Oliver Mears, Director of Opera, Royal Opera House: In Conversation (UK)

Steven Hadley

Chapter 10

Oliver Mears is The Royal Opera's Director of Opera. Mears studied English and history at Oxford University and began his career assisting playwright Howard Barker. In 2004 he cofounded London-based opera company Second Movement and directed numerous site-specific productions for the company, including several UK stage premieres. He was Artistic Director of Northern

DOI: 10.4324/9781003390725-10

Ireland Opera from the company's foundation in 2010 until 2017. In 2012 Mears was nominated for the UK TMA Achievement in Opera Award for his leadership of Northern Ireland Opera, and in 2013 was nominated for the International Opera Award for Best Newcomer (Director). He joined The Royal Opera in March 2017.

This conversation took place online on 21 September 2020.

STEVEN: It's a challenge with interviews and where we are in the world right now with COVID to think about how we might both discuss and try to extrapolate out from this immediate context. What are your immediate thoughts?

OLIVER: I think what the crisis will inevitably do is accelerate various trends that were already happening anyway and sometimes in a good way, so.

STEVEN: Okay. Do you want to elaborate on that now [laughter]? What are the trends?

PRODUCTION AND ECONOMIC MODELS

OLIVER: In my first years at the Opera House, I was reaching towards an aesthetic, if you like, which was perhaps rather more distilled than was traditionally regarded in the opera world. Which is, of course, associated very much with very lavish sets, and so on. And what I was interested in was whether the power of the theatrical and musical experience could be just as well harnessed via more minimal means in terms of how people perform on stage in terms of sets, in terms of costumes. And I think because of the financial difficulties that every opera company now finds themselves in, I think there is a logic to that aesthetic as well as an artistic imperative if that makes sense?

And I also think that one of the things that was I was questioning is – well, I mean, I guess, let's be honest, opera is often regarded as a very decadent art form. I'm sure that would be your opinion as well. And there's sort of several aspects to that decadence aren't there? There's the kind of obvious visual aspect on stage. The fact that because you've got 100 people in costume, and if you're doing something in period then suddenly it does become something which is this lavish spectacle, then you've got the fact that the very top singers are on very large fees. The fact that the opera industry depends on people using air travel. Mass air travel is really a kind of key factor of opera performance but also co-productions. And I think that it would be irresponsible for any artistic organisation not to look at the current situation, and in particular, the relationship between the pandemic and man's relationship to nature, and whether we need to be more aware of that, and whether this reliance on mass air travel is responsible, ethical.

So it's interesting, the way in which the opera model, in particular, is under a special pressure at this time, not surprisingly, given that it depends on the voice, and we're in the middle of a respiratory pandemic. It was never going to be straightforward. But I think there could be some constructive learnings from it as well.

STEVEN: Is that providing you with – unfortunately, in terms of the context – an opportunity to accelerate the potential opportunities for that kind of change?

OLIVER: I think so because we could be forced to, and the financial impact of this is borderline cataclysmic for us in particular. And the very, very sudden and drastic loss of what is being described as between £3 in every £5 of our income more or less overnight, is forcing us to re-evaluate how we make shows, how we operate, how large our staff is, what our environmental footprint is. All of these things we're really at the hard end of talking and thinking about, so I think that we do have to move fast because the implications are very, very serious. I mean, there's been quite a lot of talk about what the different opera companies are doing at the moment, this autumn. And it's very difficult because not only have you got all of the health aspects of getting singers together in a room, the protocols of opening buildings and so on. But you've also got the fact that the majority of the staff are on furlough. We're going through a restructure, which is being forced upon us to enable us to survive because of the loss in income that we've experienced. So making work is really, really hard at the moment. So it's that thing of using the difficulty, acknowledging that the way in which one works is extremely circumscribed and constrained in a way that it never had been before, but using that as a starting point for rethinking how one works in the future, which could creatively be quite exciting.

EXCELLENCE AND ELITISM

STEVEN: I wonder how far away such an un-staged or non-lavish production would be from the notion of excellence, which was implicit in the pre-COVID model of the Royal Opera House?

OLIVER: I think excellence is not the same thing as extravagance. I think that's really, really clear. I mean, it's interesting that one of my predecessors as Director of Opera was Peter Brook, and he was putting shows together in the late '40s with Salvador Dali and various other people. And of course, Peter Brook famously moved away from any extravagance on stage and in *The Empty Space* most famously. And ultimately, what is intrinsic about the theatrical experience is someone on the stage and someone in the audience. And that's all you need really. Now, of course, in opera you do – you need the music as well. You need someone to play the music. And that doesn't need to be – to be live and – but beyond that I think that one of the difficulties is that it is audience expectation, of course. And what we've got at the opera house is this extraordinarily opulent building which is stunning in all sorts of different ways. It's a beautiful, magical portal which is appropriate because when you go through those doors you should be transported to another place. But that can be done with relatively simple means. It can be done through fabulous acting. It can be done through fabulous lighting as long as the level of performance is absolutely top-notch. What is excellent in the performance? Well, it's people doing things that only they can do. It's someone singing an aria that really only four or five people in the world can sing. It's a high wire act. And that is not only down to time but also down to years and years and years of training. And while we would never want to be described as elitist, I don't think we should ever be apologetic for being elite in a way that elite sport is elite. In elite sport again, you have many years of training and practice to the point where you can excel beyond what is the norm. And that will be something the Royal Opera House should always be.

But it doesn't always need to be about frilly costumes and frocks. [laughter]. The other thing to say about the opera house is that we've got dozens of productions which are old productions. So only about one-third of the operas we do in any season will be new productions. And the rest will be productions that might be 10, 20, sometimes even 30 years old. Now, we simply cannot afford to replace every single one of those productions. A lot of those productions are ones which the audience really, really love. And they have all sorts of kind of shared memories attached to those productions. So it will inevitably be an evolution. It's very difficult to enact a revolution when the store of productions that you've got represents not just one aesthetic but several aesthetics going over certainly one generation but maybe even two generations. So that's another challenge.

STEVEN: A lot of what you're articulating in terms of the building, the audience and the implicit cost base within the ROH model often results in very high ticket prices and salary levels. By necessity you need to maximise box office income and bring in philanthropic money. Are these systemic blocks to a wider ambition to democratise more people's engagement with opera?

OLIVER: Well, it depends what you mean by democratise. From all the research that we've done, it isn't the new productions or the modern pieces that appeal to new audiences. The democratising piece, the pieces that young people want to see, what first-time opera goers want to see are the big, traditional opera. They want to see *La traviata* or they want to see *La bohème,* they want to see *Carmen.* And, if possible, if you ask them, they want to see them in traditional productions. And that's not in doubt. I mean, years and years and years of research have proven that. And so when asked this question, do you give the audience what they want? And there's quite a strong argument to say yes, you do. Or do you try to educate the audience so that they can be bolder in their choices? Difficult that, because those pieces that they're attracted to, they're famous for a reason. Because they have the famous arias. Because they are bringing the theatrically. Because they offer great roles and characters that people can relate to. So there's that aspect of things.

In terms of whether we are constrained by the structure – well, we're constrained in the sense that opera is incredibly expensive. Because often people do say, "Oh, well. Can't you just make cheaper sets?" Well, yes, you can make cheaper sets. But it's not just the sets which are the expense. The huge expense is in the people. And if you're doing a Wagner, for example, you might have up to 100 chorus on stage as well as 10 principals, on top of which you might have 120 people in the orchestra and you might have dancers which are specified in the score. We're talking many hundreds of people working on one particular show. And we'll do between 18 and 20 productions a season. And that's why we've got normally a permanent staff of around 1000, but all the freelancers we use as well.

Apart from the BBC, we are the biggest employer of artists in the UK and I think that's a good thing, personally. I think that some artists can have a degree of security and there's also freelancers that are offered opportunities to develop their practice and their art. So the number of people is a factor in the structure that's built up and that the ticket prices are what they are and, of course, there is a huge variation within those ticket prices. Everybody talks about the kind of the headline top price tickets, but we also sell tickets from £10 and upwards. 40% of our tickets are below £50. So there are opportunities to see work at a decent price. And I think that one of the assumptions in that, yes, opera's very expensive with the ticket prices – yes, it is a higher ticket price if you're sitting in the stalls and you're seeing Jonas Kaufmann. But on the other hand, think about what you're getting. I mean, for me, cost is not just about cost, it's about value. What are you getting for your ticket price? And when I talked about lavish opera just now, I don't think it's bad value to spend £200 on a ticket for that. With all those people at the top of their game, most of whom have been in training for years and years and years to get to that point offering you a kind of experience that will be literally unforgettable because it's live. I wanted to take my kids to go and see *Joseph*. I mean, it was £200 a ticket.

STEVEN: I hoped you were going to say Beyoncé [laughter].

OLIVER: Well, I'm sure Beyoncé's not cheap either. And a football season ticket is also really expensive. I prefer to think not just in terms of cost but also in terms of value. What you're getting for your money.

STEVEN: I'm glad you said lavish opera's incredibly expensive [laughter].

OLIVER: Now, well, basically, it's expensive to make. I didn't mean it's expensive to enjoy.

STEVEN: We can loop back here because as you said at the start of the interview, not necessarily. It's not necessarily expensive because you, yourself, have produced opera that was not incredibly expensive.

OLIVER: Well, yes. With opera, you're talking about multiples. I mean, even the productions that I did that were very minimal in terms of cast members and orchestra and so on they still had 10, 15 people in the orchestra. And they've all got to be paid. And you've got to put them somewhere. You got to find a space that's big enough. So there are intrinsically many more people involved in opera. Of course, there's a handful of pieces which might be a piano and one singer. But there aren't very many of them. And they're not the pieces that most people want to see. When people want to go and see opera, especially for the first time, they want that invigorating feeling of riding the crest of a wave which you get when you see one of those great operas for the first time.

AUDIENCE EXPECTATION

STEVEN: There's a constellation of concepts in this argument. The idea of the audience is doing quite a lot of heavy lifting here: "the audience want this" and "the audience need that". Of course, "the audience" in potential, if not actual, terms sit on a vast demographic spectrum. I think we need to be careful using that term. I would say for some decades these concepts have become self-reinforcing in an argument that says, "Well, here. When you really think about it it's like this and it's very expensive. And the audience want this. And it has to be excellent. And these people are at the top of their game." And once you enter into that self-reinforcing logic it all makes sense within that conceptual structure. In many instances I don't disagree with what you said. But it is a self-reinforcing logic and I want to go back to your personal belief about the potential for many more people to engage with opera.

OLIVER: Well, there's also starker reasons for why opera's not where we want it to be in the UK in particular. I mean, I've said many times that in this country opera is very deeply associated with the class system and very particularly associated with snobbery. Now, the reason I think that there's hope still that we can maybe one day get beyond that is that in other countries that's not the case. And certainly, in Germany and Italy opera houses are an intrinsic part of their communities. And going to the opera is not a function of how rich you are, but how much you love the art form and how devoted you might be to particular operas and also, to your particular local opera house. But, unfortunately, that hasn't been the case here. And, again, that links back to the fact that opera is so expensive to put on and somehow it has to be paid for. And opera will never really pay for itself. There might be kind of three or four operas that can be put on in the Albert Hall where you can pack them like sardines. Now, on the continent, because opera is really an expression of civic pride and community, that money comes from taxation. It comes from subsidy. Overwhelmingly so in Germany and France. Might be a mixture between kind of federal and local subsidy. In England, we have this mixed model where we have our box office, we have our Arts Council grant, and we have philanthropy. I think that's maybe quite a good model because it means that we have to be responsive to various different constituencies.

On the one hand, the Arts Council encourage us to take artistic risks. They encourage us to be at the forefront of conversations about diversity and inclusion. And our audience put their money where their mouth is. If they don't like something, they don't come. And I think that's useful. Whereas, in Germany or Scandinavia, they approach productions as more disposable. So if something does work, you can put a ton of money into it, and then it's fine. You just do another version of it. But here, where so much is at stake – because we really do have to keep an eye on the box office – we think we have a more responsible approach in that sense. And, yes, philanthropy is helpful. I mean, of course, there's also different types of philanthropy. There are the more conservative donors. But actually, the majority of trusts and foundations and donors tend to put their money towards the riskier projects rather than the more traditional ones. It's very rare that someone will say, as they certainly do in America, "I will support this new production of *La bohème,* but only if it's traditional." No one ever says that to us. The mixed model is under pressure at the moment for reasons outside of our control. But it feels like, in some ways, healthier than an overreliance on subsidy or an overreliance on philanthropy.

STEVEN: I would happily agree with you. Having multiple stakeholders to be responsible to creates a healthy debate within organisations. The push to make organisations less reliant on subsidy and generate more of their income in the market has now come back to haunt us as the organisations that are more reliant on earning income in the market are now the one's most at risk. Are there certain artforms that should not be in the market but have nonetheless inexorably been pushed that way?

OLIVER: Yeah. I do agree with that. But on the other hand, I mean, yes. I mean, all the big artistic organisations have been encouraged to diversify their income streams. I don't think that's necessarily a bad thing. But also, I don't think that there's anything implicit in that that suggests that if the worst came to the worst, and the world is confronted by an unexpected catastrophe like this one, those organisations would be allowed to go to the wall. I mean, I would never be able to answer that question about whether the RSC or the Royal Opera House or the National Theatre would be allowed to go bankrupt. I think probably they wouldn't be. And I think that's kind of important to acknowledge as well. That even though organisations may have been encouraged to be more independent, that doesn't mean to say that they would literally die by the sword. I think there's still a sense that they're organisations that are worth saving, ultimately.

STEVEN: I've always sensed, working in the cultural sector, the idea of an arts organisation closing is somewhat of an anomaly. And you can understand that. But if you work in the market should you be subject to the rules of the market?

OLIVER: I mean, we saw what happened with the Nuffield in Southampton, and there will be more, I'm sure. And also, what's happened with the Southbank. I mean, that really is a kind of a warning case, isn't it, for what can happen? Not only in terms of what can happen if there's an event like this, but also the response to that. Is the response to go 90% commercial? I'm not sure.

STEVEN: I want to loop back to this idea of excellence, just because I'm intrigued to know where and to what extent you think excellence can be found in the cultural sector?

OLIVER: I think it's difficult, isn't it? I mean, how do you quantify excellence? And I know this is kind of the holy grail for the Arts Council and has been discussed in terms of the metrics and so on, but I think, in some ways, opera is in a slightly stronger position than some other art forms. So it does depend on which art form you're talking about because I think that there is a degree to which opera singers do something that is so outside of the norm and does require so much training and when it happens, well, is so overwhelming for anyone who experiences it. That means that it is more quantifiable than, for example, the theatre, because everyone can argue whether someone can act or not, but at the end of the day if they speak their lines they're speaking their lines. But not everyone can sing and excellence in opera is something that, I think, many people would be able to recognise, even at quite a basic, primal level. And it does require talent, it does require training and the development of practice. And so to that extent I think the excellence is something which can be recognised.

How do you measure excellence? It's difficult. I mean, I'm with you in that at the moment excellence is measured by the press and we can talk endlessly about the fact that it tends to be this echo chamber of the same people making the same judgements from the same demographic. No question about that. But, ultimately, it comes down to the extent to which the audience acknowledges whether it's excellent or not. How far has the experience been transformative for people in the audience? I mean we're using the NPS[1] at the moment which is a pretty blunt instrument to be honest. I'm always trying to measure it myself when I've been in a theatre and you kind of sniff it, you sniff it out, whether people have really loved it or not. I think that's ultimately the determining factor whether something is excellent or not is whether the audience love it. But, again, that's a very subjective measurement.

STEVEN: With excellence I think, who is it for? Because I could probably go into your quite mediocre production and think it was amazing and have those emotionally transformative effects. So I'm just wondering where the ratio or relationship sits between this often abstract and arbitrary notion of excellence and these human responses. Because I'm not sure that they're geared in the way that they're often understood.

OLIVER: I mean, this is it. An example of this is lighting. So because of the way in which our schedules are so tightly sprung, it's very often the lighting directors who complain about the amount of time they get to work on the lighting because there normally isn't enough time in schedules to allow it. And so I always want to try and make it happen for directors and ensure that the standards are as good as they can be. And I can tell you that the difference between a show that's had 10 hours of lighting and a show that's had 20 hours of lighting is really substantial. And sure, an audience might not be able to put their finger on why a performance was better, but there is something indefinable about the superior experience of a show that's well lit, as opposed to a show that's badly lit. And it's the indefinable that makes for outstanding artistic experiences. And often, it is a function of time. I mean, it's a bit like saying "Well, The National Gallery and the Tate, why don't they just store all those valuable paintings in their cellars and put copies up. They'd be much more secure. No one would notice." Well, no one would notice, but I mean, they might, actually. There will be something in the experience.

STEVEN: Let's pluck a number out of the air and say 99.5% of the population wouldn't notice. But 0.5%, i.e. the people with art history degrees and rarefied elements of a kind of educational attainment and specific social backgrounds, would notice. But on that basis, who were those pictures on the wall for?

OLIVER: I don't think it's just the 0.5. Going back to the first-time experience that an opera goer will have, because opera is this art form that depends on all these different aspects working together, if a first-time punter goes to see a performance of *Tosca* and it's brilliantly conducted and the orchestra play it well and there are no mistakes and the person singing *Tosca* is one of the best singers in the world, then I think that they are far more likely to have enjoyed that experience and to go back to an opera and to love opera from that first experience than they would be if the conductor had been slow and mediocre and if the singer had been below par. I do think that the level of performance does have a much bigger impact on the audience experience and their openness to more experiences.

STEVEN: In a hypothetical scenario, where Tony Pappano[2] had a twin or a double, who was sent in to conduct at the Royal Opera House, what percentage of the people in the audience would notice? Does the answer rely on the audience have these aesthetic skills of differentiation?

OLIVER: No. No. No. No. No. No. No. That's not what I'm saying at all. I'm saying the opposite. I'm saying that the enjoyment of an opera should be a visceral experience. I mean, that's what Tony's so good at, it's the level of passion that he brings to all his performances. And the nature of that visceral experience is not only fidelity to the score and what the composer intended but also, the degree to which that person can create an experience which gets you in the gut. And not everyone can do that. And that's why the best conductors are the best conductors.

STEVEN: This reminds me of the debates around chief executive pay in the corporate sector, where the exponential differential between base levels of pay at the bottom of staff tiers, and CEO and chief executive pay have lost all relationship to one another. Yet is it possible that somebody could go to the Royal Opera House, and see the best singers in the world with Tony Pappano conducting and be bored senseless?

OLIVER: No. That's right. I mean, you can say that about anything. You can say there are lots of people who would go into the Louvre or The National Gallery and be bored senseless there. But that wouldn't make the argument for having a building in which you can put these works of art any less credible. You can say the same thing about books. I mean, personally, I really love *Ulysses* by James Joyce, but I know I'm in a minority. Most people find it deadly dull and difficult. But I get a lot out of it. And I guess, ultimately, isn't it about kind of creating a situation where it comes back to that same thing. Creating experiences that you have enormous faith in, that you think will be intoxicating, overwhelming, moving, and so on and so forth, for as many people as possible. So at least they do get that opportunity to experience. Even if some people don't want to come back, some people will, and thereby, you renew the audience in that way. Opera faces a challenge in a way that none of the other art forms does, due to the fact that there are these kinds of encrusted cultural baggage associated with opera. It is a real problem for us. Yet the fact that we do have certain titles that everyone can understand, every word of what's going on. The fact that there is no etiquette. These are things we somehow need to communicate more effectively than we currently do.

STEVEN: But not smelly trainers, obviously [laughter].

OLIVER: That was a long time ago.

STEVEN: What you're articulating, going back to that UK class-snobbery context, is that of all the art forms opera is the one that has most utility value in creating that social capital. People want other people to be excluded from it. But it's difficult to democratise something that people engage with specifically for its undemocratic rewards. It becomes problematic when you have public subsidy in the equation. Do you then have an imperative to reconcile irreconcilable impulses?

OLIVER: Well, I think there is a tension there. I mean, I think you're right in a way. I mean, in all my time, in two and a half years at the opera house I've never heard anyone say that the reason they like going to the opera is because the proles can't go. Now, it may be the case, that they've been very fortunate in their lives to be given the experience of going to an opera probably when they were very young and that their families could afford to take them, and so on and so forth. But equally, there are many many many audience members who I've spoken to whose first experience of going to the Royal Opera House was paying £5 to sit in the balcony many years ago. And there's always been that opportunity for people without much money to go and see our work.

I think that where the tension is though comes back to the building. I described the building as this kind of magical portal, and it is that. I think it's one of the most beautiful theatres in the world and that's great for all sorts of reasons if people take it for what it is rather than take it for being what it may have been in the past, which is this kind of intimidating marker of wealth and status. And somehow the relationship has got to be between the art which transports you irrespective of who you are, and the place that you arrive at to experience it.

STEVEN: Of course, you need to be in possession of a significant amount of social and cultural capital in order to buy the £5 ticket to go to the Royal Opera House. It's not solely a financial issue. Is one man's magical portal another man's iron gate?

OLIVER: The assumptions can be damaging on all sides, and if people have an assumption about what kind of experience they're going to have, which is actually quite far from the truth then, that's something that we need to work on as well. It's not just us. Many people get their idea of what opera is from adverts and cartoons, not primarily reality. And so that's the cultural climate that we live in, that we've got to somehow challenge, but not all of the responsibility can be placed with us because it's a more complex picture than that.

There's a film online. It was made by Opera Holland Park, but they went into a South London school and got them interested in opera, brought them in. They'd never seen an opera before. I met some of them. And they were just completely overwhelmed by that because they had no kind of baggage or they probably thought opera was for snobs, for posh people. But they came in, and they loved the building, and they found the music just totally incredible. I think that people do need to go with an open mind, and there's a limit to what we can do in opening their minds I think.

CULTURAL DEMOCRACY

STEVEN: I want to talk about cultural democracy, the pre-COVID move in the Arts Council's *Let's Create* strategy and wider conversations such as the academic work done around everyday creativity. What resonance, if any, have those debates had within the Opera House?

OLIVER: Well, it has because it's starting to be reflected in Arts Council strategies. And there was a lot of discussion and debate about the draft Arts Council strategy, as there was in the wider media and what its implications were for London-based large cultural institutions. None of them seemed to be good implications for us, to be quite honest with you. But on the other hand, I think that it was useful in the sense that it emphasises something that we knew already, which is that for us to have any future we do have to be a genuinely national organisation. And the fact that we have this beautiful building is an incredible advantage for all sorts of reasons. It's a unique place to experience opera. We've got this incredible broadcast capability. I think it's significant that we are in the middle of cosmopolitan diversity in London and we have to be responsive to that. But as soon as we go out of our building the costs rocket. It's difficult for us. And people are always saying we should go on tour. We'd be ruined if we went on tour, we just can't afford to do it. But, fortunately, we do have this ability to broadcast our work and it's seen up and down the country in cinemas. And we do have this excellent learning participation department which is really focusing now on building relationships with music hubs and communities all over the country. So there are ways in which we can be more national. I think there is progress but I think that all of us are probably a little bit anxious about the idea that face painting in a village hall is of the same type of art as what we put together at the Opera House.

STEVEN: I think you've gently sashayed into what I would probably term as "the democratisation of culture" when you're talking about the screenings and so on because that is still the "We do what we do and we take it to other people and other places," approach which is not, I think, what's at the heart of cultural democracy.

OLIVER: It is.

STEVEN: There is a particular section within the Arts Council strategy where they very explicitly say that no art form has any more value than another art form. The potential implications of it are very significant for the subsidised cultural sector.

OLIVER: Well, that's a negative interpretation of that. I mean, of course, you can argue it the other way and say, "Well, if no art form is more or less of value than others, then some art forms should carry on being supported in the way that they've been traditionally supported". That would be one way of interpreting that. Ultimately, the value that you place on a work of art is dependent on the person experiencing it. We can talk about strategy for as long as we want, and what the Arts Council thinks, and whether there's any intrinsic value in anything, of course. But ultimately, it depends on what the culture, the wider culture, and what the audience think about the art forms that they're experiencing. And ultimately, I think that most people will recognise that a picture made by a child, which is put up in the village hall, may be of all sorts of emotional importance and relevance to the child and the family and the people who are seeing it in that village hall. But it is different in kind, not

Steven Hadley

necessarily in quality. Different in kind to an opera that requires hundreds of people, who have had thousands of years of training between them, putting on an opera, which is expensive. And it's a different type of experience. One is not better or worse than the other, but it is different. And if we're saying that both are of equal value, then we have to make sure that the latter survives and a way that the former can be promoted, too, I think. It's not a zero-sum game.

STEVEN: Is it a zero-sum game when we're talking about Arts Council?

OLIVER: Well, it isn't. Because I totally agree with what Helen[3] said, which is that what's very corrosive is that the pot is too small. It means that every arts organisation does see it as a zero-sum game and thinks that if the Royal Opera House goes out of existence, then somehow that money is going to be distributed. That would never happen. All that would happen if the Opera House didn't get any money is that there would be less money for the arts in general. And what needs to happen, instead, is a complete re-evaluation of arts funding in this country. And the situation at the moment, whereby the opera houses in Berlin are seeing more Arts Council subsidy than the Arts Council of England give out in a year, is something that should make us sit up and think about the relative value that we put on culture in general, irrespective of whether you think that art should be generated from communities or whether it should be made in opera houses. It's about what value as a society do we put on culture.

CLIMATE CHANGE AND SOCIAL JUSTICE

STEVEN: I'd like to close by addressing the growing consciousness around issues such as climate change as well as racial and social justice. Do you feel that cultural institutions such as the Royal Opera House need to be seen to more explicitly incorporate these ethical concerns in how they approach funding their work?

OLIVER: Yes. I do. The Black Lives Matter moment has been very influential on us for all sorts of reasons in the way in which we're within the process of producing an antiracism statement which I think will go live quite soon, and even in the way in which it has impacted on our programming for the autumn has been really, really significant. I think that, as I said before, we have a responsibility as a national institution to absorb the environmental concerns many of us have and take action on them. And I've been pushing for a while, for example, for us to have solar panels on our roof because we've got this unique roof and it's not even about how much power it will generate. It's what statement that will be making about the importance of environmental issues to the arts.

I mean, in terms of funding, this is quite a tricky subject. The Royal Opera House can't be the answer to all of the problems that were raised by companies funding the arts or oil companies in particular funding the arts.

STEVEN: I wonder whether you think arts organisations have a responsibility now to take a stand much more explicitly as regards what we're seeing in terms of the rise of populism and the far right?

OLIVER: Well, I think there's a danger of becoming too politicised. And what we wouldn't want is to be asked our opinion on every single political issue of the day because I mean, that would obviously be totally impossible. But I think there are fundamental principles that affect the way in which we work that are relevant. And I think that the question of diversity is something that we have on the forefront of our minds because we're based in a city that's 45% non-white now. If we can't reflect that in the way we make work and on our stages then we've got a real problem. So it feels right to make a statement on a question like that. And in terms of the environment, I've talked about that before. I think that we're all assessing the way in which mankind interacts with nature. I think we all have the responsibility to do our bit to improve the situation individually and as cultural institutions. That's another area where we can actually do something. We can change the way we make work productively, constructively. But I think Brexit is an example of something that it would be very hazardous for us to make a comment on, no matter what our personal views might be on Brexit. It's something that's really polarised the country, that people have very strong views upon. And I think it will be folly for us to make a statement about whether we supported Brexit or we didn't support Brexit when really our role is to make work. And it is to proclaim the values of internationalism and cosmopolitanism that we've always had actually but without making any overt statement on the rights and wrongs of Brexit.

STEVEN: One of the criticisms at the moment is that cultural organisations virtue signal. They'll make statements about these things without enacting actual change. You can *perform* social justice. Is there anything that we can close on about how either the Royal Opera House or the sector could enact change rather than simply signalling towards it?

OLIVER: Well, I think enacting change for us means diversifying the workforce. It means diversifying the people who are on stage. But it's about making quite significant statements in terms of who makes work in the Royal Opera House. For example, we're putting on a show next month which will be the first opera by women of colour directed by a woman of colour on the main stage at the Royal Opera House. That will be a very significant moment for us especially as it turns out in Black History Month. I think it's about signal statements. It's about just doing it rather than as you say just making statements which anyone can do and just getting on with it. I'm quite wary of making lots of proclamations about how one is diversifying and doing this and doing that. But I think ultimately, it comes down to the work that you're producing and who's producing it, simple as that.

STEVEN: That feels like a suitable note on which to close, thank you.

This interview has been edited for length.

ACKNOWLEDGEMENTS

With special thanks to all those who suggested questions and topics for discussion.

Notes

1   Net Promoter or Net Promoter Score (NPS) is the percentage of customers rating their likelihood to recommend a company, a product, or a service to a friend or colleague.
2   Sir Antonio Pappano is an English–Italian conductor and pianist. He has been music director of the Royal Opera House since 2002.
3   Helen Marriage: In Conversation (Hadley, 2020). www.tandfonline.com/doi/abs/10.1080/09548963.2020.1801329?journalCode=ccut20.

The Global South and Cultural Leadership

Julieta Brodsky, Minister of Cultures, Arts and Heritage: In Conversation (Chile)

Tomás Peters

Chapter 11

DOI: 10.4324/9781003390725-11

Julieta Brodsky is Chile's Minister of Cultures, Arts and Heritage. She is a social anthropologist and former research director of the Observatory of Cultural Policies of Chile. She was one of the professionals who led "Proyecto TRAMA" in 2012, a project financed by the European Union whose purpose was to improve the working conditions of cultural workers in Chile to provide financial support and generate cooperation amongst the various actors in the creative sector. She has authored various writings, such as "El escenario del trabajador cultural en Chile"[1] (The Scenario of the Cultural Worker in Chile), "El papel de las politicas publicas en las condiciones laborales de los musicos en Chile"[2] (The Role of Public Policies in the Working Conditions of Chilean Musicians), and "¿Cómo se sustenta el Teatro en Chile?"[3] (How Does Theatre Survive in Chile?). In March 2022, she was appointed Minister of Culture in the administration of Gabriel Boric, a student leader and the youngest president in the history of Chile.

This conversation was held on 28 December, 2022 at the Santiago headquarters of the Ministry of Cultures, Arts, and Heritage of Chile.

TOMÁS: To begin our conversation, I would like to go back 20 or 30 years. The return of democracy in 1990 opened a new chapter for cultural policy in Chile. And the National Council of Culture and the Arts, the first major cultural institution in the country, was created in 2003. Since then, many debates and concerns have emerged that you, as a researcher, analysed and included in your studies. How do you see this history, this process?

JULIETA: This year marks the 30th anniversary of many things. Balmaceda Arte Joven[4] turns 30 years old, and so does the National Television Council. Even the radio station Rock & Pop is now three decades old. Looking back, one realises that 1992 marked the beginning of a new cultural era in Chile, and new cultural institutions started to function. The Book Fund was created in 1992, and then the Fund for Cultural Development and the Arts (FONDART, Fondo Nacional de Desarrollo Cultural y las Artes[5]). And since then, perhaps, the first public policies in culture started to take form, not yet with institutions, but a movement could already be observed. Looking back from today, I feel they were initiatives that are quite good. Having said that, the external eye is always more critical, and from a research perspective, we saw that public cultural policies tended to be heavily based on competitive bidding and the creation of public funds. Indeed, it was a policy of creating competitive funds, and also of outsourcing public policy, in the sense that many private institutions subject to private law were created that, ultimately, had a public role, yet under a private legal framework. And this was the form or formula for creating cultural institutions that started in the 1990s.

TOMÁS: In fact, back then, we were coming out of the dictatorship, and there was an explosion of "social desire", both in the private and public sphere, to resume cultural work. Returning to the arts after the "cultural blackout" experienced under the dictatorship felt like a historic task.

JULIETA: Of course! I feel that public policies began to form as a sort of jigsaw puzzle. Maybe it's not the right metaphor, but this way of incorporating different elements that joined a mass of initiatives that didn't necessarily have a common plan – but were important initiatives and major projects – and were extremely ambitious. They had an ambitious goal. In this sense, I now value them much more because I understand how hard it is to carry out cultural initiatives. And there was a conviction that great cultural centres were needed. In fact, great progress was made in cultural infrastructure, and there were major infrastructure programmes. The cultural centres programme for municipalities with over 50,000 inhabitants, for instance, is an impressive public policy, despite all the problems they subsequently had in their management or operation. These are great programmes and great initiatives that require significant resources and need substantial coordination between institutions. And it was a state policy that persisted beyond the various administrations, until the target that had been set was more or less achieved. But, of course, in other areas, there was a great tendency towards competitive bidding. I feel that this obviously brought about a lot of issues in the long term, especially due to the inequities generated in access to the competitive funds; because it generates many barriers, many gaps in terms of access to these public policies, to these resources. But also, because it generates a cultural production dynamic that also ends up adapting to this tool. Instead of the tool adapting to the cultural production dynamics, the cultural production dynamics end up adapting to the tool. And there has been a complexity in this aspect that is very difficult to undo, or from which it is very difficult to come back today, so to speak.

Another aspect that I find complex in terms of what cultural policies have been like in the past 20 or 30 years is hypersectorisation. I find that this tendency towards hypersectorisation has been one of the most complex issues, which is very difficult to address today. Because, of course, we've had a tendency to create funds specialised by area, by discipline, but then, within each discipline there are sub-disciplines. And today, those sub-disciplines also want to have a specific space within the discipline, and each sector, if you will, wants to have its own law, it wants to have its own competitive fund, it wants to have its own programme. And this ultimately leads us to a sort of dead end from which there is no turning back. Today we ask ourselves: What about projects that are interdisciplinary? What about everything that doesn't fall into these categories, that doesn't fit into these little boxes based on which we have determined that this is audio-visual, this is visual arts, this is performing arts? What about media arts? What about other types of languages or proposals that are more interdisciplinary, or more cross-cutting things? Or: What about cultural management as a cross-cutting concept?

So, I feel that we have also fallen into a trap in this sense, from which it is very difficult to come out. Because in the end, if you say that you feel we should not continue to move forward with hypersectorisation, the sectors that couldn't be part of this progress, or this process, so to speak, will feel excluded and discriminated today.

INEQUALITY AND CULTURAL DEMOCRATISATION

TOMÁS: The National Council of Culture and the Arts was created in 2003. It originated as a result of several debates and commissions, and a scheme that was copied or transferred from the French model, with some English and Mexican elements. One of the council's central themes was the idea of "cultural democratisation", and access to the arts was one of the major focal points of this new institution However, access to the arts continues to be an issue in Chile. How do you analyse the problem of inequality in access to the arts? What does the idea of cultural inequality mean today, after all these years?

JULIETA: Inequality is a very profound issue in Chile. And cultural inequality is a problem that we still haven't managed to resolve, despite the cultural democratisation policies, which I believe were important to carryout. Cultural democratisation policies in terms of cultural infrastructure were required. I mean, infrastructure is also an element that enables access and the generation of certain things. Then, we also need to work on other aspects to provide this cultural infrastructure with content, to bring it closer to people, etcetera. But still, infrastructure is often a necessary condition. Art education policies and heritage education policies are also important. Furthermore, now we need to try to expand the focus to other cultural education sectors, such as heritage, or other topics that are also relevant to incorporate. But that inequity or inequality in the cultural field cannot just be reduced to an access perspective, which has been the tendency. I believe that inequity and inequality in culture also have to do, for example, with the possibility of pursuing an artistic, cultural, or heritage activity. In general, the same precariousness that emerges in cultural work means that only a few ultimately decide to pursue it. Inequality is also related to, for example, an understanding of artistic forms of expression. But it not only has to do with understanding but also with closeness, with the *feeling* of closeness, the feeling that this is something that concerns me, that it is something I am interested in learning about, and that's where there's a giant barrier.

TOMÁS: The issue is that despite everything that was done with the implementation of policies, plans, infrastructure, and all the competitive funds, there is still a strong – and basal – logic of structural inequity.

JULIETA: I think so. I believe that it still exists. And well, the data proves it. I mean, the most recent National Cultural Participation Survey in 2017 continues to show this gap: it shows that, ultimately, it hasn't been reduced. Efforts to eliminate that entry barrier have been unsuccessful. And this continues to be steady over time in all the measurements we have made since 2005.

TOMÁS: Do you remember when we waited for the surveys? And we were always like "Give me the data so I can analyse", or "Now we will show something new". And it was the same thing over again: high inequality and social reproduction.

JULIETA: Of course. Perhaps the only interesting thing in this regard shown in the last National Cultural Participation Survey that was new, refreshing, was the aspect of the public space: the different forms of cultural participation and how, amongst these different forms of cultural participation, some were more unequal and others more egalitarian. And I believe that what was shown, for instance, is that this "spontaneous participation" that takes place in the public space was the only one that was more egalitarian. All the others kept maintaining access barriers. So, I think the policies that have been created have been very useful. Maybe if all those policies hadn't been created, the scenario would be much worse, obviously. But at the end of the day, the policies we have implemented have been insufficient in eliminating this barrier, in eliminating this gap amongst some sectors in terms of closeness to the cultural event, and particularly the artistic event. But I also think that inequality is reflected in what we understand by culture, or what we understand by cultural manifestation. And that is also reflected in how all of this is measured. I mean, the cultural consumption and cultural participation surveys themselves already define what cultural participation is or which types of activities are worth culturally participating in and which aren't. And some cultural manifestations are egalitarian in terms of access because they are also more cross-cutting, such as music concerts, for instance, cinema, going to a religious festival or participating in a crafts fair. So, in the end, having a definition of access that says "Well, a theatre play is the form of cultural participation I expect from citizens" is already defining that that's the valuable cultural manifestation to you. And no, it's not like that. There are thousands of activities in the popular cultural world, or other types of activities that are also cultural participation.

TOMÁS: In Chile, the idea of inequality has been circulating for decades in the social and economic domain. And certainly, it also transfers to the cultural world through very specific indicators. We have published about the topic and shown the historic inequality in terms of cultural access in the country. But this "structural inequality" reached a crisis point in 2019 with the "social outburst",[6] and a sort of social explosion of "We cannot go on this way" took place. And this has significant consequences in the cultural field. What is your take on what the outburst, the riots, and then the pandemic meant in the cultural field? What discussion is generated in this regard that may be interesting to think about from a Chilean perspective?

JULIETA: First of all, I think that everything was questioned during the outburst. All the foundations of the society we had built were shaken, and there was tension there, in how public policies had been made in the past 30 years. And I think that in the cultural field it was also observed that these policies hadn't managed to reduce or overcome the inequality occurring in Chile in every aspect, including culture. I also believe that the arts and culture sector felt the need, so to speak, to take to the streets, to be part of this process, but also to feel that what they were doing also made sense to everyone else, to the collective, because there's always this impulse in the cultural field to serve the collective, to serve the community, if you will. Nonetheless, the social outburst also showed that this wasn't necessarily being achieved. Despite the fact that, in many cases, the cultural sector strives to generate a more community-based, more collective, more crosscutting cultural sense, it is still an endogamous sector. It's a sector for which it has sometimes been difficult to speak to others.

And it is there that we have many challenges regarding how we can make a cultural dialogue with citizens in general, how it can be something demanded by citizens, where people say, "We want more culture, we want more cultural manifestations, we want to participate more culturally". I don't know, it would be wonderful for citizens to be able to demand this. It doesn't happen in Chile like it does in other countries. But yes, for example, there are still some cultural manifestations that are demanded: look at what happened when "La Tirana"[7] was cancelled? Because then we do have a citizenry that goes out and says "Hey, I demand my right to participate culturally, to manifest my own culture". So, that's where we also have a challenge as a ministry. For instance, why are we as a ministry of cultures, arts, heritage, not involved in these types of localised celebrations? That is where I feel that we should transition towards.

CULTURAL DEMOCRACY

TOMÁS: After the social outburst and the pandemic, there was an extremely important discussion at a national level. The political agreement for the creation of a new constitution was signed, and in December 2021, Chile elected Gabriel Boric, a left-wing student leader and political figure as president. In parallel, the cultural and artistic world was severely afflicted by the effects of the pandemic and organised itself through cooperatives to chart a new course for state action in the cultural field. And the need for a new institutionality emerged. You arrived at the ministry, and a new banner was taken up called "cultural democracy". How is cultural democracy conceived from a Chilean perspective?

JULIETA: Well, what we were talking about earlier has a lot to do with the concept of cultural democracy: with how we ultimately understand inequality based on what we understand by culture and cultural manifestation. So, cultural democracy implies eliminating those basic biases that we have and trying to look at the country's cultural scene and saying "Well, all those cultural manifestations that exist in our country are equally valid!" Why must I only promote one type of cultural manifestation that is not accessible to all and not say all cultural manifestations should be accessible to all? So, it's also about giving value to that which happens in places where a traditional town festival – generally held in contempt and looked down on by some sectors – plays a fundamental cultural role. Perhaps, of course, all the resources are spent on bringing one big show. But at the end of the day, they are expressions of popular culture and Chilean traditions that people want, and people ask for, and that they like to have. Their town festival is the memory of peoples. And it is a moment in which the community gathers, and they generate collective practices and express their identity and feel part of a community. Why wouldn't that be valuable compared to other manifestations? I don't want to make the same mistake again and say this is good, this is bad, but why has there been so much contempt in our public policies towards certain types of cultural manifestations versus others? Cultural democracy also means being able to take account of these types of manifestations, being able to also give them a certain dignity, and being able to promote them and show the enormous cultural diversity we have in Chile.

TOMÁS: Several of these debates, such as cultural diversity and cultural rights, have been pillars of political-cultural work in Latin America. How do you feel about this sort of synchronisation amongst debates that some countries in Latin America had already thought about, and which Chile now sees as an opportunity to implement? How do you think that programmes and actions such as the "Puntos de Cultura" (Points of Culture)[8] could be rethought and implemented in the country's territories? How is "cultural democracy" carried out as cultural policy in Chile?

JULIETA: It's not an easy task. In Latin America, there are diverse experiences of the "Points of Culture". There are experiences in various countries, and each one is quite different. The design and implementation are very particular. Under the umbrella of what we call "Points of Culture", there are different views and different ways of addressing this. But that's where we have the challenge, obviously, of creating our own programme, with our own style. And it has been very challenging work. This year, we've had a very intense participatory process to define how to implement the programme, and the truth is that new cultural needs emerge as well as new community-related organisations. We've discovered many new organisations that perhaps weren't on the radar that have joined this process, and obviously, we have a great challenge because there are many points of culture. So, we need to be able to somehow reach all of them. But I feel these are cultural policies that make a lot of sense in the communities because we know they are organisations that have been working for many years, that generate various social and community benefits, that have a lot to do with the aspects that we want to work on as a government, such as safety and the recovery of public spaces.

TOMÁS: Cultural rights, which have been a crucial element for Chile, are present in all those aspects.

JULIETA: Exactly. That is in addition to the work with children, memory, human rights, and the environment. These are organisations that are generally involved in these topics, or that work on these themes with the community in some way, but they do so without any help. Therefore, on one hand, this means facing an existing historical debt in public policies, and, on the other, it means addressing topics that we want to work on as a government indirectly through "others" – like the third sector – because, as the State, you quickly realise that you cannot do it all. I mean, you cannot reach every corner of the country because it is impossible. So how do you do it? I think the best way is through the communities: to give them tools and resources so they can do this community insertion work. But it is an important challenge, and it is a very interesting policy, even though it obviously generates some resentment in the arts sector because they think that now the public policy focus will change, and it will no longer be as focused on professional artistic work but rather on everything community-related. And this is not really so. It's also been difficult, I mean, it is important to communicate well so people understand that one thing does not substitute the other, but that we are growing institutionally. We are growing in our public policies, and therefore, incorporating new sectors, but we are not leaving anybody behind.

RESEARCH AND CULTURAL POLICIES

TOMÁS: You and I come from research backgrounds. On the one hand, what role does knowledge play in decision-making? How do you see the role of data, of information, how does the gathering of studies and knowledge on cultural policies contribute to decision-making? And, on the other, how are theory, evidence, and practice balanced? In other words, as a researcher, how is a decision in cultural policy ultimately made?

JULIETA: Well, at least for me, due to "professional distortion", and also because of all the knowledge I have accumulated over years of research and studies I have conducted, this research and theoretical corpus, so to speak, has been fundamental. Such work has helped me think about and design new public policies. But it is not a regular practice institutionally, not because there isn't an interest but because this knowledge is not subsequently processed or disseminated well. The Ministry of Cultures, Arts, and Heritage has been developing knowledge and research around cultural policies, and this has been very helpful. But we have an important challenge there in terms of how we make the results of this research known to everyone, because I believe they are fundamental. in general, everything we do is based on evidence, although we often don't have much time to review it.

TOMÁS: One of the most evident challenges when designing and implementing a policy is having the ability to process knowledge.

JULIETA: To process it, of course, because it is a fundamental tool, and many times these tools are also not enough. I mean, we often need more figures, more immediate figures, because it generally happens that we get the figures a year or two later, and by then … I mean, with the level or speed of what happens in here, you need to be constantly monitoring data to make decisions, or to be able to show the impact of your decisions. And this is something we are lacking. For example, we have conducted a great deal of work for the reactivation of the cultural sector this year that has been very important, but we don't have figures about it. We can't say that the number of cultural activities increased by X%, or that we managed to generate employability for X number of people. Although we might have an approximate figure – which we gather in the most rudimentary manner we can – we don't have monitoring that you can regularly check online like others sectors do: how it grows, how it happens in real time. And I think this is a great deficiency. For example, in a few days, we will launch the Cultural Statistics Report of the National Statistics Institute of Chile, but it is from 2021! So you are ultimately getting the data you need to have today one year late.

CULTURAL POLICIES IN CHILE

TOMÁS: So, how do you come in, with your conceptual theoretical background and all these elements, and negotiate a budget increase or negotiate coordination with other agencies such as the Ministry of Finance, the Ministry of Education, and the Ministry of Labour? How is a different or more prominent role achieved in the Ministry of Cultures, Arts, and Heritage versus the rest of the ministries or the rest of the decision-making spaces? How do you see this based on your experience as a minister?

JULIETA: I think that is the great challenge of a sectorial ministry like Culture, and of all sectorial ministries in general: to be able to convince people of the value of culture, of the social

Tomás Peters

value, the political value, the economic value, in short, of all the values that the sector on which you focus may have. All those arguments help to promote budget increases, to promote exchanges with other sectors, to generate public policies. in this sense, you look back on the administrations and say "Well, this administration had a cross-cutting conviction, there was cross-cutting support, or there was a perspective that placed value on this and not on this". You eventually start to notice in which administrations there was political conviction and in which there was none, so to speak. And it is very clear, for instance, that the administrations of Ricardo Lagos and Michele Bachelet[9] were administrations in which there was conviction. There were many very important and very interesting public policies in those days that, unfortunately, ceased to be implemented or were later shut off for various reasons. Others remained and are fundamental today. But one does notice that there was an ability to negotiate, to make resources available, to implement major programmes, develop large infrastructures, etc. And in others, you realise that conviction was not there. this is very important, the conviction that the President of the Republic might have about the value of culture. At the end of the day, the role of the president sets the tone. They say, "This is important, this is not important".

TOMÁS: In that sense, how do you see it now?

JULIETA: We have a good scenario, in the sense that culture matters a lot to the President of the Republic. And this is where the conviction of the other ministries to also incorporate culture into their policies emanates from. this has been very positive in the sense that, for example, we are working with the Ministry of the Interior, which is something that had never happened before. For instance, the Ministry of Cultures is currently working on the recovery of public spaces and public safety issues. We are seated at various tables and joined the National Security Council. We are working with sectors with whom we didn't have much of a relationship before. With the Ministry of Labour, we are also co-building the status of the cultural worker. I believe that those two ministries, for instance, didn't have a close relationship to Culture before. Others did, with Education there was a long-standing relationship. We are also working with the Undersecretariat for

Children. And the same is happening with other public agencies that didn't use to be addressed from the perspective of cultural policies.

TOMÁS: So, there has been an insertion of the Ministry of Cultures into unprecedented sectors for Chile's cultural policies?

JULIETA: Unprecedented, yes. Evidently, we continue to work with other sectors, but this relationship has deepened. But overall, I feel there is much willingness and openness to work in an intersectoral way in this administration. And I feel there is also an openness to address problems with a more comprehensive perspective in general.

TOMÁS: This is key, because public policy is being conceived at a multifactorial level in which culture is not a superfluous complement but a social intervention factor.

JULIETA: Of course, multifactorial. What's interesting about this is being able to include various actors in the conversation to have a different view and a design that really changes the way of doing things. I think that there is also a conviction today that there are things that were not being done properly, or ways of doing things that were not producing the expected results. Therefore, we have to be more innovative, be more creative, and rethink this way of doing things. And to this end, you need to include new actors in the conversation.

TOMÁS: What lines of research do you think are unexplored in the field of cultural policy that researchers should pay attention to?

JULIETA: I don't know whether I would speak of unexplored sectors because, of course, I feel that you could say "Well, I think we need more knowledge in X areas", but maybe, it is you that hasn't been able to access that type of knowledge. Indeed, there is a lot of research. I feel there is a great production of knowledge in many different areas, but maybe we are not aware of all that. I know that not only in Chile, but in the world in general, we have a lot of evidence about many topics. However, I feel that sometimes, the research field's problem is that it doesn't consider the more rudimentary issues of the public apparatus, and that it is ultimately there where you often find the obstacles. By that I mean the slowness of the public apparatus, and the number of actors involved in decision-making. Because you make a decision, but that decision has to include the Budget Office of the Ministry of Finance, the Ministry General Secretariat of the Presidency of Chile, the Congress of the Republic, and a series of actors.

TOMÁS: You have to convince many actors in order to be able to implement it?

JULIETA: And not only convince them, because many times it is not only about whether those actors believe in what you are doing or not. It's about whether you are a priority at the time or not, whether there are other things at stake or not, the economic and social context at the time, the political negotiations in between, whether the person in front of you wants something and you can give them something in exchange for what they want. So, in the end, I feel that research manages to generate a lot of knowledge and evidence. But when it comes to designing and implementing public policies, there are many other factors involved, and which are not present in scientific research. And that is the art of doing politics. There are even emotions involved, more personal issues related to how people feel, to how the sectors feel, whether they feel excluded, invited, whether they feel they are participating in decision-making or not. Additionally, there are so many sectors and so many individual actors functioning in this:from public officers to union leaders. And MPs must also be considered.

TOMÁS: It's a sum of infinite people.

JULIETA: It's in finite. And all those people have to somehow support you so you can implement what you're doing. So, of course, research is important, evidence is important, and it is important to use it for decision-making. But, ultimately, how to implement, or how to achieve certain public policy objectives depends on many other things. And not only on what is good and what is bad, what is correct, what works and what doesn't, but also on how you manage to balance the needs and interests of different sectors. Achieving what you need to achieve is not only up to you.

TOMÁS: What can other countries learn from Chile in terms of contemporary cultural policy? As a country, what could we say or share with others about international experiences?

JULIETA: At the international events in which I have participated, such as Mondiacult or the inauguration of the

International Decade of Indigenous Languages, and others, I feel there is a lot of interest in what is happening in Chile. Because, on one hand, Chile is also an example of cultural public policy, in various aspects. For example, in terms of art education, there is a lot of interest in what is being done in Chile. Chile is one of the few countries to have celebrated Art Education Week for ten years, for instance, to have carried out continuous work in certain areas. The hardest part in the different administrations is often giving continuity to cultural policies, and I believe that continuity has been achieved in Chile in many aspects. So, an interest in what Chile is doing emerges, for example, in education. There is also an interest in what we are currently doing around the Cultural Worker Statute and the decent cultural work agenda. In Chile, addressing the precariousness of cultural work has been fundamental. Because, additionally, we have an outlook on the cultural worker based on a much broader concept; in the world, there is only talk about the status of the artist. The perspective is very focused on the role of the artist. We are expanding to other dimensions that are much broader than the role of the artist in itself. We are talking about technicians, intermediaries, managers, and promoters. Therefore, our approach is wider, and this generates much more interest.

Additionally, the National Cultural Funding System is something that generates interest regarding how new tools are being conceived for cultural financing. The Points of Culture also generates interest. Although this is not something of our own – as they exist in other Latin American countries, – it is something we are considering in its situated condition. In this sense, Latin America is proposing innovative cultural policies to the rest of the world, and we are also promoting coordination amongst the ministers of Latin America and the Caribbean to have a position towards the world, and a cultural policy proposal for the world, especially now that Mondiacult and international summits will be held every four years. So, as Latin America, we have to attend these summits prepared with a common stance, with a joint position, because we have cultural policies that are very common, very specific to this region.

I also think that Chile is being watched in terms of the creation of a new institutionality. As the ministry's name suggests, the area of Heritage is also considered and brought together. We are currently generating a real conversation between the former Directorate of Libraries, Archives, and Museums (DIBAM, Dirección de Bibliotecas, Archivos y Museos) and what used to be the National Culture and Arts Council. The two institutions were merged after the creation of the Ministry of Cultures, Arts, and Heritage in 2018, and when we assumed the ministry in 2022, there was no dialogue between them. They were two completely separate institutions that had no coordination whatsoever. So, what we are trying to do now is to make the departments converse, to get public policies into dialogue, programmes into dialogue, because there is one sector that has the infrastructure (museums and libraries, for example) and another sector that has the (artistic) programming. So, we need to generate this exchange. For example, for the first time, an art education policy and a heritage education policy are being generated jointly, which the two sectors are discussing. And well, there are different experiences. The issue of cultural infrastructure is also something that other countries are observing with interest in Chile. Competitive funds themselves generate interest in other countries. But also, the lessons we have been putting together based on this experience with the competitive funds is also something we can show the world. We can tell them: "Well, there are many positive aspects, but be careful, try to avoid what happened to us in these areas: do not generate those gaps, do not hyper-specialise". We can share that experience. And I also think that something that has generated a lot of interest is how we are coordinating inter-institutionally as the Ministry of Cultures with other ministries and public policy bodies, as I was telling you earlier.

TOMÁS: Of course, when you were telling us about the role of culture in other spheres of society?

JULIETA: Exactly. How, at a state level, we are working on safety issues through culture, how we are working on care-related issues, also through culture, how we are thinking about public spaces. I think there is also a very interesting perspective there related to how Chile can start to generate innovative models and approaches in those areas.

TOMÁS: Julieta, thank you very much for this conversation. It is a great contribution to thinking about contemporary cultural policies *from a Latin American perspective.*

JULIETA: Thank you as well.

Notes

1 See https://ec.cultura.gob.cl/wp-content/uploads/2020/10/0_50_El-Escenario-del-Tra bajador-Cultural-en-Chile.pdf.

2 See http://biblioteca.clacso.edu.ar/clacso/becas/20140110083830/TrabajoFinalClac soKarmy BrodskyUrrutiaFacuse.pdf.

3 See www.observatoriopoliticasculturales.cl/wp-content/uploads/2021/05/fondart-teatro.pdf.

4 See www.balmacedartejoven.cl/.

5 For an historical analysis, see Hamdaoui, S. (2021). Enhancing elite autonomy: the role of cultural policy in post-authoritarian Chile (1990–2005). *International Journal of Cultural Policy*, 27 (7), 853–865. doi:10.1080/10286632.2020.1825404.

6 See Garcés, M. (2019) October 2019: Social Uprising in Neoliberal Chile. *Journal of Latin American Cultural Studies*, 28:3, 483–491. doi:10.1080/13569325.2019.1696289.

7 Fiesta de la Tirana is an annual festival held in the locality of La Tirana in the Tarapacá Region of northern Chile. La Tirana is the biggest geographically localized religious festivity in Chile. For a contemporary analysis of La Tirana, see Valenzuela, E. A., Aranis, D. P., & Coquelet, J. A. (2019). Transformations of religious consciousness at a Marian shrine: The case of La Tirana, Chile. *Social Compass*, 66(4), 579–595. doi:10.1177/0037768619868612.

8 See https://cdn.gulbenkian.pt/uk-branch/wp-content/uploads/sites/18/2018/03/The-Point- of-Culture-2nd-edition.pdf.

9 Ricardo Lagos was president of Chile from 2000 to 2006. Michele Bachelet was Chile's first female president. She was elected in 2006 and then reelected in 2013. Both politicians are center-left.

Cultural Policy and Cultural Leadership

Kenneth Kwok, Ministry of National Development: In Conversation (Singapore)

Michelle Loh

Chapter 12

Kenneth Kwok was Senior Director of Service Quality and Community Engagement at the Municipal Services Office, Ministry of National Development (MND). He started his career as a Literature and Drama school teacher, Vice Principal and Assistant Director of Curriculum Policy under the Ministry of Education. He

DOI: 10.4324/9781003390725-12

left teaching to join the National Arts Council (NAC) as Deputy Director of Arts Education, and then Director of Arts and Youth. His work involved school programmes, and community-based youth programmes like the Noise Festival for emerging artists. He also oversaw Strategic Planning, Research, and Capability Development, eventually becoming Assistant Chief Executive. Kenneth was also a performing arts reviewer as co-editor of online arts journal The Flying Inkpot which ran for 19 years. A writer of short stories, creative non-fiction and essays, Kenneth has been actively engaged with writing and publishing in print and online. An experienced arts educator, administrator and policymaker, he remains a strong arts advocate and enthusiast.

At the time of publication, Kenneth has taken on a new appointment as CEO of the Singapore Symphony Group effective from January 2023.

MICHELLE: You have served in the public civil service throughout your career and your latest progression was from the National Arts Council to the Ministry of National Development, the latter managing public feedback on municipal matters. How did this progression happen, from working with the arts to working with public infrastructure, public transport and the public environment?

KENNETH: Within the government, there is a very strong agenda for leaders to move around different agencies, to be in different sectors in order to develop new partnerships. You may have a very strong passion and expertise or domain knowledge in one area, but it helps when you have a wider network, wider experiences beyond the arts. If all the art lovers say, "oh I love the arts so much, I'll go to the National Arts Council", we become very insular in our way of working.

That was the reason why I chose to go to the Ministry of National Development when the opportunity came – and I should clarify that I am on attachment so I will return to the arts sector eventually. The Ministry of National Development oversees infrastructure which I felt would be very different from the arts sector, but there are points of intersection between community spaces, public housing and non-arts spaces can be activated for arts and cultural usages.

We should look at movement in the other direction as well. The arts should invite people from other agencies to come into the arts, so people who may not have an arts background can come in and then hopefully be converted. They can go back out again to their own sectors, be it tourism, social and family development, or even economics, trade and industry, because then, the arts will have more friends outside the arts circle. They can open doors to other types of opportunities, they become our connection there. Consolidating or congregating all the art advocates and enthusiasts all into one arts agency is probably not the best way to operate. We do have partnerships with National Parks Board,[1] Housing Development Board[2] and People's Association.[3]

We should see the different agencies' agendas as complementary, not as exclusionary or competing. If we can have more resources for all of us to work with, why not? That is why I've always felt that we need applied arts practitioners and arts managers in our ecosystem too. That is not to say that we diminish the importance of artmakers and artmaking, that remains the core, but I think helping people reimagine the place of the arts in society can create new opportunities for the arts sector, open up resources and get more public support precisely so artists can thrive.

ARTS IN THE GOVERNMENT

MICHELLE: What is the place of the arts in government? How open are the other ministries to using the arts in this way?

KENNETH: We have a Ministry of Culture, Community and Youth, and a National Arts Council. In some countries, culture is with education or tourism. There's no right or wrong, but, for myself, I'm glad the arts are placed with community, where it's about people, connections and relationships. Of course, working with other agencies is always an educational process, because not everyone necessarily appreciates the various dimensions, shapes and forms that the arts can take. Many say they don't understand the arts because they can't make art themselves, or failed art and music in school. But I always say, you don't have to be good at something to be able to just enjoy it or see its intrinsic value. That's the journey we need to take people on. We need to help them see the possibilities of what can be done through the arts.

They may have misperceptions about the arts as too abstract, too intimidating, too out there or whatever. Just helping them understand that the arts also include photography or storytelling or cinema, things they can identify with easily, that's a start. I think we also cannot discount the fact that some people are just never going to like the arts, no matter what we do. Just like some of us don't like mathematics or sports, and that's just the reality of life.

So we need to engage them, whether by going into their space, or inviting them to come into ours, in good faith, and with patience and openness. I believe that there is a very important role for all of us to be ambassadors for the arts, to be strong advocates for the arts, to encourage attendance, support and even fundraising for the arts. More of us need to do that. For example, we need to be bold about speaking passionately about the arts whenever we can, like, during inter-ministry meetings. I was talking to someone about how Members of Parliament (MPs) do their rounds and listen to citizens. Most of the topics arising from such conversations tend to be centred on cost of living, public health and infrastructure. How many residents give feedback to their MPs about government policies on the arts? This is not a usual topic when people meet their MPs. That's why I tell my friends that when the MP comes around, tell them that you are interested in the arts, tell them that the government support for the arts is critical, and we should have more opportunities for art programmes for families. Let our politicians hear it.

If we love the arts, we should talk about the arts. That's why my social media still highlights the arts events that I attend, even though I have left the NAC. I want my uncles, aunties, cousins and friends from school to see that there is this show going on, or this exhibition, or this great new book is out by a local author. I think it's important for us to be proud of the fact that we are in the arts, and let others know that there are people like you and me out there. It's normal to like the arts!

I really believe in the outreach and promotion of the arts, and that all of us, including artists, must play our part. Of course, the artists' fundamental role is to create work, to create art. That is why we need other types of people in the arts sector besides artists per se, who are spending their time creating works. We

Michelle Loh

need arts managers, arts administrators and the National Arts Council to be that supporting force around artists to help bring support in from the wider community.

MICHELLE: Don't you think that your case is unique? You came from NAC. If someone else came from a non-arts agency but decided to do arts-related projects, wouldn't that be infringing on what NAC is doing?

KENNETH: I think people are more open now. For example, we have partnerships with the Urban Redevelopment Authority because they look at activation of spaces for communities and enlivening spaces. They partner with NAC so the arts are a means for them to engage the community in the spaces that they want to activate. Same for NParks. For the Ministry of Education, arts come into the contexts of arts education, citizenship and character education. Same goes for the other governmental bodies, such as Ministry of Social and Family Development, or Ministry of Health to use arts for community building or rehabilitative purposes. The arts have become part of their agenda, and we benefit because more people are having positive encounters with the arts. I think this is the link. We need to see connections across agencies, across sectors and purposes. It creates more space for the arts, rather than say that the arts are a thing by itself and only for arts lovers.

MICHELLE: Cross-agency partnerships may have different priorities. Are there priorities that are set above others?

KENNETH: Definitely. For example, with the NAC, one very high priority has always been the development of audiences. The other is to advocate for the arts, so that more people become audiences. Different agencies will have different priorities and rightfully so, but it's about how we all go about achieving those agendas. For example, public housing is about building and constructing homes for people, but we also have to think about estate management, public hygiene, cleanliness and neighbourliness. When we talk about considerate public behaviour such as do not litter, picking up after your dog, there's a public education aspect. Once you go into public education, the arts can play a very important role. In MND, I worked on public wall murals as well as music videos involving professional artists to encourage residents to think about how their actions as individuals impact community living. Some may say it's not high art in a concert hall or museum, but it's still art, and still creating work for artists. Different agencies definitely have different priorities, but there is always common ground to be found. In the end, all government agencies want the best for citizens, to help them have good lives. As long as both sides focus on what makes society better, I'm confident we can find ways to bring the arts into health, into community engagement, into education, and, at the same time, use that to build appreciation and audiences for the arts, which is our priority as an arts council.

MICHELLE: Singapore is small. It seems like a lot of the decision-making that affects the arts is always related and connected with other ministries. Do you think that the development of other industries is closely linked to the arts in Singapore?

KENNETH: The National Arts Council's agenda is to develop the arts and to promote the arts, but yes, always within the larger agenda of government since we are part of the public service. I think that in any country, the tangible things like housing and roads, or education and defence will inevitably take priority. Just look at our budget, for example. We are certainly not at the top of the funding totem pole. When a public survey[4] was conducted in the midst of the COVID pandemic, artists were voted by people as the most non-essential job. Obviously, this aroused many emotions, such as frustration and anger, from the arts community. To be fair, though, this survey was done when people were thinking first and foremost about health and daily living issues like sanitation. I think the reality is that air, food and water are truly essential. The arts are not the most essential thing, but that is not to say that the arts are not important. Multiple things can be important even if not essential, and even if they are at different levels of importance at different times. Having said that, it's also about reframing society's understanding about the arts, and the role the arts played to preserve our mental health during the pandemic. The arts brought joy and hope and entertainment, and there is great value in good entertainment, and also the arts gave people avenues for activity and self-expression.

Michelle Loh

ARTS AND CULTURAL POLICY IN SINGAPORE

MICHELLE: Do we give enough time for each cultural policy to be fully actualised before coming up with the next cultural policy? Do you think that we push out cultural policies too quickly?

KENNETH: In Singapore, things are changing all the time. Maybe it's because we are a small country. We are able to react and respond quickly, and so we do. We like things fast. But I agree, perhaps we don't always give ourselves enough time for things to settle. For instance, *Our SG Arts Plan 2018–2022*[5] is a five-year arts plan. This means that the next one will come out after five years. But the work for the next plan has to start before that, so only 2–3 years into the current plan, and we will need to start reviewing and planning for the next one. So, yes, there is probably scope for our policies to be given more time to settle so we can really understand their impact. Because every new policy is very significant. It begins a new phase of our cultural development. I don't know what the magic number is, whether it should be 5 or 10 years, but I know we shouldn't rush it. I am a realist. I don't think we always need to reach our destination tomorrow. It's sufficient for us to be aware of where the destination is, and make sure we are facing the right direction and moving towards that destination. It's also vital we take the time to really gather different perspectives, that we hear public feedback, hear how policies are really affecting people's lives and practice. It's clear the government as a whole has become more consultative though. We can see that in all the various engagements like Our Singapore Conversations, Conversations for the Future, community dialogues for public housing, Singapore Green Plan 2030. There are more advocacy and civic groups now, so it is also easier for the government to organise public consultations through these ground-up collectives to hear these diverse voices. Technology has opened up more avenues as well.

MICHELLE: When the next policy comes out, does it mean that the last policy is obsolete?

KENNETH: Well, if nothing else, it has informed the thinking of the people who are now developing the next one. Each policy, whether you agree with all of it or not, will hopefully spur passion and advocacy for the next policy to be better. As a former teacher,

I take a generational approach to things. I believe the people affected by the cultural policies of today will become the artists, policymakers and advocates of tomorrow. Everything matters because every change becomes a bigger change, everything builds upon what came before. That's why education is so important. We are where we are today because of everything that happened 20 years ago.

MICHELLE: Does each policy need to be in sequence, or, could they be in parallel and overlapping as well?

KENNETH: Not everything is so neat or linear, sometimes you have to jump sideways, learn mistakes and then jump back. That's why the direction must be very clear, so that you are more or less always moving in the right direction. You will never know for sure if you are 100% right. A policy may be right at a certain time, but wrong in another time. Hopefully everything evens out over time as long as your true north is clear. When I was a teacher, I would tell my students that it's okay to make mistakes, you learn from your mistakes. But we don't always allow that in adult life. We can be very unforgiving. Having said that, if your policies have a very significant and immediate impact on people's lives like health policies, then it's understandable that there's a lot of pressure to not make any mistakes.

Thankfully, the arts aren't life and death, at least not in the same way. But this is why regular consultation and feedback is so important, so that we can course-correct if necessary, and there should be no shame in that.

ARTS FUNDING DEVELOPMENT

MICHELLE: Can you talk to me about how policies around arts funding have developed in Singapore?

KENNETH: One thing that I've always been passionate about is that we need to differentiate and customise funding to a range of roles, aspirations and challenges. When I was in the National Arts Council, one of the projects which I was involved with studied how grant funding can recognise the roles of various intermediaries in the arts sector. Not just art makers. The funding structure became more differentiated, and funding goes beyond just giving grants. The roles of intermediaries become very important in terms of providing support for art making, providing

Michelle Loh

support to reach out to audiences, providing criticism, providing spaces, providing platforms, opportunities and so on.

We worked on differentiated tracks for funding. It is not a perfect system by any means, but it was just a way to signal that the Arts Council was cognisant of different types of art groups out there and they needed different kinds of support. I think that we could have differentiated it further, but we wanted to make a start.

MICHELLE: This is very interesting because the funding structure seems to have become more complex, yet more comprehensive at the same time. There seems to be many different areas that the Arts Council is focusing on. Before the trend to fund intermediaries in a local context, it was the Renaissance City Plans focused on funding and exporting made-in-Singapore content. Any thoughts on this?

KENNETH: I am an ACSR[6] boy. In Singapore, you do have these phases according to which policies were implemented at particular periods in time. We have very clear, distinct phases and periods tied to particular policies, such as ACSR from 2012 to 2018 and Our SG Arts Plan from 2018 to 2022. The Renaissance City Plans were specific to 2000 to 2012.

Some artists will be in the right time of a particular movement, some will be ahead of their time. You can create works that are not appreciated now but appreciated in 10 years' time. In the past, going digital was seen as new or faddish. Now it is fundamental. The council has always tried to be comprehensive in our funding approach, but certain choices have to be made at any given point of time because funding is limited. Giving more money to artist X means less for artist Y, there's no escaping that. Whether it's supporting established groups vs. new groups, encouraging new works vs. re-staging of previous works, staying local or going overseas, prioritising is necessary. Unfortunately, this means some artists and arts groups may be out of sync with the priorities of the day, and then maybe they find themselves in demand only a few years later.

One of the problems in Singapore is the over-reliance on government funding. As a country, Singapore is quite centralised. We turn to the government for a lot of things like education and municipal services. In other countries, the arts are very much supported by the people. That is not to say that the government should not provide funding for the arts. The government must always ensure a certain base support and for all types of art. But we need to have more private sponsors, private donors, which is very lacking in Singapore. There have been studies on how much of philanthropy in Singapore goes to the arts, and the percentage is very small. We have not cultivated that enough. If we can do a better job of getting corporate and individual donors for the arts, these private patrons can hopefully fill in the gaps where the system has not been nimble enough to catch up. These could be artworks that are more niche, or works where there aren't enough critical mass for the council to support. If we can achieve that, it will fundamentally change the way that the arts system works in Singapore. I remember reading something once, this was not about Singapore, but a study was done where they asked people if they believed a national art museum was necessary, and everyone said yes. But when asked if they would contribute to the building of the museum, everyone said the government should do it. In the 1960s, Singapore built its National Theatre by getting the people to contribute a dollar a brick. Would this work today?

The problem is that the arts are still not a priority for most Singaporeans. This goes back to what I talked about earlier on the need for advocates. Many of my family members still don't really understand what I did every day in the council, and they don't watch arts productions. They don't attend art events in Singapore, although some make an effort when they go overseas. When they go to London, they may watch a musical, or visit the MOMA in New York. But why don't they go to the National Gallery in Singapore? If Singaporeans don't even go to the National Gallery or the Esplanade, I cannot imagine them going to the more niche or smaller, independent arts spaces. The arts are something people take for granted, or don't see as part of their daily life. The arts are only for playtime with their children or when it's a holiday.

And so everything then goes back to government funding, to the National Arts Council. It puts all the weight on the one, single source of funding, and that is the government. That is why all the attention, scrutiny, criticism and unhappiness get focused on government funding. If the arts could also get funding from somewhere else, I think everyone would be happier. If you can find a funder who is more aligned to your priorities and your

Michelle Loh

agenda as an artist, that's fantastic. I was speaking to a visual artist who had a patron who was very supportive of her work. She acknowledged that she is one of the fortunate few. Patrons can support the creation of artworks for a specific vision or audience. These patrons are potential funding options for artists and arts groups, and they will help to release a lot of the pressure that is now on the arts council. Although it is one of the arts council's priorities to cultivate more private sector philanthropy, it is admittedly a tough time since the pandemic and the impact on businesses.

MICHELLE: Do you mean that once artists find a patron or a group of loyal supporters who invest in their work, they are then free to create?

KENNETH: Certainly more so, and I'm sure many artists would appreciate that freedom. I had the same conversation with another artist whose works are not mainstream. I asked if he is applying for funding for his next project and he said, you know honestly, I don't need the funding, because he has a personal patron. He does not apply for funding because firstly, he does not need it and secondly, he would rather someone else gets it. His name and works are strong enough to get published. He is privileged enough to create the work that he wants to create.

ARTISTS AND GOVERNMENT

MICHELLE: Do artists come to the Arts Council to pour out their grievances and complaints?

KENNETH: Yes! Over the years, I've spoken to many artists who have reached out to me. One artists called me and said hey, can we meet for lunch and have a talk. After lunch, she said, you know we are very lucky in Singapore because we are such a small country. I can just call the Assistant Chief Executive of the National Arts Council and meet him for coffee. I don't think I could do that in another country. Our size helps! But, yes, it is important for the council to stay very much connected with the community. I'm glad that there are many people in the arts council, I would like to think that I am one of them, who are involved in the arts in our own private capacity or have a background in the arts so that we continue to have relationships with the arts community. The other thing that I would like to say is that many artists have contacted me just to talk. They know that nothing would change after they talk to me, but they just needed someone to talk to. This is important because every conversation that you have helps to clarify things. These informal chats may not immediately change a policy decision but listening to artists helps the council identify their real needs for the next policy decision, even before the formal consultation sessions. Beyond that, however, it is all about building real relationships, orientating all of us back on the same side.

MICHELLE: What you seem to be saying is artists are not actually looking for changes, nor do they expect you to make a change even if they contact you. Even if they tell you the problems that they're going through, do they not have any expectations?

KENNETH: That is what I realized, to my surprise. I thought that they were trying to change my mind about a decision that was made by the council, but actually they really weren't. Sometimes, it was just for them to understand a bit more about the council's position. It was also a chance for me to explain why things are done in a certain way. Conversations do not always need a purpose. There is value in conversations for their own sake.

MICHELLE: Do you think that our artists are very obedient?

KENNETH: No, and I'm glad artists are not. If every arts or cultural policy is universally loved and adored, then something is wrong. That is not how the arts sector works. I do expect some artists to push back. I do hope that artists give the council some differing views, to help us for the next round of changes. Artists should question and provoke. They should be ahead of the council.

Some artists will say to me, why is the Arts Council always one step behind the arts community? I think that is to be expected. The government is the establishment. How can the government be ahead of the artistic community which is the segment that is usually the most progressive and creative in thinking? As long as the arts community feels that the council is moving with artists in the same direction, that is the right path. At the end of the day, I am not a professional artist and can't claim to be one. I am part of an institution. I would never really understand what it is like to be a freelance artist out there, struggling to create my work, getting it produced, performed and worrying about my livelihood. But I'm on the same side as the artists, part of the same community, because we all ultimately want the same thing: for the arts sector be healthy, strong and vibrant. I hope we can work together.

The Arts Council, being part of a government, would have to balance many factors. The National Arts Council's agenda is to grow the arts sector and to promote the arts, but all these are within the larger agenda of the government. This larger agenda considers the economy, public safety and land use policies. If I'm an artist, my one allegiance is to the art form, to the arts alone. It is always going to be different. The artist has only one thing that you're fighting for, whereas the government is trying to fight for many different things.

For example, my job as Director of International Relations was to position Singapore globally, to look at international opportunities for Singaporean artists. There were certain areas that I could not move as quickly because I had to be aligned with the interests of other agencies, such as the Singapore Tourism Board. With the inter-agency relationships and the resources I had, we could move forward one step in this direction, but artists would ask, why don't we take two steps forward, or why don't we go that way instead? I had to say no, because there were other factors and players I needed to consider. There are constraints for any agency because of having to deal with multiple perspectives.

MICHELLE: Do you have any examples of consultative processes that we might close our conversation with?

KENNETH: Consultation is not always easy. There are existing disagreements and fractures amongst the arts community. There is usually no clear single message from the arts community on what is the best approach. If the ten leading artists can all agree on one thing, then the council can be assured on what and how to implement that one thing, and it will have the support of all ten leading artists. But if there is no collective agreement, then the council will have to choose the strategy or the policy which has the support and mutual agreement of at least a few artists. If the ten leading artists could all agree on one thing, that would make things much easier. One example was when an agency[7] conducted public consultations on a co-regulatory partnership with the arts sectors and was seeking feedback on self-classification.[8] The artists came together and did a video. I remember Kuik Swee Boon, Mrs Santha Bhaskar, Ivan Heng, etc. were all in it, and they collectively expressed their disagreement with the concept of self-classification. I am not here to debate the right and wrong of this policy, but that was where the arts community gave a very clear signal with respect to possible policy. With their unified decision, it was clear that self-classification was a no-go.

However, this was not the case with the closing of The Substation.[9] There was no one, unified view from the arts community. Different factions of the arts community have different views, which are understandable, but it made decision-making challenging as there was no clear position from the arts community on the best way to move forward. Consultation work can be tough. All we can do is to just have as many consultative sessions as possible: big group sessions, small group sessions, one-on-one sessions and then attempt to pull together something that makes sense and is reasonable and which allows you to sleep at night, knowing you have tried your best. In the end, you have to accept that you cannot please everyone.

Notes

1   National Parks Board (NParks) is a government agency overseeing urban ecosystems, greenery, biodiversity conservation, wildlife and animal health, welfare and management and the overall living environment (source: www.nparks.gov.sg).

2   Housing Development Board (HDB) is Singapore's public housing authority. HDB oversees public housing estates, builds homes, provides commercial, recreational and social amenities for residents (source: www.hdb.gov.sg).

3   People's Association (PA) is a statutory board that aims to promote racial harmony and social cohesion in Singapore (source: www.pa.gov.sg).

4   *The Sunday Times* commissioned a public survey in 2020 to find out which jobs are most crucial during COVID-19. Artists were named as the most non-essential job, whereas healthcare workers were listed as the most essential job during COVID-19 (source: www. straitstimes.com/singapore/manpower/8-in-10-singaporeans-willing-to-pay-more-for-essential- services).

5   www.nac.gov.sg/about-us/our-sg-arts-plan-2018-2022.

6   Reference to the Arts and Culture Strategic Review 2012.

7   The Media Development Authority was a statutory board which provided classification guidelines for the arts and entertainment industries in Singapore. It organized consultative sessions with leading artists and arts companies to gather public feedback on the concept of self-censorship in 2014. The agency has since been renamed to Infocomm Media Development Authority Singapore (source: www.straitstimes.com/opin ion/art-of-censorship-in-singapore).

8   The Media Development Authority suggested a scheme for artists and arts groups to classify their own shows according to the authority's classification code and ratings. The scheme, called Arts Term Licensing, eventually was not implemented due to the collective opposition of the arts industry (source: www.straitstimes.com/singapore/mda-removes-arts- term-licensing-from-proposed-amendments-to-act).

9   The Substation was Singapore's first independent arts centre which prided itself as a space for independent artists and collectives to experiment, collaborate and explore beyond conventional interdisciplinary boundaries. The centre closed down permanently in 2021, despite repeated calls by the public as well as artistic communities for government to retract its decision.

Cultural Diplomacy and Cultural Leadership

Mark Katz and Junious "House" Brickhouse, Next Level: In Conversation (USA)

Jennifer L. Campbell and Jill Schinberg

Chapter 13

Mark Katz, music professor at the University of North Carolina (and a DJ), founded the hip hop diplomacy enterprise Next Level in 2013. Next Level offers a novel cultural diplomacy program focused on hip hop music and dance as the mechanism to bring

DOI: 10.4324/9781003390725-13

people from disparate backgrounds together to create community, foster entrepreneurship, and resolve conflict. In 2019 Katz moved into the position of Founding Director, transferring the working directorship to Junious "House" Brickhouse, an internationally acclaimed dance educator and choreographer, who served as a participant in the program in 2015. Katz and Brickhouse are against the "love 'em and leave 'em" approach that has typically been the United States Information Agency (USIA) and the Bureau of Educational and Cultural Affairs [ECA] status quo since 1938; instead, they work to build lasting relationships with youth and artists from targeted countries, doing so through the community of hip hop.

This text is a compilation of two interviews that took place online via Zoom on 1 September and 9 September 2021 and is edited for length and clarity.

ARTS DIPLOMACY AND AUTHENTIC COMMUNITY ENGAGEMENT

JILL: There is regularly tension between the presenter who brings culture into a community, and the community itself, which might feel displaced and not supported by the presenter. What strategies are you using to engage with and connect to the communities you are visiting?

JUNIOUS: So, I'm having this conversation quite often with people. And the difficulty that I have with the question is the idea of a singular community because, often, in hip hop culture, we are multiple communities, separated by all of your obvious things. And then dance style, generation, type of hip hop music we like. And then humanity, right? All those things, right?

JILL: Are you making a distinction between a local community and a global community (global community including all humanity)? I think what you're talking about is actually the different communities within hip hop culture, and that it's not monolithic. Is that right?

JUNIOUS: That's correct.

JILL: Okay. So, what about when Next Level shows up in a particular place and geographical location? And what about that community? Or are you bypassing that all together?

JUNIOUS: I'm bypassing it all together. Today, I had a planning visit with Barbados. And when we start our planning for every residency, we recognize that we are talking directly with the embassy or consulate and their representative. That may not be a community of practice, right? These may not be people who are into hip hop culture.

So, we also know that there's a huge divide between government officials, US government officials, nonetheless, and communities of practice in the arts, right? So, I don't think I ever did anything through the lens of "we're going to meet the hip hop community in this country" because there are always people on the margins. We know that hip hop culture is not something that is readily accepted by the establishment or our governments, right? So, that creates this thing of a subculture that we don't really go into things with the same intent. I'm not going to make you learn this dance move. I'm not going to make you learn this song. I'm just trying to talk to you about how we do it where I'm from. And I'm going to show it to you, knowing that you probably do it differently, mostly because you came in, you look different, you sound different, you use different equipment. I know I'm dealing with someone who's different. I know they have their way of doing this culture. So, what we're going to do is we're going to engage. And that's supposed to be reciprocal. I'm supposed to give something, and I'm supposed to receive something. And that's what makes it different. That's what makes hip hop culture our tool of choice when we're talking about cultural diplomacy.

We're trying to fit into this cultural diplomacy space. But the language is sometimes problematic. And it's also problematic that a lot of us are new to the space. So, while we're trying to engage, and engage responsibly with other communities, we're still dealing with old language that really, well, it's not really our language. It's not the language from hip hop culture. So, we use it sometimes when we're speaking to people who speak that language. But we also have to flip it when we talk to people in communities of practice because they won't understand what we're talking about.

MARK: First, I would say there is absolutely no way to guarantee that outsiders going into a community will not both displace them and somehow fail to support them. I can't think of any set of

Jennifer L. Campbell and Jill Schinberg

conditions that would guarantee a kind of seamless collaboration. So, first of all, we need to know that. That's actually part of the work: knowing that it's impossible to avoid introducing tension. Not simply walking into a tense situation, but actually bringing it. So, Junious mentioned these planning visits. And that's a crucial part. So, first of all, we don't just show up to a place and say, "Here we are. Let's do the work."

And Junious is doing this virtually today [because of the pandemic]. But normally, we would go to the place. And then it would be one or two people. An example is when I went to Croatia, to Zagreb, with the person who is going to be the manager of the residency. This is Jaci Caprice, who is a producer and singer. She's the Next Level alum who is going to run this residency. And so, we have a couple of strategies. One is that we ask the embassy or consulate, "Who do you usually work with? Who would you recommend we talk to?" And then we do our own due diligence, and we put the word out. Who do we know in Zagreb? And we get some names. We set up meetings. We arrive. We meet with different groups. And when we got to Zagreb, we had a couple of meetings in our hotel with people who identified themselves as part of the underground dance community. And I could see that they arrived with this certain, well, scepticism about us like, "Who are you? What are you doing here? Are you for real?" And they kind of had their arms folded literally, but also metaphorically. And so, we had to try to convince them that we were for real. But a lot of what we do is we listen. We ask them what the situation is like on the ground. We ask them about their needs. For me, it always, and I say this all the time, it always gets back to agency. So, are we respecting their agency? Are we acknowledging their agency? We're not there to do what we think is best for them. We need to find out what their interests are. And their interests, some people's interest might be that we don't be there, that we don't come. I did write a little bit about this in my book *Build*.[1] So, you may have seen some discussion about it, but I could say a little bit more. I think what we did do that was right was we asked, "Who should we be talking to?" The question is: Who should we ... fill in the blank. The answer is: You should not leave Zagreb before talking to so and so. And who are those people? And so, we did. We met someone that was totally off the radar of the embassy, but everyone in hip hop knows this guy in Zagreb. His name is Phat Phillie.[2] He was, really, as far as I could tell, universally respected. I actually was in a cab, or a cab came up to pick me up, and I was standing next to Phat Phillie. And I went in, he's like, "Oh, that's Phat Phillie." And he's like some random cab driver. So, even though we met the people that everyone agreed that one should know [in Zagreb], we couldn't convince the underground folks who identify that way that we had good intentions.

There were still problems, and that's because of resources and facilities. According to the embassy, at least, and based on what we needed, and we did ask around, there was really only one facility that could house the residency. We had very specific needs: four rooms with electricity. I mean, it's not a lot, but the underground places would be like in someone's home or a small studio. So, reluctantly, we said (and this was what the embassy said, too), "Well, we got to go with this dance studio." It's a commercial studio. They did hip hop, but it was, well, there was tension. We walked into a tense situation because there were complaints. We heard that this studio always got the grant money from the embassy or elsewhere. And they weren't hip hop. They weren't really part of the culture. And yet, we ended up going with them. There seemed to be no good option, or at least no good other option. So, I think we did our best. Phat Phillie was involved. He got a lot of people to come in. But even so, we were aware that there were people who avoided working with us because of our connection with the studio. And they didn't necessarily have anything against us. I don't know, maybe they did, maybe they didn't. But they just couldn't countenance being in the same spaces as these people.

JENNIFER: I think that's fascinating because space has politics, right? And I don't know if we're always thinking that way, but it makes it even harder if you are coming from the outside, and then you have to do all this reconnaissance to find out what the politics of the space are. And because you're from the outside, you're having to ask people at the embassy who obviously have a certain perspective, and any kind of underground situation is going to have a view on whatever the embassy and the folks in the embassy suggest.

Jennifer L. Campbell and Jill Schinberg

MARK: When we went to Zimbabwe, we did most of our stuff with this place called the Book Cafe, which was a great; it was a good space. It worked out, but people said it was kind of bougie, and that if we really wanted to connect, we needed to go to the 'hood. And so, we actually arranged for a jam at another place that was in – basically, they don't use the same term in Zimbabwe, but a township. And it was in an open, large dirt space in a community. And the people who showed up were completely different from the people who showed up at the Book Cafe. So, we do try. We also did this in Senegal, which Junious knows about. We ended up with one space, and we didn't go to a bunch of other spaces, but we did visits, or we would maybe donate some equipment to those other spaces. So, it's not always either/or. We tried to do both ends, but we still can't spread all the goodness around. And people always feel left out, or perhaps insulted, or not consulted.

ON THE COMPLICATIONS OF PERCEIVED IMPERIALISM

JENNIFER: Mark, in your book *Build*, you mentioned that hip hop diplomacy has been criticized by at least one anthropologist who described it as, "the US government's management of an imperial relationship with the Muslim world." Two pages later, you state that hip hop diplomacy's power lies in its "possibility of fostering global community." (p. 8) There's a lot of tension between one person viewing exploitation of hip hop as a mechanism of imperialism, versus another person viewing it as a community building opportunity.

MARK: So, there's tension, but there's no contradiction. So, there's a difference there. There's not a paradox. I'm not saying $2 + 2 = 5$ and $2 + 2 = 4$. Those both can't be true; only one of them is true. I think both those statements can be and are true that as – and she wasn't the only person who said this – but Su'ad Abdul Khabeer who wrote the book *Muslim Cool*[3] writes very compellingly about the potential for diplomacy and cultural diplomacy to be a tool of imperialism and to be an oppressive force. And I actually don't argue against that. I quote her and say that is possible. But that doesn't preclude the possibility for community building. And if you read her book, it's interesting because she points out this tension, and these things are happening simultaneously. My feeling is I don't dispute this possibility with any kind of diplomacy when exercised by an empire or an imperialist country or a country seeking to dominate other countries. And you could say the US belongs in all those categories, so there's no trick or way to solve this except to do all the things that we were just talking about in terms of acknowledging agency and trying to get a sense of what people want and need. But also, in addition to that, knowing the history, knowing who you represent, and being aware that there is a structural issue. So, I will say it is impossible for us to go to another country and for the history of US intervention around the world to not be part of that story.

But I would think that the position that Khabeer is saying is not that there is always going to be one outcome from diplomacy. It's just that it's an ever-present possibility. And one conclusion, a reasonable conclusion could be that I cannot support cultural diplomacy funded by the US. And I wouldn't say you're wrong to think that. Another could be I accept that, but I think it's still worth trying to do. So, obviously, I'm on that side of things. But I know people who are on the other side and say, "You could give me every example of good stuff that you do, but I just can't get around this possibility." And I would say, "I understand your concern." I wouldn't try to convince you otherwise.

JENNIFER: I think the tricky thing is that imperialism is so negative, right? And so, it's easy for the negative and the bad to overshadow the positive and the good that is often done in those local pockets. And sometimes, on a smaller scale, it gets overshadowed by the big messages and the big titles that sometimes happen in the large scale. Junious, what are your thoughts?

JUNIOUS: There was a time where I thought that any effort or any move, any diplomatic move by the US government was imperialism. Full disclosure, I'm the son of two Black Panthers, so their ideas about diplomacy, and what that looks like from the US effort is a mixed bag. And if we consider everything, every diplomatic effort from the United States as imperialism, it's a moot point, right? It's like just full stop. But I also think that there's another way to look at it. Growing up in communities that often felt invisible, I always wanted an opportunity to talk to people about my experience, what it was like being me. What it was like

Jennifer L. Campbell and Jill Schinberg

in our community. Not just doing art forms, but just what that was like as an effort to improve the condition of future children. I want better for my community. I don't want my nieces and my nephews growing up that way. I'm able to do that now. So, I have what I asked for. So, I have to acknowledge that. I can't be like, "Let's just point out all the things that the United States has done wrong as a government." And what I tried to do is I tried to live on by the mantra, "We are not our governments. We are not." In hip hop, being subculture for so long, we kind of navigate that space a little bit differently. We are folklorist. We are cultural preservationist. It's on us in this direct interaction. And we're able to get that together under the Next Level program. I'm privileged in a lot of ways because, normally, when I'm interacting with people because people have done a little bit of research, and they know that they're talking to a black man who's from this place, and I don't push around easy.

HISTORICAL SOCIAL STRUCTURES

JILL: From your point of view, what is the relationship, if any, between imperialism and white supremacy? And what about critics who suggest that hip hop diplomacy is actually using black culture to maintain white hegemony?

MARK: I'm not a scholar of imperialism, but based on my reading and thinking, imperialism always has something to do with supremacy, whether it's white or not. Supremacy seems to be at the heart of it. The imperial project requires, I think, a self-view that the home state has something that the rest of the world needs, and that the rest of the world has something that the home state needs and is going to take. So, when it comes to white supremacy, I think it depends on what the constitution of the empire is. So, certainly, the American empire, the British Empire, the French Empire, I would say, yes, absolutely, in their connections with white supremacy, because of some of the things that Junious was talking about, going into another country and say, suppressing local customs, insisting on doing things the way that they're done back at headquarters, massacring people.

JUNIOUS: If there's a critic suggesting that hip hop diplomacy is using black culture in certain ways that are adverse in nature, I would take offense to that. And I'm not saying that it can't be, right? I'm not saying that there aren't people out there using good tools for evil. But in what we do at Next Level, I don't think that would be a good fit. "Hip hop diplomacy" in itself as a term isn't very common. You guys know like I do if you start saying that in public. Definitely if you say it downtown, people are going to be looking at you the side eye. They'd be like, "What are you talking about? There is no hip hop diplomacy." But one would argue that our ways of engaging have a lot of success and are better than a lot of government programs. And I can say that with confidence. And I don't mean like ECA [Educational and Cultural Affairs] programs[4]; I mean just government efforts to engage. There are people in several countries globally whose countries do not have good relationships with the United States, but we've had relationships for 20+ years. And that says something. That says that we have a way of interacting with each other that works. And I want to continue to do that.

I do want to go back a little bit and cover something about hip hop as black culture. Based on the common speak of how long hip hop has been around, I'm old enough to have seen many different forms of hip hop culture. And my personal experience is that even though when I first started doing this I only knew black and brown people that did it, I can't say that it's the same way now. So, in order to remain fair, and especially in our programming, where we try to be intergenerational, I think it's only fair to say that there are different pockets and different communities who have made contributions to hip hop culture, and that they are not all black. And I think that's only fair. If we want to embrace Sankofa[5] and go back and get it and start acknowledging people in communities of origin properly and respectfully, we have to look at where hip hop culture is now and where it can go. I try to treat it like a healthy relationship. If you love them, you got to let them change a little bit. They're not going to stay the same. And hip hop hasn't done that. So, I'm being fair, right? And even though when we talk about cultural appropriation, and cultural practice, and practicing responsibly, and the like, I always like to acknowledge that it's a little bit awkward that we have that conversation in English, right? I'm a black man of African descent. And a lot of my history is a mystery to me, and I'm learning it now. So, when people start coming up to me and telling me the things that I feel like it's a part

Jennifer L. Campbell and Jill Schinberg

of my culture and who I am as a human being doesn't belong to me because it didn't start with me, I always take offence to that. And a lot of people that I'm speaking to internationally feel the same way. They feel like, "We know where this is from. And we acknowledge that. But hip hop promised us that we could make our own contributions."

And that's the thing about hip hop culture, it allows for some of that flexibility. Equipment is used the way that it's used right now. Who knows, maybe people will use turntables differently in the next 10 years. Maybe people will use beat machines and mics differently. Maybe people will go from handheld mics to different mics set up. Cultures change. They develop. What I'm saying about this thing, specifically about white supremacy and imperialism, is that hip hop is trying to find other ways because we know that doesn't work. And those were tools used to oppress us. So, we are trying not to be our oppressors as much as we're trying not to be our governments.

THE OVERARCHING ABILITY OF MUSIC AND DANCE TO BRING PEOPLE OF DIFFERENT CULTURES AND COUNTRIES TOGETHER

JILL: How does Next Level offer a different narrative of cultural diplomacy?

MARK: Generally, the way I describe it is it's more interactive, it's more workshop based, it's more one on one or small groups rather than presentational, large concerts. On another hand, even when, let's say, [Louis] Armstrong or [Dizzy] Gillespie and others were touring, or [Aaron] Copland, probably, for that matter, there was a lot of stuff that wasn't planned, but that was one on one or after hours of people jamming. It wasn't sort of named as the primary vehicle. So, I don't want to lean too hard on the claim that we're doing it different. I would say part of it, and I realize this could come off as self-aggrandizement, but I think part of it is that we're well aware of history. I mean, like tried to read the history and do research on how things have been done before and learn from the past and be aware of the wrong that the US has done. I don't think it was as acceptable, let's say, in the 1960s for a foreign service officer to acknowledge all the coups that the US had supported or the death squads that the US had paid for, the assassinations, and so on. I think there was maybe a stronger sense of American exceptionalism. I think one of our approaches is that we're never anti-American, but we eschew the exceptionalist rhetoric and viewpoint. It's often hard to avoid. We hear it. I think part of it is about practice, but part of it is also just about attitude, and trying to just walk in with humility, and an understanding of the risks of this work. And the potential for us to do things, the potential for us to make things worse. Now, there's a fine line because that could be self-defeating. And I don't want to make the opening speech at our Barbados residency an hour-long flagellation about American imperialism. That's not going to get the work done.

JUNIOUS: There's a question that I have for you guys, actually. In a lot of the things that I've read, and that I've noticed about other diplomacy programs, particularly the Jazz Ambassadors Program[6], it's like, a lot of those artists were well established and well known. I'm not a hater, but I'm no Dizzy. People, I have to show and prove. We have to show people what it is that we're about. And we walk into the spaces, I think, more on an equal playing field than someone running into Dizzy and being like, "Hey. So, you're going to perform, or you're going to teach?" I feel like in the arts envoys I've done in the past, I didn't have as much time as we have at Next Level to connect with people and build in some of the things that I now take for granted, that I was never able to do in other programs, i.e. planning visits is one of them. Being able to stay two or three days longer at planning visit so I can go to other communities and meet people that the embassy doesn't know. But I've been able to contact my friend who lives in New Orleans, who hooked me up with some-body that lives there. And I'm going to have dinner with them and ask them about their community, like that kind of stuff. I haven't been able to do that in other programs. And I appreciate it. I'm more focused on, I guess, at this point, what we haven't done well, and what we can do better more than I am on what makes us different, and what makes us great.

MARK: Junious, I just want to add something that reminds me of a phrase to throw in. I remember what someone who had participated in some other cultural diplomacy program said. [The person] used the term "artist centered program," and complimented Next Level for being an artist centered program,

Jennifer L. Campbell and Jill Schinberg

meaning that we cared. We don't work people to death. We make sure that they have time to learn, to benefit from the experience. And so, I think we can give ourselves some credit for that. The interesting thing is sometimes that runs into tensions with the embassies because they want to squeeze in one more media visit, or one more tour, or one more interview, or whatever. And we kind of hold the line. So, in some way, maybe one thing that makes us a little bit different is that we said we're a little more willing to push back, and that we're actually fairly independent instead of just sending three artists who have never had any experience, and/or group of artists who've never had any experience working with a state department, and their main liaison is a foreign service officer.

JUNIOUS: There's a lot of things that you can do. But without the foundation, without multiple think tanks around how do we do hip hop culture, without something that helps us sustain it, it just goes back to what people said it was 45 years ago. They said that it was just a fad; it would come and go. But I would argue that hip hop is American culture. It's an American art form that has branched out to global art forms done in many languages. And it came from this small unseen community. At Next Level, if there's some things that we can do better (and I'm sure there's a long list of them) right now, I'm still drunk on the opportunity, so to speak, to be honest. And it's time to strike. We have an opportunity to do something good. And, of course, we spend a lot of time thinking about how we can mess that up. But in the words of an old wrestling coach of mine, "Lead, follow, or get the hell out of the way." We have this opportunity. So, I think we need to take all of this work that we've been doing in communities of practice and center it, make some mistakes, adjust, and get back to work.

CULTURAL SUSTAINABILITY

JILL: Would you be willing to give an example of one of the things that you think that Next Level is not doing well that you could be doing better?

JUNIOUS: Yeah, I wake up every morning with this, and I go to sleep at night thinking about it: cultural sustainability. This idea that hip hop is just an activity, that it's performative, that it's just something that the kids do for fun, when it's actually a very important cultural identity to a lot of us. As an American who has more than one cultural identity, that thing is important. It explains a lot about the way that I think, where I come from, and where I want to go. I know that so many other communities feel the same way. But the world outside of our communities only seems interested in the entertainment of it all, and people's attention span to be entertained is pretty short. So, how do we sustain when this isn't a popularity contest? I'm not saying that Next Level is doing a bad job at that; I'm saying that is our charge, and that's what we're trying to do. We're not just having residencies where we go and we perform. We're planning ahead of time and trying to connect with multiple communities, and we're also teaching people our languages and our ways of being at the embassies, consulates, and the State Department. Hopefully, we can help all of them continue to do what they do a little bit better with the right language. We've instituted several reporting processes, not just at the end of the residency, and our site managers are writing multiple reports. We also have something called a student assessment tracker based on the curricula that each artist educator has. Cultural sustainability takes a concerted effort. It's not going to happen because we showed up and we did a concert. That's what keeps me awake. And that's our goal, and the State Department is helping us with that. We've come a long way. And I think what's important for me is how do we sustain that? How do we keep improving that?

JENNIFER: You talked about how you're not Dizzy Gillespie, so I'd like to go back to this idea of sending big names and big groups to represent big ideas on behalf of government interests, what might be called celebrity diplomacy, and as part of it certain things are already financially viable. But now you have regular people doing great work who have forged their own reputation, and it is about who they are and the art that they are making in community with others, which is a very different mindset than what has sometimes historically been supported.

JILL: Junious, cultural sustainability, as you are describing it, you're actually talking about preservation and sustainability of a part of culture. Food, music, dance. All cultures have dance: all of them. So, if hip hop is part of American culture, then establishing and sustaining that piece of American culture is something separate from promoting it, or using it as a type of propaganda, which is something that Jennifer and I have been talking about.

JUNIOUS: I lived in Germany from 1997 to 2005, and I was in the military at that time. I got out [of the military] in 2001 and came back as a civilian working with a NATO unit. One of the things that I'm so grateful for about that trip was that I learned so much about American culture in Germany. Things that I took for granted because I grew up in hip hop communities, I was like, "It's no big deal." But I got there [Germany] and people knew names; they knew dates; they had video; they had letters; and there was so much information [about American hip hop]. And they had preserved it from the early 1980s. So here I was looking at myself, and the communities that I come from, through the lens of a bunch of German people, and I'm so grateful for that. And I was a soldier; they knew why I was there.

In Bulgaria, there's a group called the Sleepwalk Kings with several of the members from different parts of Bulgaria, and they have traditional dances based on their natural environments (people who are by the rivers, people who live in the mountains, and people who are on the plains). They have different counts to their movement and their traditional dances. When they're breaking, they're doing it in the rhythms of their traditional dances. So, when Americans are watching it, we're like, "They're off beat," but when [the Bulgarians] are doing it, it's on time. They're saying, "This is my culture, my community doing this thing." I tell those two stories simply because it's flipped on its head. When we go to these countries, a lot of times, they know more about us than we do, and it's a learning experience and that is humbling. It's enough to make you sit down and shut up, and just listen to what people have to tell you about things that you didn't know. I had no idea hip hop was that large and respected when I got there. And as time has passed, that's another part of why we're working so hard to get this right because it's long overdue. It's long overdue to represent these cultures and these communities in a way that's respectful, and that is not a stereotype that doesn't belittle them, or make them out as second-class citizens because they do something that isn't traditional, or isn't thousands of years old.

IN CLOSING ...

JENNIFER: I do want to ask about Afghanistan, while the moment is present, given your work and your connection with the country. You've been there, you know artists there. And then to have the withdrawal occur in the way it has – well, the outcome that it has, right? I'd like to record your thoughts. Junious, do you want to go first?

JUNIOUS: It's tough. There's a lot of artists that we know, and some that we don't know, that are up and coming whose growth has been disrupted. People who had an Olympic dream to compete in 2024 representing Afghanistan who are now running for their lives, hiding. I'm angry. I think that's how I feel. I'm angry. I hate the contradiction of war. And I hate how it's impossible to leave a war with everything okay. Yeah. It's tough. I know this sounds bad, but I wish that there was effort with hip hop culture that could be legitimized. That people could see what happens when people don't know each other or don't even like each other, what that could look like through the arts. I know that's a big ask. It doesn't seem realistic at the moment, but, man, it's better than what we got because what we got right now is a mess and a shame.

JENNIFER: Mark, what do you think, maybe in relation to the artists that you've worked with? You guys supported or connected with some artists there?

MARK: One interesting thing is the proliferation of connections and how small the world is once we do all this traveling and meet people. I got an email from an Indian sitar player, who we had met through Next Level in Calcutta. He had been a OneBeat[7] fellow, and he had gone to the US. When we went to Calcutta, we looked up to see if there were any alumni of other programs. So, we hung out with him and got to know him. And I've been keeping up with him over the years. This was 2014. He wrote to me a month and a half ago. Just before the withdrawal he wrote that he had a student, a young woman who studied sitar with him in India but is now back in Kabul. And she's a member of the women's orchestra of Afghanistan. And he says is there any way you could help? And so, we've been trying and trying. Trying everything from just connecting her with graduate programs in the US and so on.[8] So, that's one element. And I don't think Junious is aware of that, but then something that Junious is more aware of than I am is that these Bboy crews who had to leave Kabul and are now somewhere in Pakistan, basically, in hiding. And I don't exactly know the exact connection, but I got a message from a Bgirl in Colorado asking about this. So, it's just kind of this wonder that we're so interconnected, but then we're also powerless in some ways, or in many ways. I've done nothing to help this young woman, but I've done everything I can. And she sends me these messages through WhatsApp saying, "I have no hope. Please help me," and I'm throwing out every suggestion, calling every State Department person I know. I mean, we want to do good through art, and yet, these cases show the limits.

JILL: It feels really intimate to hear you both talk about this. Thank you for sharing it. It also feels like a very strange way to end our time together today because it's heavy and not particularly hopeful.

JENNIFER: It is. But to counter that real fast, that's what cultural diplomacy is. That's the work that you do. And the danger of doing it right is that you've actually connected with the people as opposed to someone who goes in and presents a program. You have connections. You have people who have connected to the people. And so, it hurts when countries make these kinds of complicated, awful decisions. It hurts the individuals and the people who have connected. So, I think it speaks to the work that you're doing, though, right? Because you care.

JUNIOUS: To be honest with you, that's the thing that I'm hoping. For me, that's the next step. Mark and I have talked about this time and time again, but why are people only talking about cultural diplomacy at the grad school level? Kids can get into the Reserve Officers' Training Corps (ROTC) and middle school and learn how to be soldiers. I'm one of them. It's the options we give people. We can teach people to think with violence, or we can teach people other ways to de-escalate and transform conflict. And I think all of the tools are there. I hope the State Department can truly embrace the power of the arts, because there's not only a lot of soft power there, but also there's a lot of powerful ways of thinking about people and connecting with people. It's not just posts or deployments, but also people who were brothers and sisters in life, and not established by borders on maps, but connections that we make personally. That stuff is lifelong. My students are able to connect with students all over the world through cultural diplomacy, through things that I've been able to do. My sister made a joke the other day that I laughed at. You might think it's funny, but she was like, "The project we grew up in got royal, got way bigger." We never thought that we would get out; we never thought that we would be traveling the world doing art and culture. And that's saying something. There's a lot of power in that. And a lot of potential. And in the military, they say you want to – what's the term that officers use? What's it called? They want to escalate success, and we can do that in a lot of ways. It doesn't have to be combative.

ACKNOWLEDGEMENTS

This project was made possible in part by the generous support of the Office of the Vice President for Research and the College of Fine Arts at the University of Kentucky.

Notes

1 https://global.oup.com/academic/product/build-9780190056117?cc=gb&lang=en&.
2 https://twitter.com/phatphillie.
3 https://nyupress.org/9781479894505/muslim-cool/.
4 https://eca.state.gov/.
5 An African term of Ghanaian origin meaning to retrieve. https://www.berea.edu/centers/carter-g-woodson-center-for-interracial-education/the-power-of-sankofa.
6 www.hup.harvard.edu/catalog.php?isbn=9780674022607.
7 OneBeat is an ECA program: https://exchanges.state.gov/non-us/program/onebeat.
8 As of December of 2022, we learned that the woman to whom Mark refers was able to connect with other members of the orchestra. They're now in Lisbon, and Junious and he got to meet her in person while they were in Lisbon in October, 2022.

References

Bureau of Educational and Cultural Affairs, Promoting Mutual Understanding. (n.d.). https://eca.state.gov/.

Eschen, P. M. (2006). *Satchmo Blows up the World: Jazz Ambassadors Play the Cold War.* Cambridge, MA: Harvard University Press.

Katz, M. (2019). *Build: The Power of Hip Hop Diplomacy in a Divided World.* Oxford: Oxford University Press.

Khabeer, S. A. (2016). *Muslim Cool: Race, Religion, and Hip Hop in the United States.* New York: NYU Press.

OneBeat. (n.d.). BUREAU OF EDUCATIONAL AND CULTURAL AFFAIRS Exchange Programs. https:// exchanges.state.gov/non-us/program/onebeat.

The Power of Sankofa: Know History. (2017, November 20). Carter G. Woodson Center. https://www.berea.edu/centers/carter-g-woodson-center-for-interracial-education/the-power-of-sankofa.

X, formally known as Twitter. (n.d.). https://twitter.com/phatphillie.

Mega-Events and Cultural Leadership

Philippe Blanchard, CEO Futurous and Former Information Director, International Olympic Committee: In Conversation (France)

Beatriz Garcia

Chapter 14

DOI: 10.4324/9781003390725-14

Philippe Blanchard is the former Information Director at the International Olympic Committee and was in charge of overseeing a major reorganisation in the way knowledge was managed and technology understood within the Olympic Movement. Philippe also acted as advisor to the Dubai 2020 World Expo. By 2021, Philippe was working on the launch of a new type of mega-event, Futurous. This conversation took place in August 2021, at the time the postponed Tokyo 2020 Olympic Games were being held, during the COVID-19 pandemic and prior to the Russia-Ukraine war.

This interview uses the Olympic Games vision and hosting process as a leading example of cultural leadership challenges and opportunities. The issues raised here have relevance for those in the culture sector aspiring to grow the international significance of their practice – or those weary of the potential downfalls.

WHAT IS THE VALUE OF MEGA-EVENTS? ARE THEY PLATFORMS FOR GLOBAL CULTURAL LEADERSHIP?

BEATRIZ: Let's start with the overarching question about how you understand mega-events. What intrigued me during our last conversation[1] was your claim that the definition of a mega-event may be getting diluted by representatives of the culture sector, which consider initiatives such as the European Capital of Culture, international art festivals or, in the UK, new events such as the UK City of Culture, as cultural "mega-events".

PHILIPPE: As you remarked in your public lecture, despite over 100 years of mega-event hosting, the world of sport, the world of art and the world of culture are not coming together to the extent they could have. I think it is a big loss because for me, mega-events … have the opportunity and the responsibility of bridging these different worlds and bringing different communities together. But let me make this clear: I have a very narrow or rather, strict, view about what a mega-event is. In your lecture you posed the question: how do we define mega-events? And in the discussion, many stressed that for them a European Capital of Culture or the Edinburgh International Festival count as a "mega-event" because of their *complexity.* It is true that events of various sizes in terms of magnitude, face similar functional areas: all of these events have to deal with transportation, communication issues, security or crowd management. But the point of distinction for me, when we talk about mega-events, is not just about complexity, but to have at the same time a *geopolitical responsibility* and also *accountability* for bridging local with universal concerns; bridging art, culture, sport all together. So I have argued that in order to be referred to as a mega-event it is essential to meet at least three criteria: the first is to have *a governing body* that aims to represent and engage different countries and different cultures across the globe – so, we have the International Olympic Committee (IOC), FIFA and the Bureau International des Expositions (BIE); the second thing is the *complexity* dimension (i.e. a broad range of functional areas); the third is the *magnitude* in terms of size, number of participants, outreach and budgets. Events that can deliver global reach, complexity of operations and magnitude of scale give us the possibility to address the concept of universality.

This takes us into the question of exploring universal values, which should be at the heart of any mega-event mission. I understand universal values as the values *of* humanity and the values *for* humanity. What it means, in mega-event hosting terms, is not that we are going to put all cultures together in a blender and have something which offers a similar look and feel for everyone. On the contrary … it is about putting into perspective the different cultures of the world, something the World Expo focuses on, although it may be missing with the FIFA World Cup and, partly, the IOC's priorities for the Olympic Games. In this context, a mega-event should be an opportunity not to be shaped by the western vision of the world – but having multiple voices on an equal stage.

THE NOTION OF UNIVERSALITY

BEATRIZ: The notion of universality needs careful interrogation. If we think of the Olympic Movement and the IOC as examples of a governing body with the capacity to lead or shape this "universality" conversation, do you think they are rising to the occasion? How do you get IOC marketing teams to accept increasingly diverse host city proposals[2] to shape the event's core narrative – from opening and closing ceremonies to city dressing and event branding – if they divert or challenge the standards that have become established?

PHILIPPE: There are many elements I want to comment on. The first one is to go back to history. For instance, think of

Olympic opening ceremonies and the big shift that happened in 1992, not in Barcelona but in Albertville with Philippe Decouflé, which influenced as well what was done by Barcelona. Before [Albertville] the opening ceremonies were mainly about bridging physical activities with some element of visual choreography; I am thinking of Berlin 1936 and what was done by Leni Riefenstahl, so you had this celebration of [the human] body which is one[3] of the two films that she shot for the Berlin Olympics. In 1992, Philippe Decouflé decided to revisit completely the opening ceremony by bringing performers celebrating an element of French culture but also elements of modern and contemporary art such as the Bauhaus movement, and performers were not only dancing or evolving in a two-dimensional plane but also bringing in a third dimension, with elastics and acrobatic movements.[4] ... This was a very strong summoning of arts into a sport competition and sport environment.

Fast forward to the opening ceremony of Beijing 2008 and the closing ceremony of Vancouver 2010: you have the storytelling of "we – our territory – are inviting the world", in the opening ceremony and, in the closing ceremony, "our territory is handing over the opportunity to another part of the world". To me this is critical because it is about relating universal values. The universal values are not the same but there is something that is essential: the recognition that we have specificities and the necessity to accept these specificities and differences because our humanity is fifty shades of [laughs] emotions, of different palettes of stories, of histories, of philosophy, of religion. So, if we go back to the role of the governing body, my concern is that in order to manage the complexity involved in any mega-event hosting, they [the governing bodies] have shifted from and an obligation to advance universal values to an obligation to focus on essentials, on basic operational needs. So instead of saying to respective event hosts: "you need to explore and showcase the specificity of your culture and you have a wild card to do so", they are more and more stringent on their demands and are more and more directive about the core messages that should come through. This means they are no longer providing a platform for diverse interpretations of what the mega-event stands for.

Beatriz Garcia

You mention the role of marketing departments. To me it is extremely interesting that now, within the marketing department of these governing bodies you have lawyers, more than marketing people or more than creative people. This means that the creative people are working under the direction of the lawyers. So, they are working within a legal space instead of being granted the possibility to challenge, to provide a different perspective. And to be fair with these structures (I mean the IOC, FIFA and BIE) they are also evolving in a world which is more and more concerned or worried about cultural differences. You have the development of cancel culture, of woke culture which means that instead of accepting differences, accepting the fact that the past is the past, and the moral considerations of the past were different from the ones we have today, instead of that, woke and cancel cultures are imposing a revisitation of history and are extremely castrating, if I may say so, in terms of cultural expression.

So, what does that mean for art and culture within mega-events? What it means is that instead of providing a platform where artists can tell their stories, can demonstrate the specificities of their culture and show their willingness to welcome the world, and to be – to quote the Tokyo 2020 Olympic motto – "to be united by emotions", now it is as if they are extremely cautious about what people may say, that is, "are we boasting too much about our own culture?", "what is the biggest common denominator we can focus on?" … For me this is a cultural nonsense. Mega-event governing bodies should not be focusing on showcasing the biggest cultural denominator, we should be demonstrating the differences.

If we have a look at what is happening in the Tokyo Olympic Games[5]: we have no fans, we have not a mixture of culture, the activities in the Olympic village are extremely monitored, the activities of journalists are extremely monitored as well, so instead of showing the profusion and blossoming of different perspectives we are de facto experiencing a one-size-fits-all event. For me this is a huge mistake. This is something we are working on with Futurous[6] as a new form of mega-event. We want to make sure our competitions are staged in historical places, because this is about offering opportunities for peripheries to demonstrate themselves, to tell their own story. This is also about opportunities for the athletes, the visitors and the fans to have other experiences and hence we have those values for humanity, instead of having a tight closed box.

WHAT IS MISSING IN CURRENT EVENT POLICY FRAMEWORKS?

BEATRIZ: This is an important point. The concern for many is whether aspiring to celebrate what is "universal" means that we should focus on common denominators. You are suggesting that if universal means "we are all one", "we are unity", then there may be a dimension that is empowering but there is also a dimension that, in your words, is "castrating", because it is about trying to get rid of anything that breaks the mould. How do you break that tension? How do you avoid the mega-event and its host city becoming like an airport, a "non-place"?

PHILIPPE: Exactly. But as I usually say, this is not just the responsibility (or the fault) of FIFA, IOC, or BIE. It is also a common worldwide trend where we are replacing the notion of liberty with the notion of security. So, risk management is more and more important. You now have security by design when you manage a mega-event, which means everything is assessed in terms of potential risk. Further, because of the financial importance of sponsors and broadcast right holders, there are more and more constraints and we are shifting the experience from an Olympic city into an airport, as you say, where everything is standardised and done to create a Hollywood-style approach where you are creating emotions but the emotions are following a recipe, whatever the culture.

Mega-events have been staged in Asia for over a decade now. In terms of sport, it is very important to remember that the concept of sport as competitive is definitely a British concept,[7] it is not an Asian concept. For Asian people sport is about "He", it is harmony and balance, it is about martial arts … So the relation to the body, to the sportsman or the sportswoman, is completely different. This is a world view and interpretation of sport and culture that could have been more prominent in recent mega-event editions. Going back to the Tokyo Games, I was interviewed by a French TV channel alongside two medallists in canoeing, and they were telling me that, as soon as they finished their competition, they were requested to leave the Olympic village and return to their

Beatriz Garcia

countries. So, what that means is that the sportsperson is no longer considered a citizen of the world, but only considered as a product: you come, you do your work and as soon as you are finished, you get out because we do not need you any more.[8]

I am not blaming Tokyo, I am not blaming the IOC, because they are also suffering from the zeitgeist.[9] It is not their sole responsibility to avoid this efficiency and security-driven approach to event delivery. But for me what is interesting is to see that the IOC had the opportunity to challenge that, but they were not interested or not able to do it probably because they were being held accountable of diverting the safety measures, the health and safety conditions of the Games [in pandemic times], so they did not take any risks. That proves that instead of celebrating sport and universal values, the only thing that really mattered when hosting the Games was the "show". This is clearly a loss …

You were mentioning the importance of "getting lost" in the Olympic city. I love that expression. I remember Guy Debord and *The Society of the Spectacle*. He used to get lost – and get drunk, a lot [laughs] – in the city as a wanderer, going from one bar to another, meeting different people, to be in contact with different people. Athletes in the Olympic village are not allowed to get lost, they are not allowed to leave the village. When athletes are prevented from going to the host city and exploring, when instead they are held in a close environment, only transported from their competition venue and then back to their room, we are definitely showing the bad side of the society of the spectacle.

ALTERNATIVE MODELS

BEATRIZ: What are the alternative models? The value of your background is that you understand how the IOC operates and can have sympathy about the challenges they face as an organisation. Mega-event governing bodies may ask themselves: what are these events for? Are we hosting the Games in order to be safe, or are we hosting the Games in order to inspire humanity? Are athletes from 206 nations gathering in a single place, against all odds, in order to get a medal or are they there to demonstrate what is possible in an event that aspires to intercultural exchange? What is the bottom-line, the part of a mega-event experience that must be protected at all costs? That is the big question.

PHILIPPE: This is not just the big question but the *only* question. There are some territories in the world where they have understood the value of mega-events and they have linked these values with domestic and geopolitical considerations. I started working on the concept of Futurous as a new or alternative mega-event format three years ago and I was fortunate to be working with a former Olympian who used to be the CEO of the US Olympic and Paralympic Committee. He has a high level of cultural understanding. We were discussing the first amendment of the US constitution, which states that every man and woman has the right to pursue happiness. What does it mean? It does not mean that you have the right to have happiness, what you have is the right to pursue it; what this implies is that everyone has the right to be empowered and have the opportunity to do his or her best.

I think it is the same with a mega-event. It is not about defining a fixed framework where the governing body is imposing what you can or cannot do – it is more of a collaboration, or may I say a tango dance with the host city. The host city can indicate "these are my specificities, these are my values, these are the stories I can tell", and may request "you mega-event, you provide us the possibility of being proud of our country, being proud of our culture, of our history" but without meaning that the host city's culture or history is better than the others. It just means that they are proud of it and are happy to welcome other people to live and experience something that is not necessarily linked to their own culture or to their own history. So, let me stress: in terms of universal values, this is for me the gold standard. How do you define and create an organisation whose main task is to protect the vision of the host territory? That means that you cannot get rid of art, you cannot get rid of culture, you cannot get rid of history. In the case of Futurous, this has forced – and helped us – as a governing body, to engage with different territories in the Middle East, in Asia, in Russia, where they are proud of their culture and they want to share what they experience, what they have done, who they are. If we articulate a vision that emphasises the necessary coexistence of art, culture and sport, this means that the mega-event governing body needs to articulate the objective of promoting sports excellence but taking into consideration the natural beauty and the history of the host territory.

THE RESPONSIBILITY OF MEGA-EVENTS

BEATRIZ: This brings me to ask about the "responsibility" of mega-event governing bodies. When you allow culture to express itself freely, sometimes what one culture wants to celebrate feels wrong to another culture. You seem to suggest that if you give the chance for hosts to share what they value (no matter what this is) in an environment that feels safe and offers them sufficient space to have a say, maybe there will be a chance for other cultures to understand, even if they disagree with it?

PHILIPPE: I think the key is respect … and being able to have an honest communication where we have differences, we have men and women coming with different cultures and religions, but this is the beauty of our humanity. It is in this respect that mega-events must be extremely cautious. The idea is not to move from one territory to the other in order to optimise financial considerations; the idea is to provide the opportunity for different territories to express themselves. And this is something that was critical for [modern Olympic Games founder] Pierre de Coubertin and [former IOC president] Juan Antonio Samaranch. I think it was also important for [former IOC president Jacques] Rogue, because they understood that there was a trade-off between the profitability and all the constraints linked to the hyper-capitalism of mega-events, and the opportunity to give different cultures the chance to express themselves.

The question is how do we recreate this agora, how do we use the mega-event as a platform to recreate these public, open-ended, intercultural exchanges? I know it is complex. I was flabbergasted, very disappointed when I saw how the UEFA 2020 competition ended up with British fans beating Italian fans. This situation suggests that there are people who need to be re-introduced to notions of respect and this may be one of the responsibilities of any mega-event initiative. Art and culture offer the opportunity to explore different perspectives. It is tautologic: art and culture are not only a name but also the means to reflect on the diversity of our humanity. But I am not naive,

I know there is money at stake and that we live in an ongoing culture war in the sense that some countries or some cultures are trying to impose their views because there is a question of colonialism, big money, etc. For me, it is clearly the responsibility of mega-event governing bodies to grasp that essence, spirit and make sure they are protecting it.

BEATRIZ: You are offering examples of ongoing contradictions and challenges. Many commentators are questioning the value of mega-events and remain unconvinced that they can address their universal value and intercultural exchange aspirations. In the wake of the COVID-19 pandemic, do you believe there is still a need for mega-events? If so, what is their value and what is the way forward?

PHILIPPE: In a more and more standardised world, we need more mega-events, i.e., platforms where different cultures can come and present themselves; where there is respect and complementarity, where people are happy to talk about themselves and are also happy to meet and to mingle. This is clearly the beauty of what the Olympic village is supposed to be for. Going back to the city as non-place or airport metaphor: we can have standardised, sanitised environments, we can build safe bubbles … but this will not help us become more tolerant or understanding of each other. This is the beauty of continuing to bring in mega-events and creating contemporary "agoras". We need to have the possibility to engage different communities, presenting themselves and learning from the others.

This brings me to the notion of *interactivity*, very important to what I am doing now. The mega-event should not be just a demonstration of sporting excellence, it should be an opportunity to engage with the fans. The fan is part of the mega-event: the visitor, the offline visitor, the online fan. They are part of the movement, they should not be treated as just statistics. They must be given the opportunity to express themselves and learn from each other. In the Futurous event, we are using sport to talk about technology and also talk about sociology. It is about how people can interact with technology and with one another. The emphasis is not on a streamlined commercial proposition but is about trying to embrace complexity, avoiding the one-size-fits-all model of other event hosting.

COMPLEXITY AND INTERACTIVITY

BEATRIZ: You talk about interactivity. In culture circles the new dominant keyword is cocreation. But co-creation is often highlighted when operating at a small scale. The challenge for you seems to be how to make this possible in a grand scale. Is it possible to be "mega" and at the same time truly interactive, building on a co-creative approach? It sounds very good on paper but, how can it materialise?

PHILIPPE: You are touching on the core of what keeps me awake at night. That is ... how do we translate the efficiency of the mega-event in terms of promotion and respect of universal values, as well as promotion and respect of individual cultures? Does that mean that we need to have a quota? Does it mean that we need to make sure we do not go in too deep? My team and I are working with companies like Microsoft, Facebook and Telegram. I think social media give platforms for people to communicate about them-selves – it is the materialisation of Andy Warhol's "fifteen minutes of fame" claim. I believe in humanity, and I think the next stage will be truly co-creation, as you say. It will be truly providing platforms and opportunities for many people to have their say simultaneously.

At Futurous, we are spending a lot of time with social media, we are working with philosophers and technologists and we know about the trolling attitude, the bad side of social media, where people think they can do things they would not do in real life. But I am seeing trends such as trolling at the infancy stage. I believe there will be a common understanding that this is not intelligent, that you are not creating value by just being sarcastic or indeed, destructive. I would say, "yes, criticism is interesting but, what do you propose"? For me, the next stage in mega-event hosting is all about the management of this complexity, the management of this magnitude. Complexity and magnitude should be at the core, which means that we must work with the organising committee, we must work with the host institutions so that they clearly understand the objectives and they also accept the risks that are related to that ambition. You may have seen that some people are not interested in what we are doing, and they see us as something conflicting or contradicting their perspective, instead of it being about delivering a different perspective. This means that the liaison between us [the Futurous governing body] and the host territory is critical, and we need to invest time and make sure that our concept of operations is sufficiently sensitive so that there is a common understanding. We must allow time to engage with the different communities, including the arts and culture communities – not only the ones in the host territory, but also those from other territories. So, the plan is that we have this ongoing dialogue and we end up creating a mega-event that has all the benefits of the Babel tower [laughs] without the negative dimension.

THE ROLE OF PHILOSOPHERS, SOCIOLOGISTS AND ARTISTS IN MEGA-EVENTS

BEATRIZ: What I take out of what you are saying is that the future of mega-event hosting involves a significant reappraisal of their bottom-line priorities – or raison d'être – and associated governance model. You have mentioned the involvement of philosophers, sociologists and artists as part of the governance approach for your new ventures. So is it really possible to have an alternative mega-event model that takes seriously the idea of the philosopher and the sociologist being part of the core team, and of the advisory group? How do you make this happen?

PHILIPPE: What is important is to create a balanced model that provides us direct access to some countries. We have been working with UNESCO which was extremely prestigious indeed, but it was also extremely constraining because you need to have unanimity to be able to proceed with every decision … and you cannot reach unanimity every time. This is why we have decided to create a first stage of Futurous with forward thinking countries. The discussions we have had so far with the French, with Monaco, with Singapore and with Russia have been extremely interesting. They have told us that they understand our philosophy. Obviously, we have our own agenda, but we also respect the agendas of our territorial stakeholders. We have discussion where we "agree to disagree", so to speak. We are discussing the different priorities and agreeing a framework where the different territories and our different communities of interest can make their voices heard. Because this is what I understand is critical in the middle to long term.

As a mega-event governing body, you need to reconcile your activities with the political vision – political in the Greek sense of the "life of the city". We have been fortunate to work with very insightful people who were challenged by the same questions as my core Futurous team. The work I did with the Dubai government in the context of the World Expo [2020] or the work we are doing currently with the Saudi government is extremely interesting because yes, they have their official positions – addressing short-term considerations – but they are also working on something new, they see new types of event like Futurous as an opportunity to advance mid to long term objectives, where they are spending more time, more money, more resources helping their domestic communities but also engaging with international communities. I am really confident that we have found the right partners and we have set the right methodology. On the methodology front: our concept of operations is heavily investing on the definition of KPIs, of objectives, and making sure we have a clear alignment. We have also clearly identified who are the stakeholders we want to work with, and how we are going to inform them, which gives us the possibility to minimise the relative weight of risk management. This means that we are not putting risk management at the core but rather making it one element of the process, so that we are not constrained by making our first or top priority consideration the avoidance of all risk.

BEATRIZ: With such a model, do you have room for the qualitative? If so, how do you develop indicators that are qualitative while also providing a framework to verify whether you are reaching your goals?

PHILIPPE: This is … [chuckles], I am smiling, because you are touching on another key issue. It is so easy to have an agreement on quantitative elements … but our governance model involves more than 100 experts including political leaders such as Pascal Lamy, from the World Trade Organisation. I have also met Princess Al-Saud, who was the Head of Sports for Saudi Arabia and is currently an IOC member; we have been working with Carlos Moiras in the European Commission, he was the commissioner in charge of innovation and technology. We have been working with them and everyone said what you have just said, i.e. "please do not focus only on concrete quantitative elements, but rather make sure you share the same philosophy, make sure you have room for arguing, because *shit will hit the fan* … ", pardon my French [smiles], because of the complexity of the event, because of the ambitions of the event; and very often you will face a willingness to step back and go back to your comfort zone.

What we have been doing over the last year and a half, working with the Russian government, was to meet extremely involved persons who were able to leave their "official jackets" at the entrance of the meeting room, and explained, considerately, what they were expecting. It was the same in the UAE, in Saudi Arabia, it was the same in Singapore. We had some discussions as well with China and India. And it was extremely interesting to explore the possibility of speaking very freely, in closed rooms, and with the formal commitment of everyone that what was said in the room would stay in the room, and would not be used in short sighted, instrumental ways. So, to answer your point, what does it mean? It means that instead of having a limited amount of time to define your projects and then rolling out the planning and the implementation, you need to have a very strong governance model, where you have access to the key decision-makers; it means that you have always on sight the political perspective, the steering committee and the operational constraints that you are facing.

This ultimately means that the model that is currently existing for the Olympics or FIFA … I think we can propose something alternative. We have seen it with the extension of the preparation times for the Olympic Games or the Expo. You need to have enough time, but not have too much time – because when you have too much time, people start wandering, people start justifying the responsibility. They want to have more resources, they may start pushing for things that may not be relevant [to the original event vision]. For me, what is critical is to make sure that yes, we are working under pressure, but we are not over-investing in … closed phases. You need to have a process where you can always readapt and make the most of new opportunities. Now, thinking of your British colleagues, an example: the beauty of London 2012 was initially, when the bid was presented to the IOC in 2005, with the assessment of [consultancy company] Arup,[10] the bid was supposed to be around 2.9 billion pounds.

As you will remember, in October 2012, after the Olympic and Paralympic Games, the British government announced that the Games had been 8.9 billion pounds. What struck me was that, one year prior, in June 2011, the official budget was 9.8 billion, which means that the Brits, the organising committee were able to create a structure which was evolving and they were able to seize the new opportunities as they arose and as they were facing the constraints. So, this notion of flexibility is critical and it what we want to achieve here [at Futurous].

This is why we have been discussing our plans with people from the government and we have met sponsors, we have met media outlets, to explain what we were considering. Throughout this process, these stakeholders were also changing their views on us, and not considering that we were coming with a fixed toolbox, imposing things and establishing "you do that, I do that, and we are working with lawyers". Not at all. Instead, we are working with philosophers, we are working with politicians, we are working with people who are committed to deliver together. And, as a result, we are not experiencing what maybe other big structures are currently experiencing. Am I clear? [Beatriz assents].

GOVERNANCE MODELS, BEYOND A "RADICAL MONOPOLY"

PHILIPPE: Something that was also stressed in your questions … I am a huge fan of [the philosopher] Ivan Illich,[11] he was working on the concept of "radical monopoly". This concept says that when you are setting a structure, when you are setting a technical tool to answer a situation or a problem, the answer which provides satisfactory solutions at the beginning may need revisiting, because there is a stage when the answers you have originally proposed become counterproductive. The most obvious example is the evolution of automobile usage: we created cars in order to travel faster, but when you have too many cars you realise that they are actually blocking the efficiency of travel. What this means is that we have to be very cautious not to institutionalise the answers [to a given challenge, such as a mega-event hosting process], but to share a common thinking, a common philosophy where event governing bodies are respecting the authorities, the responsibilities of the different structures existing (the transport authority, the policy authority), and where they are also sharing their own "answers" to the challenge, consolidated with other "answers", so to speak. And it will be the role of the steering committee to make the arbitrage. So, it is a big mind change, because it means that instead of competing with one another, the "answer" to a situation, such as a mega-event, needs to be put into perspective with other answers, by a range of stakeholders and not a single entity. Making the parallel with COVID-19: several territories decided to put medical answers aside, or something that was no more a medical issue but became a political issue. This is what we want to avoid. We want to avoid one field of activity becoming prominent over the others and taking over.

To sum up: the role of the mega-event steering committee, our governance model, is extremely important because our diverse event stakeholders need the arbitrage. That means that the relationship between us, as a governing body, with the host territory needs to be completely different from what has become common practice. We need to provide expertise and tools, but the implementation of these tools needs to be done based on the host's respective objectives, because the political side, the geopolitical side is critical. The tripartite collaboration between the host country, the host territory [usually, a city or region] and the governing body leads to a more harmonious relationship or symbiosis, where we, the Futurous team, which owns the event, provide expert analysis and elements of reference but at the end of the process, the hosts also become part of the Futurous movement. This gives them a stage, [not only during the event itself] but in the mid and long term.

BEATRIZ: The big question myself and other posed back in the late 1990s was whether mega-events could operate successfully at both a global and local level. What we have observed since is the need to account for *time*, for long-term cycles; the need to allow enough time for processes to evolve in a manner sensitive and inclusive of different stakeholder needs. So how do you plan for a mega-event, if you accept that you do not have all the answers from the get-go, that you need time to actually understand each other at each edition? How do you account for what you are not yet ready for?

PHILIPPE: Your whole point is critical, because in contemporary societies we do not have "time" anymore, we want all things to be fast and furious ... When we talk about the Olympic Games as a mega-event, we see them as they are now, in 2021, but we forget that the first edition of the Games, in 1890, was staged two years after the launch of the Olympic Movement in La Sorbonne in 1894. At that time, the participants were from 14 countries, while by 2021, there are 206 competing nations. Our governance model is something we are building with the host territories. This is something we are co-designing – you mentioned co-creation earlier. We are bringing different expertise – I would not say "experts", because when we talk of experts it is always associated with external authority, with the "I know better because I am the expert". This is not what we want to do. We want to collectively agree on things. What I want to stress is that our governance model is not overly institutionalised, otherwise we have this tipping point, outlined by Ivan Illich, where we are creating a "radical monopoly" and we are no longer communicating with each other; it is no longer a conversation but two monologues in parallel. Or several monologues with different stakeholders.

BEATRIZ: Thank you Philippe.

DISCLOSURE STATEMENT

No potential conflict of interest was reported by the author(s).

Notes

1   Public Lecture: Garcia, Beatriz "Can we live without mega-events?", University of Liverpool, November 2020: www.liverpool.ac.uk/communication-and-media/news/stor ies/ title,1237256,en.html.

2   After having had three editions of the Olympic Games in Asia (Pyeongchang 2018, Tokyo 2020 and Beijing 2022); and the World Expo taking place in Shanghai (2010) and Dubai (2020).

3   Leni Riefenstahl "Olympia", www.youtube.com/watch?v=H3LOPhRq3Es.

4   Philippe Decoufle, Albertville Olympic Winter Games, opening ceremony segment, www. youtube.com/watch?v=d1zdyrHtST0.

5   This is a reference to the postponed pandemic-times Games edition, taking place in August 2021 instead of 2020 under heavy COVID-19 restrictions for all involved. As noted, this interview took place at that time.

6   www.futurous.org/.

7   What we understand as Olympic sport, which involves competition and medal winners, follows internationally accepted rules and set definitions of sporting practices. Blanchard refers here to the common belief that such rules and definitions were mostly

informed by sport codification practices taking place in the United Kingdom in the 19th century (i.e. the Rugby School).

8 The formal IOC request for athletes to vacate the Olympic Village as soon as their competition was over was due to time-specific COVID-19 rules in Tokyo 2020. Blanchard is also referring to a growing trend to shorten the period of stay at the Olympic Village, particularly amongst the most successful athletes. See: www.latimes.com/sports/olympics/la-sp-oly-athletes- village-20160818-snap-story.html.

9 This refers both to the previously mentioned "trend" to make health and safety measures the lead priority in mega-event hosting, and to the time-specific added pressures resulting from the COVID-19 pandemic.

10 In common with all mega-events, the calculations for the London 2012 forecasted budget differs, depending on how figures are presented – and to which stakeholder. The House of Commons.

11 https://en.wikipedia.org/wiki/Radical_monopoly; Illich, Ivan (2020-06-29). "Tools of Conviviality" (PDF). *Cornell University.*

Beatriz Garcia

Index

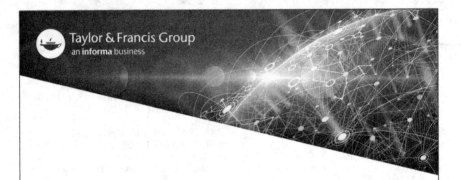

Printed in the United States
by Baker & Taylor Publisher Services